Get Wallet Wise

Recover from Money Missteps
Create Positive Money Habits
for
Everyday People

Ken Remsen

*To my wife Noreen,
son William and daughter Natalie.
You are why I do what I do.*

Table of Contents

Get Wallet Wise

Part Two: Taking Control of Your Finances

Introduction

"Money is better than poverty, if only for financial reasons."

Woody Allen

Remember, I am speaking to you in the firm loving voice of a teacher...

"Ken, do you think it is possible for me to get out of debt?" I hear this time again during my financial coaching sessions. I tell my clients that with determination, discipline and hard work, they can get out of debt and build a nest egg. The key is to spend less than you earn. This is common sense, however, in our complex world of money, many of us do not know where we stand financially. We have a hunch, but we are not working from a budget, we are not balancing our checkbook, and we are not reading our credit card statements. Everything financial is on autopilot because that may be the path of least resistance. The best way to spend less is to have a "Low Threshold for Excitement." Buy a car you can afford. Buy a house that is less than you can afford, etc. Introduce yourself to inexpensive fun. It is unnecessary to spend your hard-earned money on fun until you have paid off your debts and started saving for the future.

I wrote *Get WalletWise* because of the numerous financial conversations I have had with family, friends, customers, and vendors. "It's a Jungle Out There" in the world of money is an understatement. My goal is to help you, and if possible, the world become financially literate. I believe financial or money illiteracy contributes to wealth inequality.

Before the Global Financial Crises of 2007-2008, I taught a personal finance math class in high school. In those classes, I learned that there was a desire by the students to learn personal finance. In class, I created a mock car salesroom and split the students into two groups: the salesperson and the customer. It was hilarious to see the normally shy students transform into confident negotiators.

I taught them as I want to teach you, The Seven Most Important Words in Negotiation. *"Is that the best you can do"?* I promise these seven words will save hundreds, thousands of dollars, maybe more depending on your situation. Not only did I teach them what to say, but also how to say it, and whether to say the words while negotiating or even better, while walking away from the salesperson, heading for the door, ready to leave. If you are unable to strike a deal, my next favorite seven word phrase is, *"Let me know if your situation changes."* As it was occurring to their family, a student asked me about the meaning of foreclosure. Another student gave the book, *Maxed Out.* Written just before the 2008 Financial Crises, this book showed me that the consumer finance world is more "dog eat dog" than I knew. The book and its movie tell the story of how consumer lending and credit card companies make oversized profits while bleeding customers dry. The movie introduced me to the concept of debt collection brokers! Adding this to the many stories of personal money struggles from my friends and family, I knew I should do something positive for you. I wrote a book for you about managing money.

Who is this Financial Book for?

I wrote this book for those who need a financial literacy boost. Do you owe unpaid balances on your credit cards? Are you borrowing personal loans to pay back credit card debt? Are you maxing out your company's 401k? At the end of the month, is there more month than money?

Everyone's financial literacy could use a boost. Believe me, I know. I have made many of the mistakes discussed in this book and learned many lessons in the "School of Hard Knocks". Many of the lessons were very difficult, but I would not trade those well-earned knocks for anything. That history gave me the knowledge and strength to sit down and write this book for you. Fortunately, I also received friendly advice. A mentor told me, "It is best to learn from other people's mistakes." I heartily agree. From my personal experiences, I share my observations with you.

Are you in the...?

1. The Trapped Class

2. The Treadmill Class

3. The Freedom Class

Writer Ramit Sethi invented this description of the present day American economic class structure. *Get WalletWise* shows you how to move from the Trapped and Treadmill Class to the Freedom Class.

One financial advisor told my father that D a d 's nest egg did not have enough money to qualify for his advice. Another "advisor" later sold him unsuitable financial products. This book is for people like you, who make their living driving for UBER, work in a hotel or restaurant, or any type of hard-working job. This book is for young people who are learning how the world works. This book is for the working-class poor, who have jobs, but along with 50% of Americans, have no net worth. They have no equity in their house or car and have unsecured debts (credit cards mostly) that exceed their assets. I have been there myself, gotten "over the wall." N o w I want to help you achieve financial security.

Why this Financial Self-Help Book?

In an interview with the well known business tycoon, Jamie Dimon (chairperson of JP Morgan Chase) declared that the citizens of our country are having two distinct experiences. Half of Americans work for large thriving corporations, and the other half of Americans work in less stable industries. It's like a Tale of Two Cities. Dimon said, "It is absolutely obvious that a big chunk of (people) have been left behind. Forty percent of Americans make less than $15.00 per hour. Forty percent of Americans can't afford a $400 bill, whether it's medical or fixing their car. Fifteen percent of the American population make minimum wage." Dimon also added that the education system is broken and sometimes a college education is worthless. I discuss the student loan crisis and how you can navigate these scary waters in Chapter 5 of *Get WalletWise*. Dimon also mentions that 70,000 have died because of opioid abuse. In Chapter 9, How Addictions Affect your Finances, *Get WalletWise* focuses on the financial tragedy that drug abuse causes.

That interview took place in March 2019. Just think how many more people in this country are in trouble since the COVID-19 pandemic. In November 2020, 26 million Americans said they did not have enough to eat.

There are genuine problems in the American economy. You cannot afford to be frivolous with your money. Unlike most self-help money books, *Get WalletWise* discusses the money pitfalls that will trip the unwary and vulnerable.

You learn that Attorneys, Financial Advisors, Car Sales People, Landlords, Bankers, Employees, Employers... Fill in the blank... MAY not be looking out for your best interest. You will develop the skills to know whom to trust. This book is the first step for you to get on the right track of money management.

Avoid Calamity

Get WalletWise discusses the consequences of not saving for retirement or paying for a tattoo instead of paying the rent. I discuss the financial damage caused by drug use and DUI. I discuss why some people consider the Lottery as a retirement plan. I discuss car title loans, payday loans, and student loan debt. The pitfall of not having a budget frequently leads to many other stresses that affect our ability to manage our finances and ultimately find true happiness. We don't know what lies behind the next corner, so it's time to get our financial house in order.

Conclusion

Learn from my successes and failures in personal money management to steer a straight course to your debt free financial success. The process of becoming debt free will probably take you out of your comfort zone. That is okay. Anything worth achieving requires sacrifice and hard work and I know you can do it. Let me teach you how to manage money. You can definitely achieve a debt free life and I am happy to show you how to do it.

Chapter 1

Credit Card Debt

I love money. I love everything about it. I bought some pretty good stuff. Got me a $300 pair of socks. Got a fur sink. An electric dog polisher. A gasoline-powered turtleneck sweater. And, of course, I bought some dumb stuff, too.

Steve Martin

Pandemic Update

With layoffs skyrocketing during the outbreak and lock downs, Americans have been piling on more credit card debt: forty-seven percent now carry balances, up from forty-three percent in March (2020), and nearly a quarter say they've taken on more card debt amid the corona virus downturn, a CreditCards.com survey found.

In an interview with Warren Buffett by Yahoo! finance, Turning to credit cards because of financial hardship is one thing, but Buffett says some people use them as "a piggy bank to be raided."

He recently told his company's shareholders about a friend who came into a windfall and asked for advice on what to do with it. She also had credit card debt — at 18% interest.

"If I owed any money at 18%, the first thing I'd do with any money I had would be to pay it off," Buffett said he told her. "You can't go through life borrowing money at those rates and be better off."

https://finance.yahoo.com/news/warren-buffett-says-financially-survive-204400784.html

You Should be Careful with Credit Cards

Credit cards, by design, are financial products that exploit our human nature to be happier. Credit cards are very convenient and may help enable an instant-gratification mentality.

"Young people are threatened... by the evil use of advertising techniques that stimulate the natural inclination to avoid hard work by promising the immediate satisfaction of every desire."   Pope John Paul II

The more emotional a seller can get you through advertising about a product or service, the more you will spend on impulse. When convinced a particular purchase will make us feel better, we will make the purchase. If a business can convince us that the purchase makes us "seem" successful, then we will buy more.

Businesses encourage us to use our credit cards for the purchase because we do not suffer the same psychological pain we do when we pay with cash. We are paying with a magic plastic card! We feel no pain for our purchase.

The greatest test to determine if you are overspending is carrying a balance on your credit card. Do you carry an unpaid balance on your credit card? You may be an over spender. If you are not an over spender, then pay off your credit card balances monthly and avoid the interest charges. If you don't pay off your balance each month, your credit card bank charges your account nosebleed interest rates usually above 18%. The average credit card interest rate is 16.44% (at the time of printing). Besides the interest rate, banks charge you overpriced "over the credit line" fees and "late" fees. Another reason why I wrote this book is to help you save money by avoiding these high fees.

Credit Card Solutions

I have created three different approaches to managing your credit card accounts depending upon your ability to pay the balance in full each month or if you carry a balance.

This is awkward:

Next, I ask you to ask yourself a few important questions. This exercise will require you to be completely honest with yourself. How do you feel about credit? Are you responsible with credit? What is responsible credit use? Do you make impulse purchases with your credit card? Do you pay your credit card balances in full on your card monthly? Do you make your card payment on time? Are you assessed late fees or over the limit fees on your credit card accounts? How many credit card accounts do you have? Ask yourself these questions and connect with the applicable level below. Level One starts with folks who are losing control of their finances.

Here is a simple form to begin the journey to having a zero credit card balance.

Download from: https://www.walletwise.org/downloadableresources

Credit Card Debt List				
Creditor	Debt Amount	Monthly Payment	Interest Rate	Months Past Due
Credit Card # 1	$	$		
Credit Card # 2				
Credit Card # 3				
Credit Card # 4				
Credit Card # 5				
Credit Card # 6				
Total Credit Card Debt	$	$		

You can start the process by collecting your credit cards. Then print your statements from your online accounts. Locate the balance owed and put that under "Debt Amount." Add the monthly payment you can afford. Find and list the interest rate. Are your accounts past due? This is an extremely important exercise. Please do not pass it by. We can use this information to decide if you will snowball or avalanche your debt as discussed in Level 2 of the following credit card debt categories.

Level One

If you hold an unpayable balance on your credit cards and are having difficulty with your personal finances, and you can never pay the balance in full each month, then cut the credit cards. That's right. Get a pair of scissors and physically cut the cards in half and dispose of them. That's the price you pay for not being able to use a credit card. Can you fix this? Yes. You live by a four-letter word: **CASH!**

This is good news. Remember, I said above people do not equate wallet sized pieces of plastic with the pain and suffering you feel when you spend cold, hard cash on a purchase. You will now do a better job determining if that next purchase is a want, or a desire, or an absolute necessity.

Remember to sign up for alerts and automatic payment so you are never late again on your credit card payment and become liable for late fees. "Wait a minute," you say. "Why do I need to do this? I just cut up my cards." Just because you cut up your cards does not mean your account no longer exists. You still have the account. You cut up your cards to eliminate your ability to use them. The account still exists, and you still owe the money.

If you possess the skill to negotiate, contact the credit card company and ask them for a lower interest rate. Tell them you are considering switching to a new card with a better interest rate. This only works if you are up to date on your payments.

Cash Budgeting

1. Determine which expenses you can pay in cash.

2. List categories like groceries, entertainment, eating out, and clothing.

3. To reduce your spending only use cash for these categories.

4. Do not use debit cards, credit cards, nor check book.

5. Disconnect any automatic payments connected to your credit card.

6. Keep your debit card at home until you get a handle on your spending.

7. A simple way to keep track of your cash expenditures is to use the envelope system. Make an envelope for each budget item and put in the correct amount of cash. When an envelope is empty, then you are done spending in that category. Put paid receipts into the correct envelope to see how much money you spent in that category.

You should develop a procedure to manage your cash. Using cash may be inconvenient, but it is a great way to get a handle on your spending and reduce impulsive credit card usage.

Please see the following article to unpack this idea.

https://www.thebalance.com/how-to-switch-to-cash-only-for-your-budget-2385691

In Chapter Twelve, "Budgeting and Money Management," I will discuss how to run a ledger to keep track of your cash, which is an alternative to the envelope method.

Warning:

You should not do business with a debt relief, debt settlement, or debt consolidation company. I discuss the reasons why these are terrible ideas designed to take advantage of people in financial distress in Chapter Four "Using Debt Settlement and Relief Companies. "

How to Function Without a Credit Card:

Despite what many people say, you can function in life very well without a credit card. You should get a pre-paid debit card. The pre-paid debit card limits your liability. It's not cash, and many pre-paid card companies include fraud protection. If you travel, there are rental car companies and hotels that have payment alternatives to cash.

Start by getting a Prepaid Credit Card. One of my favorites is PayPal Prepaid Mastercard https://www.paypal-prepaid.com/. I suggest opening a PayPal account. No PayPal account? You can try MOVO prepaid debit card. https://movo.cash/

NerdWallet, the Balance, Credit Karma, the Simple Dollar, and Money Under 30 recommend MOVO as one of the best prepaid debit cards. There is no credit check and you can make quick direct deposits according to their website. I would not recommend that you set up direct deposit into this account as a replacement for your checking account. Instead, you can transfer money from your checking account to this prepaid card for planned incidental expenses. Your money is safer because you only risk the money in the prepaid account and do not risk your money in your checking account.

"But Ken, I need a credit card to rent a car." **Not True!**

https://www.daveramsey.com/blog/rent-a-car-without-a-credit-card

You should check out Dollar rental car. They will rent a car with a NON prepaid debit card.

"But Ken, I need a credit card to book a hotel room." Not True! Hotels will take reservations and process payment through a debit card. They will put a hold on it as a deposit for one or two nights, depending on the hotel. So, it's an excellent idea to deposit money in your account before you travel.

Remember to sign up for alerts and automatic payment so you are never late again on your credit card payment. I have repeated this same statement several times in this chapter because it so important!

Level Two If you are using credit cards and hold a balance on your credit card, remove the credit cards from your wallet and put them in a sealable sandwich bag, pour water into the bag, and place them in your freezer. Put those cards on Ice!!

Literally!

This removes the opportunity for impulse purchases. Transfer your card balance to a lower interest card while you repay this card balance. There are credit cards specifically designed with this idea in mind. I suggest contacting your local credit union for the best interest rate and professional banking services.

How to Pay Off Debt

Here's a trick I learned from Clark Howard. Pay off credit card balances faster by paying the minimum payment: divide the payment in half, then pay your credit card payment every two weeks. You want the power of compounding to benefit you. By paying more often, you receive the reward of less overall interest being charged against you. Don't pay one payment of $200 every month, instead pay $100 every fourteen days. By doing so, you can pay off your debt balance 75% faster. Another key aspect is to keep your payment the same. Just because you are making progress and the credit card says, "Now you can pay less," doesn't mean you should do so. Don't reduce your payment. You will never get ahead. Unless there is a more important bill to pay, get out of the habit of paying just the minimum payment.

The credit card statement will show you the length of time to pay off the balance if you only pay the minimum payment. The statement will also show you the inflated amount of interest you will pay.

Late Payment Warning: If we do not receive your minimum payment by the date listed above, you may have to pay a late fee of up to $40 and your APRs may be increased up to the Penalty APR of 29.99%.

Minimum Payment Warning: If you make only the minimum payment each period, you will pay more in interest and it will take you longer to pay off your balance. For example:

If you make no additional charges using this card and each month you pay...	You will pay off the balance shown on the statement in about...	And you will end up paying an estimated total of...
Only the minimum payment	17 year(s)	$9,194
$175	3 year(s)	$6,300 (Savings = $2,894)

For information about credit counseling services, call 1-877-337-8187.

If you only pay the minimum payment, you will pay $9,194 over seventeen years. The credit card company reports an arbitrary amount of $175. If you pay $175, then you save almost $2,900 in interest fees. To see how much interest you can save by paying off your balance faster, check out the following.

https://www.bankrate.com/calculators/credit-cards/credit-card-payoff-calculator.aspx

Snowballs and Avalanches Debt Payoff Strategies

Financial gurus developed these debt reduction strategies to help debtors better understand how their debt is getting smaller. In addition, some people prefer one method over the other because of their perceived speed their debt is being repaid. This can make it easier to see that you are making progress and your hard work is paying off.

Check out this amazing site to help you get a handle on run away debt.

The following notice is from their website:

"Undebt.it is a debt payment manager that will generate a plan for you to get out of debt by paying extra amounts on certain accounts until they are paid off. All of the payment plans that Undebt.it can use are all rollover plans, meaning that extra payments are rolled from one debt to the next and so on. Dave Ramsey encourages this type of debt payment system. It was generically popularized by Dave Ramsey's Debt Snowball. The two most popular payment plans are the debt snowball (paying the lowest balance account first and the debt avalanche (paying the account with the highest interest rate first which is also called "debt stacking". You can use either of those plans with Undebt.it or one of the several other methods detailed below. The debt avalanche is mathematically the most effective, but all of the rollover methods work well and will get you debt free in a similar amount of time; just choose the plan which works the best for your situation. Remember, you can change the payment plan."

Debt Snowball Calculator and Debt Reduction Assistant

Try https://undebt.it/ a free online, mobile friendly application that creates an easy-to-follow payment plan.

The "Snowball and Avalanche" debt repayment methods are favorite methods of reducing debt repayment. The avalanche method uses extra money to pay off your high interest rate debts first. This makes sense, because the longer you hold a debt at a higher interest rate, the more interest will accumulate. Pay the minimum payment on the remaining debt accounts and focus on paying as much as you can afford on the highest interest rate account first. Once you complete paying off the highest interest rate account, move to the next highest interest rate account. Repeat this process until you are debt free.

The snowball method pays off the smallest debt balance first, giving you a faster sense of accomplishment. Once you pay off the smallest debt, move on to the next smallest debt etcetera. Another advantage to this method is the fact that you will lower the number of accounts outstanding.

How to Pay Down Debt

When you carry a balance on your credit cards, there are a few additional words of wisdom that can help you pay down the balance faster. You should transfer the balance to a low interest credit card. My suggestion is to start a relationship with your local credit union. They have great rates and a no-nonsense approach to credit card customer service. For example, I just went to my credit union website, and they have a balance transfer card at 1.9% for fifteen months, no balance transfer fee (that's good and no annual fee (that's golden!.

You could get a debt consolidation/personal loan from your credit loan or bank. Another benefit is the fact the personal loan is a fixed interest payment that results in a fixed monthly payment. See Chapter Two, "Overusing Personal Loans. "

Here is the problem: Many of my financial coaching clients went to their banker and qualified for a debt consolidation/personal loan to pay off their credit card debt. The problem is that my clients never got a handle on their budget or excessive spending habits. They continued to use their credit card irresponsibly, racking up additional debt after agreeing to refinance their old credit card debt with a debt consolidation/ personal loan. Now they have "double trouble!" They have a balance on their card... Again! And now have a regular monthly payment on their debt consolidation/personal note. That is why I strongly suggest you take your credit card and put it in a freezer bag and throw them in the freezer. Get another trustworthy person to hold you accountable to stop using your credit cards until you pay the debt consolidation loan off. Pay off on the loan may take three to five years. Then use the credit cards to purchase items you can only afford to repay monthly.

Level 3

If you use credit cards responsibly, carry only two credit cards on your person. One would come in handy as backup and I will explain. Why only two? What if your wallet or purse gets stolen?

More credit cards in your wallet open you up to a possible larger fraud coverage ($50.00 per card if the card is stolen and then used to pay for a purchase. If you have over two credit cards, store the extra cards in a secure location like a safe or fireproof lockable file box. If someone steals your two cards, you have back up to your backup. You really should have backup payment cards in case of online and physical theft.

Never have a store credit card. (See Chapter Three, Pay Day Loans, RTO).

If you pay the balance of your card, every month choose a card with no annual fee and a long grace period, so you don't get charged with interest.

Level One, Level Two, Level Three

Carry a debit card as a double backup but try to never use it. Never use a debit card for gasoline purchases, hotel rooms, or rental cards because they put holds that block access to your money in your checking account. If you scheduled an automatic auto or mortgage payment, you could trigger an insufficient fund episode. In addition, banks handle debit card fraud issues differently than credit cards. If you don't report or discover debit card fraud at once, you will be liable for $50.00 of the fraud (MOST high tier credit cards charge zero) if you report within forty-eight hours. Between forty-eight hours and sixty days you are on the hook for up to $500, and after sixty days you are on the hook for the WHOLE amount!

If you lost your credit or debit card, it may be possible to freeze your account temporarily while you do a second check to find your card. You can check with your specific card company for details.

Remember to sign up for alerts and automatic payment so you are never late again on your credit card payment.

Additional Information: Credit card use opens you up to a variety of suboptimal events. Although not exclusive to credit cards, be aware of the possibility of identity theft and identity fraud that stems from the use of credit cards and credit accounts. This is another reason that it is important that you read your credit card statement at least monthly.

Identity Theft: This involves the theft of your personal financial and identification information online or offline.

Identity Fraud: Your stolen identity is used to withdraw cash, incur unauthorized charges, and open false accounts.

You must create a system to protect your personal information. Shred documents that contain personal information. You should buy a good shredder at Amazon.com. You should guard your passwords. Consider a free password control account. Try password managers Dashlane or StickyPassword. You should buy a lockable security box and store a paper copy of your passwords and important PIN numbers. Thieves can open accounts online with your birth date and social security number. Guard your numbers! Social networking has a bounty of our personal information that makes identity theft easier. Limit the amount of personal information you display on social media applications like Facebook, Instagram, and Twitter. As an additional safeguard, keep antivirus soft-ware on your computers and consider purchasing a VPN or Virtual Private Network to protect you from the bad guys.

You can Detect fraud by monitoring your credit reports regularly.

See Chapter Thirteen "Check Your Credit Reports and Credit Scores" to find out how to freeze your credit files to protect your identity.

You must review your credit card and billing statements monthly. Balance your checkbook and sign up for e-mail and text alerts. This way your accounts alert you when there is any legit or illegal activity. A thief's favorite hijack method is to change the address of your account. You can purchase AAA auto protection to receive free credit card account fraud protection with your auto coverage.

Managing Your Credit Card Account

The following Credit Card Rules conversation will help you understand how to manage your credit card and understand our responsibilities when using a credit card. This section will discuss how to read our credit card statement, collect our bonus points, manage and cancel "gray" charges, credit card disputes and more.

Did you know that Credit Card application is a contract!

Understanding these contracts is important. If you are getting sleepy, make a cup of coffee and then begin again!

Every credit card has an agreement (a friendly word for contract). I suggest you become familiar with the important items in that agreement. Credit card agreements have price information. The pricing section includes the introductory interest they charge you, separated by purchases and credit card transfers. The statement displays the APR (annual percentage rate) for cash advances. They display the grace period time between the end of the billing cycle and the beginning of interest charges.

Here is an example of a Capital One's Pricing Information.

CAPITAL ONE PRICING INFORMATION	
Annual Percentage Rate (APR) for Purchases	Introductory rate of 0% to 9.99%, ranging from 9 months to 18 months. Non-introductory rates between 14.24% and 28.24%. Some Purchase APRs may vary with the market based on changes in the Prime Rate.
APR for Transfers	Introductory rate of 0% to 9.99%, ranging from 9 months to 18 months. Non-introductory rates between 14.24% and 28.24%. Some Transfer APRs may vary with the market based on changes in the Prime Rate.
APR for Cash Advances	Non-introductory rates between 23.74% and 28.24%. Cash Advance APRs may vary with the market based on changes in the Prime Rate.
Paying Interest	Your due date is at least 25 days after the close of each billing cycle. We will not charge you interest on new purchases, provided you have paid your previous balance in full by the due date each month. We will begin charging interest on cash advances and transfers on the transaction date.
Minimum Interest Charge	If you are charged interest, the charge will be no less than $0.50.

Annual Fee	Between $0 and $39 annually.
Transaction Fees	
• Transfer Fee • Cash Advance Fee	3% of the amount of each transfer. The greater of either $10 or 3% of the amount of each cash advance.
Penalty Fees	
• Late Payment	Up to $38.

This is only the first part of Capital One's credit card agreement. The second part is the Customer Agreement. This part includes all the provisos, limitations, and addenda. The most important parts of the Customer Agreement to discuss are the credit limits or credit lines. The bank establishes these rules. The Authorized User section describes the rules involving the additional "persons" you have allowed to use your card. Remember that you are financially responsible for anything your "authorized" user does with your account. I would suggest you do not allow "authorized" users on your account. Have other "persons" get their own account. If they cannot qualify for an account, have them get their own debit card like Greenlight debit card, www.greenlight-card.com. This section also discusses the handling of disputes and a list of fees such as Stop Payment Fees on access checks, cash advance fee, transfer fee, membership fee, late payment fee, and returned payment fees.

Can you see the pattern? A lot of fees leave your wallet and end up in the credit card company's wallet. Credit card companies charge high fees for late payments and over the limit problems. I hope you can avoid them. If you don't read your credit card statement, these fees get tacked on without your knowledge. Ignorance of the terms of your contract is not a good plan or a defense.

Look at the $38.00 late payment fee you pay in the above statement! Sorry, but that is how it works. If you want the "so-called" privilege of using a credit card, then read and understand the contract.

I suggest you read the fine print of the agreements before you sign. The contract favors the credit card company and not you!

You have legal rights! The Fair Credit Billing Act protects you against debt collection harassment and abuse, credit bureau abuse, and discrimination. You should see www.ftc.gov and search for Fair Credit Billing Act.

Instead, Establish an emergency fund.

Instead of using your credit card as a piggy bank to pay for emergencies and unexpected expenses, set up an emergency fund to pay for emergencies. See Chapter Twelve, "Budgeting and Money Management."

You should be proactive with your credit card management. One of my financial coach clients shared a story where they called credit card customer service to dispute the reversal of a Sun Pass charge that was legitimate but flagged as a fraud. That's Florida's toll road payment system. They found out when they attempted to pay for gas with the card. The gas station denied the card for payment. They received no e-mails or texts. No phone call that there was a problem. A denied purchase was the first feedback they received. They went to check the account online and they could not access the account. No reason was given. They called the 1-800 number on the website and got an automated system. When they finally got through to customer service, they found the charge in question were two weeks old.

None of the charges were fraudulent. Result: Card canceled. New ones will arrive in the mail.

Take Away: Please make sure you have a backup plan in case your credit card is declined.

The easiest way to use a credit card is to only purchase items we can afford to pay for by the end of the credit card's billing cycle. This allows us to use the card's purchasing power without paying interest to the bank. If you are currently carrying a balance on your credit card account, fear not, we will discuss how to fix that problem.

In addition, you must be careful about credit card charge errors.

Just as important as reading the credit card agreement is to read your credit card statement at least monthly. It may be wiser to look at the statement weekly until you have established a legitimate system of managing and monitoring your accounts.

By reading my credit card statements regularly, I found: If ignored, the vendor would happily charge my credit card and receive my money for nothing.

a. I opened my Discover statement. This account has a small balance left over from a zero-interest balance transfer I made about 2 years ago. I paid the difference between the statement balance and the payoff balance. I noticed that now I have an interest charge on the statement. That's right, the balance transfer offer expired. Hmm. Let's check the interest rate. 21%. Really? Paying that off as soon as possible.

b. *Post COVID-19 note: At the end of January 2020, Discover sent me a letter that my account was closed for non-use. Our takeaway is that you should charge something small on a zero balance card to keep it active. I lost that credit line. Not a huge deal, but closed credit accounts can cause your FICO credit score to go down due to you using a higher credit utilization ratio.*

c. I received a text alert (Ask Trim) from Citi card. $19.99 charged by an app via Apple iCloud. I started a free financial application expecting the FREE app trial to go away as they did not have my credit card number because I did not update my credit card on iCloud. Right, I shut myself off from the app store. Nope, Apple got the new number. Four weeks after the FREE trial ended, the app charged my card to reactivate. I went online and disputed the charge, and they removed it.

My point here is that credit cards are a powerful financial tool that you must manage carefully by monitoring statements monthly.

Please, we must read every credit card statement at least monthly.

You must reach out to credit card customer service every time there is an issue, no matter how large or small! You must check your account statement and activity online every month!

Here's an example of what one of my credit card statements looks like. This a credit card I got through a relationship with AAA. The credit card company is called ACG Services. This part of the statement is the Summary.

New Balance	$102.84
Minimum Payment Due	$30.00
Payment Due Date	08/01/2019

Late Payment Warning: If we do not receive your minimum payment by the date listed above, you may have to pay up to a $39.00 Late Fee.

AAA Dollars Gas Rebate Summary	
Earned this Statement	$2.06
Earned Year to Date	$30.74
For details, see your rebate section.	

Activity Summary

Previous Balance	+	$166.14
Payments	-	$162.82CR
Other Credits	-	$3.32CR
Purchases	+	$102.84
Balance Transfers		$0.00
Advances		$0.00
Other Debits		$0.00
Fees Charged		$0.00
Interest Charged		$0.00
New Balance	=	$102.84
Past Due		$0.00
Minimum Payment Due		$30.00
Revolving Line of Credit		$24,900.00
Revolving Line Available		$24,797.16
Days in Billing Period		29

All credit cards are 0% interest if you don't carry a balance!

What this means may not be obvious to everyone at first glance. Credit card companies charge interest when you carry a balance. If you pay the balance of the card each month you pay zero in interest. This means you pay nothing for the purchasing power created by the credit card.

However, it is still possible to pay your outstanding balance monthly, but the credit card charges you an annual fee. It's like the price you pay for the credit card company to be friends with you. Don't fall for this. Get a credit card sponsored by your credit union with low or no annual fee.

Please pay your balance in full each month.

This part of the statement is the detail of the transactions.

Please note the highlighted 2019 Total Fees and Total Interest Charges.

They are 0.00. Zero is your goal! Please note the AAA credit statement credit adjustment noted above. This card with AGC Card Services (partnered with AAA) automatically credits back your points for purchasing gas with the AAA card. More on this later in this chapter, but I use this card for only paying for gas. It doubles as my backup card in case my major card is not working.

Side Bar: AAA

AAA is an amazing personal finance resource. AAA is an insurance company and bank besides being an automobile club. I'll talk about this in the "Insurance Chapter," Chapter 19, but AAA sells auto, boat, RV, life, renters, flood and home insurance. AAA is a bank. Not only do they partner with banks that issue credit cards, but they also have access to savings and checking accounts, mortgage and reputable personal loans. They also have an auto buying service. I will mention AAA in Chapter Eleven, "DUI and other Legal Calamities." AAA is a leader in teaching the public about ills associated with distracted driving, aggressive driving, as well as drinking and driving.

The next statement is from the card I do the bulk of my bill paying. I paid a little interest in 2019. Did you notice the cash advance interest rate mentioned on the statement? Cash advances are 27.49% BOO! The reason I mention the Cash Advance rate here is to let you know how expensive it is to borrow cash from your credit card account. We should not use credit cards as an ATM. Banks created credit cards to assist us in buying consumer goods. Credit card companies collect fees from both you as interest in carrying balances and store merchant fees. When you borrow cash from your credit card, you pay a higher interest rate because the credit card company considers you the borrower and the merchant. Please don't borrow cash from your credit card account unless it is an absolute emergency! You should repay the amount as soon as possible.

Interest charged

Total interest charged in this billing period	$0.00

2019 totals year-to-date

Total fees charged in 2019	$0.00
Total interest charged in 2019	$107.14

Interest charge calculation

Days in billing cycle: **33**

Your **Annual Percentage Rate (APR)** is the annual interest rate on your account.

Balance type	Annual percentage rate (APR)	Balance subject to interest rate	Interest charge
PURCHASES			
Standard Purch	12.24% (V)	$0.00 (D)	$0.00
ADVANCES			
Standard Adv	27.49% (V)	$0.00 (D)	$0.00

Credit Card Bonus Points: Do not forget to redeem your bonus points. You should apply bonus points to your balance instead of buying something with them on impulse. I've worked with multiple clients who forgot this credit card reward and when discovered reduced their balance owed!

Log on to your credit card's website and locate the procedure for redeeming points.

Do Read your statement to discover if your credit card is changing its billing, interest, or "details" about your account. Credit card companies often change the rules of the game in the middle of the game. In addition, if you see unacceptable terms, I suggest you transfer to a new card. If you have bad credit, you won't be able to apply for a new, better card.

ThankYou Points Earned This Period

2x on Dining	497
2x on Entertainment	0
1x on Other Purchases	2,390
Total Earned	**2,887**

» Visit
to redeem points or see
full rewards details.

Bonus Points may take one to two billing cycles to appear on your statement. Please refer to the specific terms and conditions pertaining to the promotion for further details.

Important Changes to Your Account Terms
The following is a summary of changes being made to your account terms. Your Citi Flex Plan APR is changing to align with your APR for Purchases. These changes will take effect on September 02, 2019. For more information, please see **"Details About the Changes"** below.

The current *Interest Rates and Interest Charges* section of the Fact Sheet (Pricing Information Table) will be revised as follows:

Revised Terms as of September 02, 2019	
APR for Citi Flex Plan	**12.24%** This APR will vary with the market based on the Prime Rate.

The current Details About *Your Interest Rates and Interest Calculations* section of the Fact Sheet (Pricing Information Table) will be revised as follows:

Details About Your Interest Rates and Interest Calculations	Periodic Rate as of 06/24/2019	For variable rates: U.S. Prime Rate Plus
Citi Flex Plan APR	0.03353% (D)	6.74%

Do you want to have a credit card? Remember, The Golden Rule says, "Those that have the Gold make the Rules". If you don't like the rules, then it's not mandatory that you must have a credit card. Please understand that credit cards are real debt contracts.

Beware of Grey charges: These are repetitive charges to your card that never go away even after you cancel them, such as your magazine, free trial, or software subscriptions among others. You can fight this abuse by checking your credit card statement at least monthly. Many credit cards allow you to dispute charges online by simply following the credit card companies dispute process. If you carry a zero balance, cancel any credit card that continues to bill you for disputed charges. Don't do business with a credit card company that does not play fair. CITI card allows you to file the dispute online with no hassle. You can also contact the vendor. You should cancel that unused, unwanted, unneeded magazine and online video streaming subscription or similar liabilities now. However, consumer aware, the vendor may turn on their heavy sales pitch to convince you to keep whatever service they are selling.

I'm a bad boy! Another way to remove gray charges is to ask your credit card company to issue a new card as if you were reporting your credit card as lost or stolen. Have your card replaced with a new card that comes with a new card number. This will automatically make most grey charges disappear. Remember, though, update any accounts that you want to keep. This strategy can help you discover unnecessary charges lurking in the background.

Updated Development I have noticed recently is that subscriptions transfer from the expired card to the new card without your permission. I told you credit card companies are sneaky!

Children with credit cards to access Online Video Games.

There are many stories on the Internet sharing the traps developed by the gaming industry. It is a free country. Adults are free to max out their credit card dressing their character in a video game. But what if I tell you that children under 18 play video games allowed by their parent and then rack up thousands of dollars in credit card bills by purchasing additional "In App" purchases? "Gaming is a World of Heavy Sales Pressure and Frictionless Theft," says Evan V. Simon. Parents discovered the charges of their children, which resulted in financial hardship for years. There are no safeguards with online gaming No cashier to stop reckless spending. There is no tangible product to return to the store for a refund.

Online gaming addiction is a problem. Free mobile games make most of their money from "In app" purchases from compulsive customers, says Simon.

In Fortnite you can buy virtual clothes to upscale your character. You can play the game free forever, but if you want "Bling" you can buy a Battle Pass or Battle Bundle. Kids racked over $4,000 in charges without realizing and created a credit card statement with many pages filled with many one and five dollar charges.

Credit Card Disputes

Credit cards have protections for its customers. If you received a good or service not as promised and the vendor does not want to remedy the situation, contact your credit card company and dispute the charge. They may send you an application to fill out to explain the product or service you purchased and the nature of your dissatisfaction. Many credit card companies give you an immediate credit of your dispute until they resolve the dispute. The vendor tells their side of the story so the process can take 30-45 days. If the credit card company agrees with you, the temporary credit becomes permanent. The letter here is an example of a credit card dispute letter regarding an auto repair that went bad. You should respond clearly, accurately and proactively when mistreated by a vendor. In the situation mentioned below, my client was told to "pound sand" by the dealership service manager. Here an independent auto mechanic verified my client's findings. The result is that the bank refunded the

Credit Card Dispute Letter March 17, 2008

RE:

As per customer agent discussion on March 12, 2008:
Please find a complete explanation of disputed charge.

Brought car to ████████ to repair oil leak. As indicated on repair estimate, I indicated an oil leak coming from the back of the engine. The service writer, Daniel, asked if I had performed very specific scheduled services. I said, no, I am here to fix the oil leak first. The service writer, before seeing the car intimated that neglecting to perform a timing chain replacement, along with certain oil seals, and replacing the water pump would stop the leak. These are all items at the front of the engine! After the mechanic Cliff, inspected the car, he diagnosed that the valve cover gaskets were leaking and that was the cause of the oil draining down the back of the engine. The mechanic stated that repairing the valve cover gaskets, along with scheduled maintenance service totaling over $1,200 would repair the problem. I considered them the experts and approved the repairs. (Please review the repair estimate. I do not have a copy that I signed authorizing a repair of the vehicle. This maybe the deal breaker right here!) 3 and one half weeks later I still had the same symptoms. I waited to see if the burnt oil smell would disappear after repairs were done. They did not. On 1/21/07 (see attached report) another mechanic verified that original problem not repaired. He discovered a leaking head gasket that had been leaking for some time. See attached 2nd opinion of mechanic indicating these initial repairs were irrelevant for the leaking head gasket. I was billed $1,200 for irrelevant repairs and to had to return the car to the dealer to repair what should have been diagnosed and repaired correctly the first time. I am paying for their mistake. In fact, I found a website www.subaruheadgasket.com that indicates that this is a very common problem with my year and model of Subaru and described symptoms exactly as mine. It would seem the experts would be aware of this problem. In fact the service manager, Rene told me, "They have been repairing a lot of these." So why was it so difficult to properly diagnose my problem in the first place?.....the experts did not find it. That's the problem. In addition when I went back the second time to Palm Chrysler Subaru to repair the head gasket, Subaru corporation participated in paying for one half (admitting design flaw) of the head gasket repair. If the diagnosis had been correct in the first place, would have Subaru Corporation helped in the overall repair? We will never know. I got stuck with the bill.

In addition, the engine overhaul was done hastily. After one week I discovered the air conditioning inoperative and a few days later, the car stalled completely with a code for a defective crank sensor. I had the car towed back to the dealership at my expense for warranty repair. I left the auto with them a week to make certain it was repaired properly. The entire time, there was no admission of wrongdoing and the statement preceded every explanation, "We will have to check to verify what your saying is true." Every time! They admitted nothing and I received no apology for their negligence!

The reason I did not report this sooner as I thought disputing the charge would jeopardize a competent repair job. They would have also refused to refund my towing bill. I also risked losing the car to the shop if the dealership considered my dispute a reason of non-payment. I could not risk either circumstance. Yes, believe it or not, a repair estimate starting on Dec. 26, 2007 was not officially completed until I received the towing reimbursement on March 12, 2007. (Please see attached check stub.)

My goal is to have the disputed charges refunded to my account. I spoke with the general manager, Troy, on March 13, 2007, and he told me to get lost! The repairs of 12-26-2007 were irrelevant to the leaking head gasket that a second mechanic had to locate. His second opinion response agrees that the Dec. 26, 2007 repairs were irrelevant and says so on his letterhead. I have done everything AAA credit card has asked to resolve this situation.

20

charges and another letter to the Subaru corporation resulted in a cash settlement.

In Conclusion

Credit cards are powerful. When used responsibly with planning and discipline, they can make your financial life very convenient. In addition, responsible use of credit cards allows you to pay for goods and services without risking your checking account balance. You should locate and visit your local credit union. Relative to other financial institutions, credit unions tend to look out for your best interest.

Chapter 2

Abusing Personal Loans

"A bank is a place that will lend you money if you can prove that you don't need it."

Bob Hope

Personal loans are the fastest-growing consumer debt product, according to lendingtree.com. The average personal loan balance in the US is $9,000. Personal Loans represent another credit product that encourages borrowers to borrow more money to pay off other debt. (You have heard the phrase, Borrow from Peter to pay Paul). Banks and Loan Companies offer personal loans for home improvement, debt consolidation, loan consolidation, or moving expenses. Unfortunately, folks take out personal loans to pay for vacays or other non-essential expenses. Paying for luxuries with borrowed money is **Not WalletWise!** Most consumers borrow a personal loan for debt consolidation of credit cards. The difference between credit cards and personal loans is that credit cards are revolving credit accounts. You pay a specific minimum payment, but not the total charge that month. The credit card balance rolls or "revolves" to the next month. Personal loans do not revolve. A personal loan has a fixed interest rate, and a fixed monthly payment allowing for easier budgeting. Personal loans, like credit cards, do not need collateral. A personal loan is a suitable tool to manage debt. The average interest rate for a personal loan in 2020 was 9.34%, which is less than the average credit card rate of 14.65%. Another advantage of the personal loan is the inability to use it to pay more expenses. You cannot carry a personal loan around with you in your pocket and buy something new like you can with a credit card. The problem is that some borrowers use their credit card again now that the credit card balance is zero.

Credit Creep

Several of my Financial Coaching clients have borrowed personal loans to pay off credit card debt. In two cases specifically, after securing a personal loan to pay off credit cards, they began using their credit card again to fill in the gap between their income and expenses. Many borrowers pay off their credit cards but never change their flawed spending habits (see Chapter One, "Credit Card Debts"). Please change your spending habits after you pay off the credit card debt. If you use a personal loan to pay off your credit card, please reread Chapter One, "Credit Cards", to decide if you are responsible enough to carry and use a credit card. If not, physically cut the card so you do not continue to spend, spend, spend. If you don't stop using your credit card, "credit creep" starts over again. If you continue to use and abuse your credit card after you have paid it in full with a personal loan, you will have both the personal loan and the credit card to pay off. In this sub optimal situation, debt ratios are too high, and you cannot borrow any more money. Your debt amount spirals higher. You robbed Peter to pay Paul, then borrowed more money from Paul. You are between a rock and a financially hard place. If you continue this pattern, then bankruptcy is a possibility (Sometimes a necessary solution).

Last Word about Credit Creep

When you consolidate your credit card debt with a personal loan to pay off your credit cards, take the credit cards, put them in a sandwich bag and put them in the freezer. That's right. You should put those cards on ice. If you cannot control your spending habits and credit card use, then cut up the cards. Please refer to Chapter One, "Credit Card Debts" for more tips on how you can manage and pay down credit card debt.

Lending Moves Online

Data from a TransUnion study, dated February 2019, shows online Fintech (financial technology companies, or alternative online direct lenders, lead the way in the record-breaking 156-billion-dollar personal loan industry. In 2018, Fintech outpaced commercial banks for a personal loan origination.

Fintech financing is popular because of the simple application process. You have access to more debt after a few clicks on your computer screen. Most online personal loans have no origination, prepayment, or late fees. That is good for you when you need a personal loan. It is also a double-edge sword because the process may help you borrow more than you can afford to repay.

Easy to apply. Easy to borrow. Easy to spend. Repeat! That's the American way! I say this because many personal loan consumers have more than one personal loan at a time.

Who are the companies in this business? One company I see advertising in this space is SoFi. SoFi looks for a minimum credit score of 680 and charges between 5.99% and 17.67% (at publication). LendingTree and Best Egg are popular. Credit Karma attracts  users through offering free current credit scores and budget tools to entice you to borrow. A top-rated company is Laurel Road. You will need a minimum 700 credit score and the interest rate ranges from 8% to 16.3%. Marcus, a new division of the investment bank Goldman Sachs, only needs a 660-credit score but charges up to 28.99% interest. Avant only needs a "mirror warming" 580 credit score charging up to 35.9% interest. That is outrageous. What is the Rule of 72? This formula calculates how long it will take the lender to double their money. 72 divided by 36% interest suggests Avant doubles its money every two years.

Checking your rate will not affect your credit score. If you chose to apply for a loan; however, we will request a hard credit pull from one or more consumer reporting agencies, which may affect your credit score." Sofi.com website

SoFi advertises if you lose your job, they will pause your payments and help you find another job. Wow, that is service!

Many legitimate lenders allow you to apply for a loan by prequalifying. Pre-qualify for the loan means to begin the process online without entering a final agreement. The lender performs a "soft inquiry" on your credit record, allowing you to compare interest rates and payment options without affecting your credit score. There is no "hard inquiry" until you think the lender is making you a reasonable offer. Then you will go ahead through the process online, and when you are ready to move forward with the final agreement, then the lender will do a "hard inquiry" to your credit report. The credit bureau reports the "hard inquiry" in your credit report, and it might affect your credit score.

See Chapter Thirteen, Credit Reports and FICO Scores.

Continue the 15-minute process if the terms are acceptable and receive your money within ten days. I plugged my information into the SoFi website to receive an interest rate quote. The interest rate offered, for a $25,000 unsecured personal loan, was between 8.77% and 10.40%. That's not terrible.

I do not recommend using online personal loan lenders. They are not well-regulated, and you may not be borrowing the money from whom you think you are getting it. Many online lenders don't lend but connect you to the lender based on your financial situation. The terms and conditions are difficult to determine.

Barbarians at The Bank: Many popular Fintech companies, by design, want you to borrow more than you can afford. In an interview, a FinTech CEO described his "typical" consumer, who is 46 years old, is an individual that has liabilities that exceed assets, and carries $15,000 plus in credit card debt. This is the definition of a predatory lender. Their business model succeeds when you become insolvent. These same people lobby Congress to change banking rules, so debt collectors can collect interest rates and penalties different from what you agreed to.

Should you consolidate your credit card debt? The answer is a firm, maybe. If you have the discipline to borrow a personal loan to pay off high interest credit cards, then a personal loan is a valid tool. If you are using personal loans to pay essential expenses or luxuries you cannot afford, then you should not use this tool.

I recommend going to your local credit union or community bank to apply for a credit card consolidation personal loan. I also recommend getting your credit card from your credit union.

Try this calculator from FICO to see if a debt consolidation loan makes sense. https://www.myfico.com/credit-education/financial-calculators/should-i-consolidate-my-credit-cards

Please do not confuse personal unsecured loans or debt consolidation loans (which do not use collateral) with home equity loans. The reason I mention this here is that I recently received this confusing flier in the mail.

The title is right. Not all debt is the same. The problem here is that they are advertising a home equity loan (which uses your home as collateral) and comparing it to the interest rates charged by unsecured personal loans. That is comparing apples and oranges. The reason personal loan debt charges higher interest is that the debt is unsecured (no collateral needed). The lender of a personal loan is taking on more risk and requires a higher payment in interest to reward the lender's added risk.

The Takeaway here is to not allow a flier in the mail to motivate you to do business with a company. Instead, you should be proactive and visit your local credit union.

Chapter 3

Payday Loans, Rent to Own and More

"Lenders, including major credit companies as well as
payday lenders, have taken the over the traditional role of
the street corner loan shark, charging the poor insanely
high rates of interest.

Barbara Ehrenreich

Payday Loans, Pawn Shop loans, tax refund advances, checking account overdrafts, car title loans, rent to own furniture stores, retail store credit cards, prepaid credit cards, store check cashing service are just some forms of "predatory" lending that hurt consumers and earned the industry over **180 billion dollars** in fees and interest in 2018.

"By definition, predatory lending benefits the lender and ignores or hinders the borrower's ability to repay the debt. These lending tactics often try to take advantage of a borrower's lack of understanding about loans, terms or finances."

https://www.debt.org/credit/predatory-lending/

These financial products are predatory because they offer us services at outrageous fees to take advantage of our desperate financial situation. These companies entice us with no or low-down payment and low monthly payments. Unknowingly we accept a financial agreement that charges us nosebleed interest rates and excessive fees. These businesses prey on people with little or no cash. We feel like there are no alternatives, so we must do business with these "sharks". Fortunately, there are positive alternatives to predatory service providers.

Predatory Shark	Positive Alternative
Payday Loans	Credit Union, or Digital Bank *Dave* or MoneyLion
Pawn Shop	Family Loan
Tax Refund Loan	File Your Taxes ASAP to get your refund deposited to your account
Checking Account Overdrafts	Don't use checks when there are no funds.
Car Title Loans	Credit Union Emergency Loan
Rent to Own Furniture	• Buy furniture cash from a 2nd hand furniture store. • Buy furniture from a Goodwill or Salvation Army retail store for cash.
Retail Store Credit Card	Shop for what you need at a secondhand shop or thrift store.

Positive Alternatives

Fortunately, there are alternatives. Instead of heading out to the nearest buy here, pay here furniture store, please check out your local thrift stores. Can you go online and check out Facebook Marketplace? You should try visiting yard sales and get necessities for pennies on the dollar. Yes, go to yard sales in affluent neighborhoods. You will find great items at a superb price. Try Craigslist. My daughter uses Craigslist's "items for free" section to give away unused furniture when moving from an apartment. You can use this service to get stuff for your crib.

Underserved Consumers (who cannot afford normal banking services), pay over $173 Billion in fees and interest to predatory lenders, according to the Center for Financial Services Innovation organization.

Retail Credit Card

I walked into a major clothes retail store to buy two pairs of slacks and when I went to the register to pay; they interrogated me about my desire to get a store retail card. I qualified for 90% off my purchase and elves would clean my house for the next month! Retail credit cards are another type of predatory lending. They offer low credit lines that put you in a high credit use ratio. This is BAD. This affects your credit score adversely. In addition, you give the store permission to bombard you with special deals only available to the credit card holder, encouraging you to buy more stuff you don't need. They come with interest rates between twenty and thirty percent. This means when you carry a balance for 2.4 years and you will end up paying double for your purchase. How's that 10% discount sounding now?

The fees collected from Retail Store credit cards top 38 billion dollars, and by a huge margin, make the most money when compared to Subprime and Secured credit cards. Seventy two percent of retail cards do not base their APR interest rate on your creditworthiness. You could have great credit and you are still getting robbed.

Your clothes shop says thank you!!

Have you ever tried to pay for gas on the side of the road with a store credit card? Um... It doesn't work. Retail store cards have limited usage. Remember, the interest rate for a credit card with no balance is zero percent! That's my favorite interest rate! Zero. If you insist on using a store credit card, pay it off in full each month so they do not charge you interest.

https://www.thebalance.com/retail-credit-card-drawbacks-961131

https://www.investopedia.com/financial-edge/0511/store-credit-card-traps-to-avoid.aspx

https://ptmoney.com/store-credit-cards/

Sub-prime Credit Card

Have you toasted your Credit Score? Is it below 600? When you need a credit card, your low credit score will limit you to a subprime credit card. These credit cards charge high interest rates (average 25%), low credit line ($200 to $300) and my favorite part... wait for it... You get to pay a security deposit. The better cards charge a Program Fee. You will get a bump in your credit line after you pay five or six months of payments on time. Most have a large annual fee between $75 and $100.

A Better Alternative

Another type of credit card is the Secured Credit Card. Your security deposit will become your credit limit. When you repay the card balance, the bank refunds your deposit. That's good. You don't need a credit score and these cards report to credit bureaus, which may help your credit score increase if you repay as promised. The better card companies link a savings account to your secured card. Your credit line is the amount you have in your savings account. We call it collateral! That is okay, too.

It is best to use secured credit cards to rebuild your credit score when your credit score needs repair. At the time of writing, Capital One and Discover offer the best in this category.

Consider a Prepaid Debit Card instead.

Why consider a prepaid card? These cards offer lower fees and serve as a replacement to a traditional bank account. They accept direct deposits. There is no credit check. That is because you load your funds on them in advance. This is a great budget enforcer too. Some companies offering these services at the time of writing include Wells Fargo, Greenlight, Simple, Fifth Third bank, and more. You should check out www.nerdwallet.com and search for prepaid debit cards for the latest information. Try Walmart's MoneyCard. This card is affordable and is feature packed.

Checking Account Overdraft

Hard to believe that financial research organizations like the Financial Health Network consider Checking Account overdraft fees a type of loan! I never thought of overdraft fees as a financial product, but vulnerable consumers use them as short-term loans. When you bounce a check, and the bank honors the check, you are borrowing money from the bank without pre-approval. Banks charge Americans (on average $35, creating $34 billion in overdraft fees in 2019.

Another sobering statistic is that eight percent of consumers pay 75% of overdraft fees. This means that these folks paid over $24.5 billion in fees to repay ten or more overdraft situations. Yes, that means eight percent of overdraft fee payers paid ten overdraft fees in one year.

Ally Financial's CEO, Jeffrey Brown said *"It is time to end them,"* in a press release. "Ninety-five percent of the consumers who paid $12.4 billion in overdraft fees in 2020 were ""financially vulnerable"" and disproportionately Black and Latino, according to the 2021 *Fin Health Spend Report."*

The Consumer Financial Protection Bureau puts it this way: Let's say they charged you a $34 fee for being overdrawn by $24, and it took you three days to pay that overdrawn amount back. That's the same as taking out a loan with a 17,000% annual percentage rate. I'm sorry, that APR is ridiculous.

Look, everyone makes a mistake, but overdraft fees are suboptimal to your finances. No one signs up for a 17,000% interest rate. Ask for the overdraft policy from your checking account bank. You must know this. Set up your checking account so that if there is not enough money to honor the check, then the bank should not pay it. Not the best alternative, because this solution supports the dangerous habit of writing bad checks, but you can sign up for overdraft protection that links to your checking account that raids your savings account when your checking account occurs an overdraft. Sign up for account alerts to help protect you from overdraft fees. You should immediately deposit the funds into your checking account to avoid overdraft fees. Some banks do not charge an overdraft fee when you immediately deposit funds to cover the overdraft.

If you use a debit card as your checking account, tell your bank to opt **out**. Your ATM will say no to your withdrawal request. Good! That's okay. For emergencies always have emergency cash hidden on your person...

Better Alternatives

Try the App *Dave*. (https://www.dave.com/ It's a bank in the form of a computer application that adheres to your budget and provides **no** interest pay day loans. It does not require a credit check. It tracks your rent to help increase your credit score. The app charges $1.00 per month. That's a good thing.

The free "Mint" App allows you to set account balance alerts. Come to think of it, so does my bank. So set an alert!

Rent to Own Furniture Store

Please do not use a Rent to Own furniture store because they charge, normally, 100% interest. That means at that interest rate, the company doubles their money in 9 months.

Your rent to own furniture store says thank you for your business!!

In fact, the rent to own furniture industry says thank you very much. Targeting low-income earners, RTO (Rent To Own stores collect over 8.6 billion dollars in revenue. The most popular items they supply are TV's, sofas, and washing machines. For example, research at one rent to own store, advertises a sixty-five inch Samsung TV for $39.95 per week rent price. It also lists six months, same as cash price of $2,184. I found it on Amazon for $1,399! Clicking view details states you will own the set after 91 payments (21 months at a grand total of $3639. And what is that TV worth after almost two years???? A used TV is not worth much.

Authorities documented and accused rent to own businesses of illegal collection practices. For example, in Florida, rent to own stores prosecuted 3000 people in the past ten years for failing to return merchandise. Because of poor RTO bookkeeping, these bogus collection practices damaged customers' credit profiles.

A 2015 Federal Trade Commission report states that some RTO stores are selling used items. They remind consumers that besides the high interest rates, RTO stores tack on fees for setup and delivery, and of course late payment fees.

Fingerhut: "Get the Credit you Deserve"

Fingerhut charges 29.99% on purchases. This is not a good way to get stuff! This company makes the bulk of its revenue from finance charges and high shipping charges. This company services customers who have little cash, or damaged credit.

Better Alternatives

If you need something like a TV, washing machine or furniture and you cannot afford it, it's time to get creative. Check out thrift shops and local Salvation Army and Goodwill stores. My mother bought my wife and me, when we were starting out, a nice wooden dining room set for $100 from a thrift store. Used furniture is very inexpensive. Check out Craig's List "Free." People are giving away perfectly good furniture because they are moving and don't need it and cannot afford to take the time to sell it. These same items maybe garage sale leftovers. That is fortunate for you. Garage sales are a great place to stretch a dollar. Check with churches in your area that may have members ready to help you fill a furniture need.

Consider trying a reputable store that will provide "in store" financing. Some stores offer ninety days, same as cash. You should also consider lay-away. You get your merchandise after you have paid in full!

When you research the item online, which you would like to purchase, check coupon sites to find codes and discounts. Go to Amazon or eBay online to find the best deals. Leave an item in your online shopping cart, but don't pull the trigger. Wait for several days to see if the vendor offers you a discount on the item sitting in the shopping cart. I have tried it and it works occasionally.

Family-Owned Furniture Stores

If you must borrow to buy furniture, consider finding a local family run business store. Some of them have credit accounts with reasonable payments and interest payments. Be careful of furniture stores referring you to their recommended lender. Their recommended lender may have similar characteristics as a store credit card. They may charge up to 30% interest rates.

Pay Day Loan

After you're done at the furniture store, you need a pay day loan because at the end of the month you may have more "month than money". That pay day loan will cost you approximately 300% in Florida. But Ken, those friendly people only charge me $12.00 per $100. That's 12%. Wrong. They are charging you 12% over a two-week period. You must repay the payday loan within fourteen days… seven days is better. If paid in fourteen days, that equates to 12% every two weeks. Fifty-two weeks per year divided by two means Twenty-six periods. Twenty-six periods times 12% = 312%! That is over 300% per year. We compare interest rates per year, not bi-weekly.

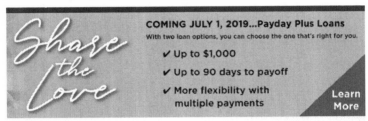

I add this friendly graphic to share with you how the payday loan industry puts "lipstick on the pig".

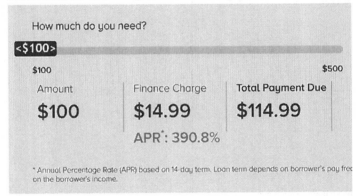

Here are screen shots of calculators from two online payday loan companies. 390% APR in red. That is not good for your wallet.

This means the payday loan business doubles its money every 3 months!

According to the Federal Reserve, twelve million adults use payday loans. The average borrower takes out eight $375 loans per year and spends $520 on interest according to the Pew Trust. Many payday loan businesses target customers encountering an emergency when, in fact, 69% of borrowers used their payday loan to cover every day recurring expenses.

The point is to not use payday loan services. If you have an emergency, it may be best to ask family or friends. This method of financing your emergency is suboptimal but is better than going to a payday loan company. Finance companies design pay day loan companies for consumers with bad credit. Customers must have a job and a bank account to pay back the loan. Beware of the debt trap payday loan companies create with their offer of extensions and refinancing the original payday loan when you find you don't have enough money to repay.

Better Alternatives

1. Ask your employer for an advance on your pay. Wal-Mart employees have access to the *EVEN* app that allows Wal-Mart employees to get a cash advance on their future earnings.

2. Open an online checking account with *DAVE, CHIME* or *MoneyLion.* They offer a cash advance feature for their account holders in good standing.

3. Ask your bank or credit union for a short-term loan.

4. Consider borrowing money from friends or family.

5. Locate the Federal Low Income home emergency assistance agency in your community.

6. Ask a local church that is willing and able to assist you with a legitimate emergency.

Pay Day Loan Online Lenders from TV Advertisements

As I am watching a sports channel, a commercial shows two buffoons staring at two flat tires when another buffoon, dressed in a t-shirt and cape from a bad Halloween costume, reports the advantages of borrowing from an online lender. They promise money to you the next day; the commercial offers a promo code. They are an online payday loan company with fees up to 600% APR. They neglect to mention that in the TV commercial.

This is not good for your wallet.

Check Cashing Service

Another financial land mine is the "Check Cashing Store". Check Cashing stores cash your government, payroll, and personal checks for an outrageous fee. The fee charged is between one percent and five percent. That equates to $50.00 for a $1,000 check! If you are in California, the fee is 12%. An unregulated state has no fee restriction. How much are you willing to pay?

Better Alternatives

The solution is Walmart. They charge $4.00 to cash a check and can put the money into a Walmart Gift card at no charge. Another alternative to check cashing business is a prepaid card program. Consider the Walmart MoneyCard Visa, https://www.walmart.com/cp/walmart-moneycard/1073524. The Walmart MoneyCard is a prepaid card program. You deposit money into the account, and they issue you a card backed by Green Dot Bank. Your card can be a VISA or Mastercard. It looks like a credit card, but it is not. You can earn cash back and get paid early with their proprietary ASAP, Direct Deposit. Walmart claims you will get paid up to 2 days before payday. There are no overdraft or monthly fees. There is no reload fee. There is a convenient phone app. Another great Walmart feature is they have a check cashing service that is affordable. They can load the money onto your MoneyCard.

Car Title Loan

Here is another popular predatory lending choice. You can hock your car title. The Car Title lending industry lends money against your debt free car title. So, if you purchased a car cash as I recommend in Chapter 15, you can give up the car title as collateral for money. The average car title loan in the US is less than $1,000. According to the Pew research group, the fees for borrowing $1,000 will cost you $1,200. Borrow $1,000. Repay $2,200! This is not a good deal! Most folks pay back their loans in four months. That is close to 300% interest annualized. Seventy percent of car title loans are renewals. You do not repay what you owe. The dealer allows you to reset the debt clock. This means you extend the original terms, incur more fees, and increase the chance of default and losing your car.

Pawn Shops

Everybody's Favorite Bank! I used a pawn shop once. I was in business for myself. I had few lines of credit. I was expecting several business projects to pay off in the next thirty days, and a popular speaker in my industry invited me to an expensive seminar that started within a few days. I pawned an expensive camera lens. I used the money borrowed from the pawnshop to pay for the seminar. I thought it was "worth it". My projects paid off, and I repaid the loan within thirty days. To the sad sighs of the pawnshop owner, I repossessed my lens. It worked out that time.

For many people, pawn shops become their bank of choice. 30 million Americans use pawn shops each year. Many pawn shop customers do not have traditional checking and savings accounts. Many go to pawn shops to borrow small amounts of money. The average pawn shop loan is $150. Have something of value to pawn? Valuable electronics, jewelry, tools, firearms and musical instruments are the most popular pawned items. You will not receive what your item is worth. You get about 20% of the item value. Interest rates range between 120-300%. The average pawn shop fees and interest are 240%.

Home Improvement Hacks.

Did you know you could finance the air conditioning system in your home with the A/C contractor? If you miss enough payments according to the contract, then the A/C contractor may repossess your outside compressor until you have fulfilled the contract.

https://wsvn.com/news/help-me-howard/can-you-repossess-an-appliance/

Personal Note

I sold my rental property to a handyman that had little or no credit. A mistake I regret. He hired a predatory air conditioning contractor to install a central air conditioning system. The contractor sold the system for little money down and a high interest repayment plan. Within a year the owner of the house defaulted on the air conditioning loan and the A/C company came and repossessed everything. They not only repossessed the outside compressor, but they repossessed the air handler inside and the **ductwork** inside the house! This left gaping holes throughout the interior of the house. It was criminal. Was it illegal to do that...? Back then... who knows? In rural America it was the Wild, Wild West.

Lucky enough to have a 401k?

Let's borrow money from our 401k account! This is a poor decision on two fronts. First, you incur high fees and second, you lose the impact of compounding on your retirement account! This is not smart! Here is an online calculator to calculate your losses from borrowing from your 401k.

https://www.bankrate.com/calculators/retirement/borrow-from-401k-calculator.aspx

Make sure you don't want to change jobs. Most employers need immediate payment of the 401k upon your departure.

If you don't pay it back, then the IRS gets into your life and treats your cash withdrawal as an early 401k distribution, complete with income tax and a 10% early withdrawal penalty.

The financial management industry collects approximately two billion dollars in fees from folks who borrow from their 401k.

The biggest drawback from withdrawing money from your 401k is that you lose the investment potential or leverage of compounding interest. If you borrow half of your 401k, depending upon the term of the loan, you could lose 60% of your accounts earning potential. This is a choice, but please find an alternative to robbing your nest egg. Don't use your 401k to prevent bankruptcy. Bankruptcy protects retirement accounts.

This book does not give you legal advice. You should consult your attorney or accountant for 401k advice. Please don't rely on this book for legal advice.

In Conclusion

You should not fall prey to predatory lenders. Even though you feel you cannot afford any alternatives to easy financing, the opposite is true. You may remain in poverty if you are not careful with your finances. You should stay away from easy, but ultimately expensive, financing. You should not purchase furniture at a Rent To Own store. You should not buy a car from a buy here "pay here" car lot. You should not upgrade the wheels of your car using a buy here pay here wheel and tire shop. Pay day loans charge up to 300% interest annually. You should not use a check cashing company to cash your checks.

Instead, you should check out https://www.walmart.com/cp/walmart-moneycenter/5433. Walmart designed its financial services department for everyday people. Walmart offers credit cards, reloadable debit cards, reasonably priced check cashing services, tax preparation services, gift cards, and domestic and international Money Transfers. Let's go to Walmart!

Chapter 4

Avoiding the Mistake of Debt Settlement and Debt Consolidation Companies

"The only man who sticks closer to you in adversity than a friend is a creditor."

Anonymous

Let's Clear the Air with a Few Definitions

Debt Settlement Company—Offers, for a fee, to renegotiate some of your debts, collect a single payment from you, and pay your debts.

Debt Relief Company—Same as Above, Debt Settlement Company.

Debt Consolidation Company—Combine and wrap up all of your unsecured debts into a new loan.

Debt Collection Company—Hired by lenders and creditors to collect an unpaid debt from you.

Debt Settlement/Relief Companies

Who are the companies advertising on the radio and late-night TV promising to reduce or remove your credit card debt? Are they legitimate companies designed to create a debt repayment plan suitable to your situation? Are these companies providing a legitimate solution to solve your debt problem.

Most are scams eager to take what little money you have left. The advertising implies that you will eliminate your credit card debt with little or no consequences. This is simply not true. Debt settlement companies charge you a fee for their service anywhere from 15 to 20% of your debt. From the beginning you, end up paying 15-20% more than you owe. They claim: 1) they lower your interest rate; 2) there is no tax implication; 3) they offer affordable solutions. Unfortunately, this is not true. Most debt relief customers do not complete their program.

Debt settlement companies often tell their customers to stop paying your debt; instead make your payments to the settlement company. Once they have collected their fee, they disappear, leaving you dealing with your creditors. Your debt is now higher because of late fees and penalties. Many debt settlement companies are scams.

Debt settlement/relief companies create a debt repayment plan, and you pay one monthly payment deposited in a savings account the debt relief company charges you for. They pay your bills. These programs deliberately default on your debt to secure a better chance to lower the balance you owe. Unfortunately, that wrecks your credit. The debt relief company then contacts your creditors after you have defaulted on your debt. The debt relief company then tells your creditor that you are one step away from bankruptcy and it would be better if the creditor settled for a smaller dollar amount than accept nothing if you declare bankruptcy. The debt relief company keeps 20-25% of your debt as payment.

Don't fall for these scams.

It is interesting to find that some debt settlement companies and debt collectors work together. In fact, there are companies with both departments under the same roof.

Debt Buyers and Settlement companies made over $3.5 billion last year settling debt. Some publicly traded companies combine debt collection and debt settlement under the same roof! Is this a conflict of interest? It may be, but this business model is legal. Debt collection companies use computer generated behavioral and statistical data to decide if you are a suitable candidate for paying your bad debt! This means they are looking for consumers who can stay afloat with as much debt as possible. Debt settlement companies consider them the best customers. When you cannot meet your agreements with the debt settlement company, they just send your file down the hallway; to debt collections. I implore you to stay away from too much debt, debt settlement companies, and Debt Collectors.

When should you seek debt settlement/relief?

Never!

- Seek bankruptcy when it appears you cannot pay off your unsecured debt (credit cards, personal loans, and medical bills) within the next five years. The total of your unsecured debt equals 50% or more of your gross income.

- Consider a Debt Management plan. Nonprofits like American Consumer Credit Counseling provide free advice and affordable Debt Management Plans.

You should seek advice from an attorney. Please note: I do not provide legal advice in this book.

Instead, connect with the Financial Counseling Association of America or the National Foundation for Credit Counseling. These are legitimate financial educators providing credit, bankruptcy, housing, and Student Loan Counseling for free or at low cost.

Check them out at https://fcaa.org/ and https://www.nfcc.org/.

What should you know about Debt Consolidation Companies?

Debt consolidation companies wrap most of your unsecured debt (credit cards, personal loans, payday loans, medical billsinto a single loan. The debt consolidation company promises a lower payment. This may be true, but they depend upon your financial ignorance to get you a lower payment by extending the term or the length of the loan. Let's say you have $10,000 in combined credit card and personal loan debt. The payment total is $361. The debt consolidation company charges 9% interest and refinances your debt for five years. Your new payment is $207. A savings of $150 per month. Here is what they forget to tell you. Instead of being paid off and debt free in three years, you will pay the lower payment for an extra two years. The good news, in this situation, is you will save interest charges.

You do not need a Debt Consolidation Company

Debt consolidation is a strategy you can employ on your own. You can combine your credit card payments, personal loans, and any other high interest rate loans into one simple loan. The idea is to have one easy payment at a lower interest rate. The combination of loans results in an overall lower payment. Another possibility is to open a HELOC or Home Equity Line of Credit at a very low interest rate i.e. if you own your home and you have equity to borrow against. The "only" problem with this method is that you are using your home equity as an ATM. This became a hobby for millions of Americans in the early to middle 2000s and was a major contributor to the financial crisis of 2007-2008. You are putting your home at risk to reconfigure your debt. That could be a very good thing, or a very terrible thing. It depends if you can manage your expenses. If you pay off your high interest credit card debt with your new debt consolidation loan, and then celebrate by using your credit card again on unnecessary wants to fill up your garage, or go on a trip to Bermuda, then you are making a poor decision. I call this "credit creep." The credit card in your pocket with a zero balance is itching to buy more stuff. If you have the discipline to cut the card, not close the account, and spend no more (online, then this may be a solution. I hope you have the discipline to pay off your unsecured debt in full and stop borrowing from your credit card again. Learn to enjoy your newfound debt-consolidated life. Put any extra money you make into paying more on your debt consolidation loan.

Check out this calculator to see if consolidation from many cards to one card makes sense.

https://www.myfico.com/credit-education/financial-calculators/should-i-consolidate-my-credit-cards

Another choice is to open a new credit card account with a 0% balance transfer card. The lender may not charge you a balance transfer fee. I prefer doing business with a credit union. They charge lower inter-est rates besides having zero balance transfer plans. Transfer any expensive (high interest rate debt to your new "zero" balance low interest rate transfer card. This only makes sense if you can repay the debt before the promotional period expires. If you don't repay the debt before the promotional period ends, you will be obligated to pay all the accumulated interest from the day you transferred the debt. That is expensive! You must have the discipline to stop using the card to buy unnecessary wants.

Debt Management Companies

You may consider a nonprofit debt management company. Debt management companies normally charge $40.00 per month. The debt management solution dedicates a person to pay your debts. You send them a single check and they pay your bills. They may also renegotiate better interest rates. A debt management program can take three to five years to carry out. Look for these reliable, low-fee, debt management companies in most cities described as Credit Counseling Agencies. Most are nonprofit.

What are the alternatives to Debt Settlement/Relief?

1) **Negotiate a lump sum t**o pay the debt in full with your creditor. Negotiate on your behalf. You will need confidence to succeed at negotiation. If not, consider hiring a credit coun-selor to help negotiate for you. Settling for 40% to 50% of what you owe is realistic. Again, you may have to pay taxes on any forgiven debt above $600. In addition, negotiate how the debt agreement is reported on your credit report! Credit Report "Accounts" are called *Tradelines*. The rating you are looking for is "Paid as agreed". When you make the call, it is imperative you keep your emotions in check and be patient. It may take more than one call and more than one associate before you get a reasonable agreement. Don't forget to escalate the call and ask for a supervisor. Make sure you have an accurate financial hardship story ready for the call. If you can realistically pay 50% then start the negotiations below 50%. If you start at 50% there is no "wiggle" room. After you agree, it is imperative to agree in writing. Make sure the terms and conditions are under-standable, including how the debt is reported to your credit bureau. Don't default on your new agreement. If you do, "It's no Deal!" You are back to square one and you owe the entire balance. Isn't that special?! Remember that the creditor will

write off (charge off) any unpaid debt. The business writes the debt off of their income statement as a loss to subtract against their profits; Lowering their tax bill. Then they sell the unpaid accounts in a package deal to a debt broker. When this happens, the creditor will not sue you. Now a debt collector owns your debt and they will collect the debt.

2) Talk to your creditor about creating a "Repayment Plan." You will lose your credit line. Your credit score will drop. Again, ask the creditor to report nice things about you to the credit bureau. Ask the bank to lower the interest rate, monthly payment, and reverse any late fees or penalty fees.

3) Work out a forbearance agreement. What is forbearance? It is a legal term that means you ask your creditor to stop a collection action against you. If your situation is temporary, like a medical situation, creditors may reverse any late payments and penalties. They may suspend payments for a few months. There is no forgiveness of debt. Many creditors offered generous forbearance programs in response to COVID-19.

4) Find a financial counselor or financial coach to create a debt payoff plan. Create a debt payoff Plan. Connect with the FCAA or NFCC. These are legitimate financial educators providing credit, bankruptcy, housing, and Student Loan Counseling for free or at low cost.
Check them out at https://fcaa.org/ and https://www.nfcc.org/.

5) Consider Chapter 7 bankruptcy before getting involved in a Debt Settlement agreement. It's the most common form of bankruptcy, and it cancels unsecured debts without collateral. Chapter 7 includes credit cards, personal loans, and medical bills. Bankruptcy will stay on your credit report for 10 years. That's not good. It will prevent you from qualifying for certain jobs. When you borrow again your interest rates will be higher and you will not qualify for the lowest auto insurance rates as statistics show you are a more reckless driver. You may feel the impact of the social stigma of bankruptcy. You will need to pass a needs test. Active military and veterans have more lenient qualification standards. Again, I am not offering legal advice. Consult with an attorney to determine if you qualify.

Debt Collection Company: Debt collection companies buy debt from lenders who have given up collecting their unpaid debts. To a lender, a loan is an asset. If that loan is unpaid, the asset is worth zero. Tax laws allow the lender to write-off the bad debt on their taxes to offset income. This tax law motivates lenders to dispose of and write the bad debt off as a loss as soon as possible. Then the lender sells their bad debts to a collection agency for pennies on the dollar. The debt collection agency then contacts the original borrower to collect whatever they can get the borrower to pay. They only have pennies invested in each bad debt, so they only need a few people to agree to pay some part or most of their debt to be profitable. Debt collectors may call you and write a letter to collect the unpaid debt. Debt collectors can sue you to collect bad debts and file default judgements that show up in the public record. Default judgements are court orders to pay the debt. They can report the unpaid debt to the credit bureaus. Collectors in most states can garnish your wages. There are state and federal regulations affecting wage garnishment in your state. You should know your legal rights if threatened with garnishment.

In Conclusion

Members of humanity, for thousands of years, have reported that debt is bad for you. Ben Franklin said it well, "It is better to go to bed supperless, than to wake up in debt." You cannot borrow your way out of poverty, but you can sure borrow your way into it.

Chapter 5

Student Loans 2.0

"For-profit, higher education is today a booming industry feeding on the student loans handed out to the desperate."

Thomas Frank

Ahh, the thrill of attending college. It reminds me of the board game Life. The Game of Life gave you the chance to attend college and borrow student loan debt you repaid later, after you started earning big bucks. In the board game, you ended up with a higher paying job that offset the increased debt load you possessed compared to the player who went straight to work. By the end of the game, the college graduates usually finished the game of Life with the most assets. Oh my, have times changed.

Note to Reader: I will discuss alternatives to Student Loans later in this chapter. The following is a must read for future college students and parents.

C o l l e g e education costs, which include college tuition, college room and board and college supplies, have skyrocketed. Student loan amounts have ballooned to keep up with college costs. Even students who receive large financial aid packages, as scholarships from the college to pay the bills, still have to borrow enormous amounts of money to pay the bills. We leave these important decisions to 19 to 25-year-old students that have (according to the same intellectuals running the colleges) maturing brains. A friend of mine responded to this statement by asking, "For those first entering college, wouldn't you say a lot of those decisions are made together with parents? They're often the ones filling out financial aid paperwork, etc.?" My response is, "No. The admission counselors deliberately whisk away students from the parents at orientation to be sold <u>classes</u> the student may or may not need." This happened to my daughter. Survive this process by having an amazing relationship with your children and having a big conversation with your student before they enter the college admissions office by themselves. Independent adult creation is the goal. Parental supervision is no longer required. We think the advisor is our friend and expert when, in fact, the adviser is protecting the interests of the college. Your student may be inexperienced at this level of negotiations. I believe in teenagers becoming independent adults who learn by making mistakes. The college is negotiating with your student, which AP, IB, and AICE classes they will accept. It benefits the college to accept none of them so that the college can sell your child more classes. This is one reason it takes six years for your student to complete a four-year program. My daughter, entering University of South Florida, went to the admissions office without us and bought a German class even though she was a Francophile. She had taken French classes throughout high school. Why not be consistent with her past classes and take French? No, German. Well, it helped her sing the German pieces in the chorus. This story is humorous now, and not a big deal. Be careful, it could be much more serious. A friend of my daughter, in a public Florida University, was in the engineering program. One semester before he was ready to graduate, the University changed the graduation requirements of the degree. I suspect the University had an unpaid bill to pay and needed to raise extra revenue. My daughter's friend ended up enrolling for an added semester of courses to complete his degree. He had no other choice, but to pay the tuition for another semester. As I have mentioned in other sections of this book. Bankers, lawyers, real estate agents, and even college admission agents are not looking out for your best interest. They work under competing agendas. Caveat emptor! That is Latin for "Buyer Beware!"

A recent Wall Street article reports that most college freshmen do not have the emotional maturity to make complex financial and life decisions alone. So, what could go wrong? Plenty! College financing is more complicated than shopping for a mortgage. In college, they redo the finance paperwork every year!

Data analyzed from the Federal Reserve's 2018 survey on the Economic Well-Being of U.S. Households, reports over half of young adults who attended college, borrowed to pay for their education. Most borrowers stay current on their payments. Many borrowers paid their loans. However, twenty percent of debtors (those who owe money) are behind in their payments. Private college students and individuals who did not finish their degree program fare worse.

Fun Student Loan Fact

According to oneclass.com, fifty-seven percent of students that take on student loans don't graduate! And yes, the default rate of dropouts is higher than the default rate for graduates.

Most students financed their degrees with student loans. Other forms of debt included credit cards and home equity loans. Debt in 2018 ranged from $20,000 to $25,000. Combining federal and private debt, the debt level equates to $30,000 per student.

Among those making payments on their student loans, the typical median monthly payment is between $200 and $299 per month. The average payment per month is $393 per month. (This statistic is skewed because of expensive medicine and law degrees

First generation college students are more likely to be late in their payment. First generation borrowers under thirty years of age are twice as likely to be behind in their payments.

I've read many newspaper articles, online news, and blogs describing the experience of going to college, searching and finding a desirable field of study only to end up with a college degree that is useless (unmarketable) and a student saddled with $50,000, $60,000, even $90,000 in debt. The graduate struggles to make loan payments while driving a $500 car and living at home and working at a minimum wage job. Where did the money go? To the ivory tower. Colleges should be ashamed at what they are doing. JP Morgan Chairman and CEO Jamie Dimon called student lending in the U.S. a "disgrace" and said, "It's hurting America". They are setting up students for failure. The "Federal Student Loan Programs" fact sheet gives sage advice under the "How Much Should I Borrow?" paragraph. The fact sheet says to research your future career at https://www.bls.gov/ooh/ and find your salary. Then the fact sheet says your student loan payments should be a small percentage of your salary after you graduate. That completes the depth of the financial advice given by the FSA (Federal Student Aid) about "student borrowing" common sense. There is no discussion of the possibility of changing your mind and then changing your major after you start college. Colleges love students who change majors. Back to the drawing board. Those physics "classes" now don't apply to your declared biology major. The student pays for the new classes and takes out more student loans. This adds to the cost of an overpriced rite of passage. Thirty percent of college students change their major at least once. Ten percent of students change over two times. Fifty two percent of students majoring in mathematics change their majors. The statistics for college graduation rates show that only 28% of students finish their four-year degree within four years. In fact, the government measures the statistic for graduation rates in terms of students completing a four-year program within six years. Why does it take students six years to complete a four-year program? At public two-year colleges, 26% of students take three years to complete a two-year degree! SAT/ACT exam scores determine the success rate of students completing college. Why don't colleges have students take a battery of emotional, skills based, and talent-based tests to better predict student success in completing college and finding a rewarding career? This may reduce college major change and college dropout rates. (At the cost of lower revenues at colleges)

College Industrial Complex

College is not for everyone. High schools crank out diplomas and en-courage (push students to go to college. Colleges recruit large numbers of academically unqualified students, not up to the challenge, to pay for their "amazing," amenity-filled campus. Do you see the irony? We, the college elite, want to produce an independent young adult. Our campus has the finest luxury dormitories, so your child will be "middle class" comfortable, though they could succeed with the basics. Your student borrows more to pay for unnecessary amenities that attract students to the college. The colleges charge higher tuition to pay for better ameni-ties, and the cycle continues. Universities spare no expense.

The total number of U.S. student loan borrowers exceed 42.3 million. That's over 12.5% of the U.S. population! Students and graduates be-tween eighteen and twenty-fine have most of the student loan debt. They owe about $1 trillion out of $1.67 trillion total. Student loan debt is the second highest national debt category after home mortgages.

https://fred.stlouisfed.org/series/SLOAS

https://www.forbes.com/sites/zackfriedman/2019/02/25/student-loan-debt-statistics-2019/#44533ab3133f

College Board estimates the average annual in-state cost for tuition, room and board, fees, books and supplies at a four-year university is $21,370. That's real money.

According to Pew Research, one-third of adults under age thirty have outstanding student loan debt.

According to NerdWallet, April 2021, the debt elevator is going up!

Medicine Dental	$201,490
School Pharmacy	$292,169
School Veterinary	$179,514
School Average	$149,877
Graduate Student	$ 82,800
Debt	

Solution:

Checkout this great resource, www.collegesimply.com for detailed real college cost information.

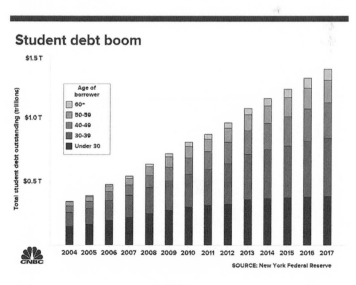

55

Parents: Discuss with your newly minted, college student in advance, how much access, you the parent, should have in their lives. Parents have no legal right to see your student's college transcript. HIPPA rules block you from receiving any health information about your over eighteen years of age children even if they are on your health care plan and you are paying the premiums. After they turn eighteen, they are 100% in charge of their finances. I suggest a Limited Power of Attorney (POA) signed by your eighteen year-old child allowing you to have access to financial matters and a health care proxy for health care. This is insurance in case of an emergency.

Students: If you don't have a working relationship with your biological parents, consider giving limited Power of Attorney and your Health Care Proxy to another trusted relative or friend. Just find someone trustworthy that will look out for your best interest.

https://www.forbes.com/sites/deborahljacobs/2014/08/15/two-documents-every-18-year-old-should-sign/#79c74d966e33

Step One to Applying to College: Fill out the required FASFA form. This establishes your eligibility for financial aid. The form includes student and family income data from the parents. The FASFA form deadline is before the IRS April 15th tax return deadline, reinforcing the country's "Fire, Ready, Aim" mentality. Brace yourself, FASFA form completion is complicated and a pain in the neck. Enroll in your local Community College and save a ton of money. In Florida, if you graduate with an Associate of Arts degree, you may walk on to any Florida four-year university to begin your degree or major study in your Junior Year. That is what I did. I went to the amazing St. Johns River Community College in Palatka, Florida. It is on the top twenty list for least expensive college in the country! I'm honored to know I went to one of the cheapest colleges in the country!

When I graduated with my AA, I went to the University of North Florida to finish my degree in business administration. I mostly lived at home when in Community College. When I went to UNF, I equally worked full time. And I went to school full time. 3.1 GPA.

ROTC: Consider a military partnership while going to college. If you cannot afford a college education, ROTC programs can provide financial assistance while you attend the college of your choice. ROTC programs reward in more ways than financial. Don't forget you get to go to summer military camp and obligated to four years of active duty.

Saving for college is a good idea. Although saving for retirement is more important. The Coverdell Education Savings Account was the original program. (ESA) The Tax Cuts and Jobs Act of 2017 makes Coverdell redundant. State sponsored 529 plans are now the "go to" tax benefit college savings plan. In fact, 529 plans allow you to save for private K-12 tuition (up to $10,000) besides college expenses. A 529 plan named (like the 401k) after Section 529 of the Internal Revenue Code is a tax-advantaged plan of saving for your child's future college expenses. Individual states sponsor 529 savings plans. In Florida, for example, you open this "qualified" account and begin selecting investments that fit your investment style. Your child's future enrollment date chooses a target style fund. The investment grows tax free like a traditional IRA. You should save automatically. You can ask your family and friends to contribute through an eGift portal. Use the 529 plan account for higher education expenses like tuition, fees, books and supplies. Use it for room and board. Use the funds for computers, peripherals, software and internet costs. The Florida plan allows you to attend any qualified educational institution nationwide or private. According to 529 plan requirements, your student must attend at least half time in a program.

https://www.myfloridaprepaid.com/

Corporate Scholarships: My son and daughter received corporate scholarships. My son received a scholarship from Wachovia. My daughter received a scholarship from State Farm Insurance. Check with your employer about benefit availability.

Work-Study: Many, if not most colleges, offer work-study programs for students with financial need. The jobs are normally easy and still allow you time to work on classwork.

Grants: Free Money for Colleges

Unlike student loans, you do not repay grants! Most grants are need based. The federal government provides grants. Your FASFA application will check your eligibility for government grants.

- Federal Pell Grants;

- Federal Supplemental Education Opportunity Grants: https://studentaid.ed.gov/sa/types/grants-scholarships/fseog;

- State Grants http://www.collegescholarships.org/grants/state.htm Research your specific state for details;

- College Grants;

- Popular Student-Specific Grants: Grants designed to aid the diverse array of students;

- TEACH Grants;

- Military Grants;

- Minority Specific Grants: African American, Hispanic, Native American, Asian American and Grants for Women;

- Women's Colleges Offering Grants;

- Industry Sponsored Grants: State Farm Insurance, National Society of Accountants, Future Farmers of America, Healthcare;

- Grants for specific studies: See the Swann Foundation fellowship for Caricature and Cartoons;

- Grants for specific Talents: Music, art and photography grants;

- Math Grants: National Science Foundation, American Math Society, Mu Alpha Theta, Raytheon;

- Sports Grants: Play a sport? Get a grant.

There are hundreds of grant possibilities. You cannot be lazy. You cannot afford to be lazy. Put forth effort and apply for the grants. It's a good idea to add a nice photograph of yourself to the grant application.

Do the research and apply for as many grants as you can. Your current and future wallet will thank you.

https://www.collegegrant.net/

Scholarships: There are many types of scholarships available.

- Academic scholarships

- Athletic Scholarships

- Minority Scholarships

- Scholarships for Women

- Creative Scholarships

- Scholarships from specific industries.

Start the scholarship application journey during the middle of your junior year in high school. Many scholarships ask for personal essays describing your dreams and aspirations. Learn to write well before you apply for scholarships. Scholarship applications have non-negotiable deadlines. Remember, deadlines are closer than they appear. Scholarship applications may need a photograph of you. Get photographed before starting the application journey. Research local businesses online to see if they offer scholarships. Electric companies, insurance companies, and any large businesses in your town may offer scholarships with no strings attached. Most civic organizations have scholarships. Apply to the Rotary, Kiwanis, Daughter of American Revolution and Lion's Club.

Check out these scholarship research websites.

https://www.anthonyoneal.com/scholarships

http://www.collegescholarships.org/financial-aid/

https://www.collegeboard.org/

https://bigfuture.collegeboard.org

https://www.fastweb.com/

Crowdfunding: Create a crowdfunding post. https://www.gofundme.com/

Employer Reimbursement: I worked for Sprint Long Distance when I started my photography business. Sprint offered a generous tuition reimbursement package to employees. Several friends attended the local community college and received reimbursement. Likewise, State Farm Insurance has a college tuition reimbursement program. Check with your employer.

Raid Your IRA: I'm not a fan of this because parents should not sacrifice their retirement savings to finance your child's education. Please don't borrow from your traditional or Roth IRA to pay for college expenses without penalty. The IRS considers education a "qualified" reason, meaning that your fund raid is not subject to tax. The IRS limits your borrowing to 50% of your vested account up to $50,000.

Student Loans - The Last Resort

Please check out www.studentloanhero.com. It is a division of Lending Tree. This site provides calculators and information about student loan financing.

There are three types of public federal student loans. For undergraduates, the federal government subsidizes the Direct Subsidized Loan program. The federal government subsidizes the interest on your loan while you attend school, resulting in less money owed. The Department of Education is your lender. Establish financial need to qualify for this loan with a $5,500 limit. The advantages of a Federal Student Loan are (fixed interest rates, income-based repayment, loan cancellation for specific careers (Teach at a Title One School, and no credit check.

The next federal student loan program is the Direct Unsubsidized Loan. Students can use this program for undergraduate, graduate, and professional degrees. Interest rates are fixed, but higher for graduate degrees. Interest accumulates during the entire period, hence unsubsidized. You can borrow up to $20,500. The Department of Education is the lender and collector. There is no credit check.

The third federal program for loans is the Direct PLUS loan. This program is for parents to borrow money in the parent's name to support their child's education. This is my least favorite choice as it puts the parents on the hook. The Direct PLUS program has the highest interest rate of the three programs and requires a clean credit rating.

After you exhaust government resources, the private student loan is the next option. Now we are back at the carnival. Many private student loan lenders use predatory lending tactics. The good news is that a few reputable private lenders exist. Students should not be shopping for private student loans until they exhaust every other source of funds for college. Suze Orman, famous financial guru, says: Avoid private student loans at all costs.

1. Discover

https://www.discover.com/student-loans/?dd_pm=none&dd_pm_cat=student_loan

2. SallieMae

https://www.salliemae.com/student-loans/smart-option-student-loan/?dd_pm=none&dd_pm_cat=student_loan

3. LendKey

https://www.lendkey.com/private-student-loans/?clickid=3tNwzNygzxyJUe3wUx0Mo382UklXrWU5ryaS0Y0&irgwc=1&sk=AFF-Investopedia&utm_source=AFF-Investopedia&utm_campaign=AFF&utm_medium=referral

Be careful of lenders offering better rates with a cosigner. Cosigning is a plan destined to fail. A cosigner agrees to be 100% responsible for the debt. Guess what happens? The original borrower cannot pay and leaves you with the bill. One third of cosigned loans goes into default. Many private student loans allow the cosigner off the hook, officially called cosigner release, if the borrower satisfies the institution's payment rules. Institutions reject 90% of private student loan borrowers that apply for cosigner release. If your cosigner goes bankrupt, the lender can start an auto-default, even if the loan is in good standing. Demand for payment is immediate. You will have thirty days to pay off the loan. If you do not pay, you are in default. Hence the term auto-default. Word to the wise. Don't cosign any loan or ask anyone to cosign your loan. It turns your college debt into a complicated legal matter. Speaking of the law, did you know that Federal and Private student loans are impossible to discharge in bankruptcy proceedings? That is why I say student loan debt takes priority over the rest of your debt.

Employers help Workers pay their Student Loan Debt

https://www.forbes.com/sites/zackfriedman/2017/09/14/fidelity-student- loans/#954170233a55
https://www.npr.org/2019/02/25/696355143/come-work-for-us-well-help-pay-down-your-student-loans

This Just In, Indentured Servitude is Back!

CNBC reports that income sharing agreements from colleges are taking shape. What are Income Sharing Agreements? Instead of paying your college education bills by borrowing money in advance, you agree to have the college pay in advance for your education. In return, you agree to have a percentage of your future salary pay your college back for your education. Sounds great, right? Here is the catch. It may lead to unregulated philandering by college institutions receiving much more money in forfeited salary than if you just borrowed the money and paid the loan back with your paycheck. In many cases, the ISA agreements ending up costing more than federal loans. The government may offer these programs. In a world of honest players, this method has merit. I am not a big fan of a government entity being responsible for deducting money from your paycheck to repay what is in essence a debt. The fine print in the contracts included mandatory arbitration clauses, banned lawsuits, and may even force you to use a particular bank.

The world of college education financing is a veritable jungle. The unprepared student and parent stand to lose money. Be a frugal student and pick a high-quality, inexpensive community college for the first two years and live at home. When you graduate with your AA, pick another inexpensive, high-quality university that will satisfy your degree and future career needs. Ironically, after you receive your bachelor's degree, employers don't care about your alma mater. Employers basically care that you graduated from college. Many people have jobs that are not in their degree field. So, you should get out there and get your degree fast, furious, and as cheap as you can!

Retirees: Retirees owe $18.2 billion in student loan debt. A 650% increase from 2005.

Social Security offsets (garnishment have increased over 500% (for over 40,000 people for seniors 65 and older according to AARP.

According to CBS News, three million Americans over the age of 60 still have student debt. The average debt was $33,800. Most incurred this debt while helping their children attend college. Other debt occurred when folks went back to school to enhance their job skills. The investment return on both scenarios failed a cost/benefit analysis.

Veterans: At the time of writing, President Trump signed an executive order that makes it easier for disabled veterans to have their student debt discharged. It is the TPD or Total and Permanent Disability Discharge. The veteran will not have to pay federal income taxes. States do not collect state income tax on the discharged debt.

Public Service Loan Forgiveness: This is another government program that sounds great when reported on the news, but in reality, is very difficult to qualify for. While you are in college the regulations could change many times before you graduate. Consider it as icing on the cake if you receive this benefit.

https://studentaid.ed.gov/sa/repay-loans/forgiveness-cancellation/public-service#qualifying-employment

Alternatives to Student Loan Debt

I never thought I would offer students alternatives to attending college. Here I am, a teacher, advocating college alternatives. One reason, according to the Washington Post, is that out of thousands of students graduating from college with desirable STEM degrees, 75 percent are working out of field. Why? There is a difference between the perception of what a STEM job entails and the reality. It does not seem to matter that there is an abundance of STEM jobs available. Second, an executive summary produced by Fidelity Investments reports 39% of the 2013 class would have made different choices related to college planning had they understood the true cost of college. Fifty percent of graduates would have researched more grants/scholarships. Sixty-Nine percent of graduates said they could have cut back on eating out. Sixty-Four percent of graduates said they could have cut back on retail spending. Third, seventy percent of the U.S. workforce do not have a degree.

Join Military Service:

The current military experience is comparable to an apprenticeship. There are thousands of job possibilities available in military service. Remember, you serve and obey their orders and fill a need for the United States military. It is not a vacation. It is an honor to serve, but make sure you are mature enough to make an important decision. The military offers you training and careers in science, engineering, medicine, and communications. I have friends who started their military career serving as a corpsman (Like a paramedic). Now they are doctors with their own practice. Any job found in the world exists in the military. Regardless of the role you serve, the experience is helpful in the civilian world. Over one million veterans and their families take advantage of the GI bill's college benefits. There are ROTC programs that pay for your college and prepare you for an officer role in the service in return for a service commitment period.

Go to Work:

There are many jobs that do not require a college education. Entry-level jobs offer the opportunity for advancement. My neighbor started in the stockroom at Walmart and is now a store manager. I have heard of stories of entry-level workers in fast-food restaurants becoming a franchise owner. While possible, success requires hard work and long hours. Many organizations have call centers that need workers with no experience. The job involves sitting in a gray cubicle with a headset around your neck during your "tour" and assisting customers on the phone with their problems related to your industry. The work can rewarding, and pay well, Many companies offer tuition reimbursement. Be careful. I have friends and family that lost their entry level customer service job because of technological advancements or because of outsourcing jobs overseas. I recommend starting your research for your dream job at https://www.bls.gov/ooh/home.htm. They pack this site with useful information. There is information about job salaries, education required, projected job numbers, and growth rate. Another going to work skill set you should master is learning the ins and outs of job search websites. Create a truthful and creative LinkedIn account. Be familiar with Glassdoor, Indeed and Zip Recruiter. Plug in your resume and wait for responses. Plug in with sites such as Flex Jobs and Fiverr. These companies give you access to thousands of contract and freelance jobs. However, be on the lookout for scams. Real employers do not ask you for money; period. Writing a paragraph on freelance work leads me to the next alternative.

Entrepreneurship:

By age thirteen, I already had a paper route in a small community and a successful lawn business. By age eighteen, I was a real estate salesperson, property manager, and appraisal apprentice. Owning your own business is very rewarding, challenging and frustrating. You must excel at math, writing, people skills and technology skills, even though mastery of these skills does not guarantee success. Starting a business at a tender age may give you the occasional pass for a mistake. That was not my experience. An elderly couple cheated me out of money for a lawn job. When I was in real estate, a crooked real estate broker had me investigated for showing property to an under qualified buyer. They dropped the charges without merit. The world is a jungle out there. When you are in business by yourself, no large corporate or government entity is protecting you from the "big bad wolf." Going into business is not for everyone. You must be self-motivated, and require no supervision. You have a burning desire to succeed, and no one will stop you. If you meet these standards, then you will discover that owning your own business is the most rewarding way to make a living. You will enjoy a sense of independence. There is no ceiling on the dollar amount of money you can earn. Did I mention no income floor either? No regular paycheck, no guarantee your marketing will work, or your phone will ring, and no guarantee that Apple won't invent a device that destroys your business. Welcome to capitalism. The World of Creative Destruction. There is nothing like it in the World!

Success depends upon you finding and using mentors, getting a job in the field you wish to start a business, (what!) preparing for failure, and getting involved in theater. Shakespeare was right. "All the world is a stage." Do not be deliberately deceitful, but "Fake It Until You Make It" is a valid strategy. Join Toastmasters to excel at public speaking.

You have situational awareness. Recognize threats to your business model, current competitors, future competitors, and technical competitors. Pursue problems in your neighborhood. For example, I continually observe our Nation's financial literacy short comings and this book is response to that experience. Look for future opportunities. Make wise choices, always watch your back. Ideally you will be successful. Failure is a success when you consider it a "learning experience". https://www. entrepreneur.com/article/300403

Associate Degrees:

If you are starting a career that needs more than a high school education, but less than a bachelor's degree, consider an Associate Degree. There are three main types of Associate degrees. The Associate of Arts degree is a general education degree to prepare you for the University experience. An Associate of Science degree prepares you for a special career. You can still transfer to a university, but an Associate of Science degree prepares you for the workforce. Types of jobs include:

Air Traffic Controller;

Computer Programmer;

Web Developer;

Law Enforcement;

Automobile Repair Technician;

Engineering Technician;

Medical Imaging Technician.

There is also the Associate in Applied Science. This category is more job specific and so the Associate in Applied Science provides training in Accounting, Web design, Nursing, Paralegal, Respiratory Care and Teaching Assistant.

Trade Schools:

Trade Schools prepare you for many careers. According to the National Association of State Directors of Technical Education Consortium, there are seventy-nine career pathways within sixteen vocational divisions. Career Tech

Education in high schools and colleges provided training for specific careers.

The most popular career training paths include:

- Personal care aides;

- Home health aides;

- Diagnostic medical sonographers;

- Occupational therapy assistants;

- Cosmetology;

- Dental hygienists;

- Medical equipment repairers;

- Medical assistants;

- Licensed practical and licensed vocational nurses.

Don't forget to consider the construction trades. Many people enjoy working with their hands. Trade Schools can prepare students for electrical, heavy equipment operation, carpentry, plumbing and welding careers. Good automobile mechanics are hard to find. Individuals with entrepreneurial spirit can gain more financial reward by opening their own shop.

Apprenticeships and Internships:

An apprenticeship is a paid, on-the-job, training program that results in industry certification and sometimes an associate of arts degree.

Please watch this video to understand the role of apprenticeships in a dynamic workforce. https://www.youtube.com/watch?v=BU1w-yxQwlk

A significant advantage to the apprenticeship strategy is the opportunity to receive your education, an Associate degree at no charge, industry certifications and a full-time job offer. This website describes the BMW program.

https://www.bmwusfactory.com/bmw_articles/bmw-manufacturing-doubles-size-of-bmw-scholars-program/

Are you a Disney "Phile?"

https://www.disneyanimation.com/careers/interns-apprentices

Do you love Universal Studios?

https://www.universalorlandojobs.com/universe-opportunities/internships/

Are you a "Space Nut"?

https://intern.nasa.gov/

Plumbing?	Apollo Home
Culinary Arts?	Boyd Gaming

https://www.boydgaming.com/

Customer Service?	Enterprise Rental Car
Technology?	Aon

An apprenticeship lasts between one and five years.

An internship is a shorter experience lasting three to six months. Internships are "paid" or "unpaid" and concentrate on career investigation. Internships do not result in certification. An internship is a long-term, job shadowing experience. Students affiliated with a college in a paid internship opportunity received a job offer 60% of the time. Unpaid internships offer an opportunity for you to shine in front of a potential employer. Unpaid internships act as a long-term interview allowing you to prove your worth.

https://www.thebalancecareers.com/what-is-an-internship-1986729

Student Loan Alternative Reality:

I ask the question: Why don't the banks require borrowers to produce their personal budget? Loan applications ask for income, but not expenses. Bankers rely on ratios derived from your application and your credit report to estimate what you can afford to repay in debt payments. The banker knows you'll eat hot dogs and ramen noodles instead of defaulting on a loan. They don't care. They have already collected their commission. In the same theme, why don't student loan lenders ask for or prepare a working budget for their student borrower? In fact, colleges should hire a full-time financial coach to teach students how to make wise decisions about spending their student loan proceeds. They could give seminars to incoming freshman (who three months before were high school seniors) teaching the students about money management. Is this revolutionary thinking? Part of me thinks the lenders would not be happy lending less money to students who may behave more responsibly. It might be bad for business.

Chapter 6

Divorce and Your Finances

"My momma told me, You better shop around!"

Smokey Robinson of the Miracles

Finances are the leading cause of divorce. Couples stressed about finances are more likely to get divorced, and that can cause more financial stress.

Here is the financial cost of a divorce: Divorce is expensive! The cost of a divorce varies. Your net worth, business ownership, geographical location, and if there are children involved, determine the cost of a divorce. The average cost of a divorce is less than $13,000. An uncontested divorce can cost, on average, $4,100. If there are child support, child custody, or alimony disputes, the divorce costs more. A divorce that goes to trial may exceed $20,000. Divorces can take on average, between twelve and eighteen to complete. The national average rate for divorce lawyers is $270 per hour.

According to the census bureau, 782,038 couples ended their marriage in 2018.

The Importance of Marrying Well

Your choice of a life partner will be one of the most important decisions you make in your life. There should be an emotional connection, but is it a suitable match? Does that sound a little Edwardian? Based upon the national divorce rate somewhere around forty to fifty percent, it might be time to rethink the impulse romance and wedding. The decision will affect your future mental health, physical health, and financial health. You are creating a lifelong partnership that may involve starting and raising a new family. Raising a family in today's chaotic world is a daunting task. That's why a monogamous relationship with one partner is a great idea. It creates a stable living environment in an increasingly chaotic world. Growing up in a happy home will create well adjusted (mentally, socially, physically, and educationally) children.

The point of marriage is to provide a practical, emotionally fulfilling and financially efficient way to live. Marriage involves an oath. Can you keep a promise? How much do you feel Americans keep their promises? According to Dave Ramsey, one-third of couples make purchases without their partner's knowledge.

Before entering a marriage, there are many "Grown Up" topics to discuss. I hope you take time to get to know each other. This takes time. Successful Marriages after a two-week courtship are rare.

Here are a few topics to discuss before marriage.

1) What is commitment? Why did you pick your spouse?

2) In the time to get to know each other, it would be well to learn how you settle arguments and decide as a couple. Can you compromise and learn how to forgive? Conflict management is very important.

3) Will you have children? How many children will you have? What are the spiritual expectations?

4) Where will you live? What are your career goals?

5) How will you handle money decisions as a couple?

6) Will you get pre-marital counseling from a counselor or pastor?

7) Do you know each other? This takes time. Successful marriages after a two-week courtship are rare.

8) Do you have friends and family you can look up to? Preferably married ones.

9) In-Laws are real. Create an In-Law plan and discuss boundaries.

Here are the Financial Topics you may discuss before getting married.

Before getting married, it is important that couples completely reveal their financial situation to each other. Besides the numbers, it is important to discuss with each other their feelings about money. Couples should discuss their money history with each other. What are your spending habits? What is your debt history? Do you both believe a budget is important? One important document to share before getting married is the sharing of each person's credit report. Yes, I know, very romantic advice. Regardless, it is very important that the couple see each other's credit report. This would be especially important if the new couple plans to buy a house. You would both want to know "everything" before qualifying for a mortgage. This is not a good time to find any surprises!

Couples should engage in the exercise of developing a list of their top three values. The couple then prioritizes their values and shares with each other. This exercise will foster a more intimate discussion of what they want to do with their money. Many younger newlyweds may have student loan debt and credit card debt. It is important that these couples create a plan to address this debt. Once you are married, "the couple" now owes the debt together.

I suggest having further discussions about marriage finance. Both newlyweds and mature couples can discuss the following topics. For example, how will you handle investments? How will you handle day-to-day expenses? How often do you update your budget?

Topics of Marriage and Finance

Easy Topics:

1. Income

2. Debt

3. Savings

4. Having Kids

Hard Topics:

1. Tax Benefits
2. Estate Benefits
3. Employment Benefits
4. Medical Benefits
5. Government Benefits
6. Death Benefits
7. Insurance Benefits
8. Legal Responsibilities & Privileges
9. Beneficiaries
10. Inheritance

Why Does "Marriage" exist?

Marriage can mean many things. Marriage involves an emotional relationship and may include the possibility of children. Marriage is also a practical financial arrangement. The legal title of marriage is the very fancy title of an "Estate by Entireties." This estate is the exclusive legal partnership of a husband and wife. (Congress is writing legislation to change the words husband and wife to a married couple, but as of August 2019 that has not yet happened. This means same-sex couples will create a Tenancy by the Entireties (TBE or Joint Tenants with Rights of Survivorship, (JTWROS This means same-sex couples will need to be very careful legally, consulting with an attorney in their state about property ownership. The big deal here is that when one partner dies, in an "Estate by the Entireties" the surviving partner at once gains legal ownership of the "estate". This ownership "structure" overrules wills and heirs' wishes without probate court involvement. free. This legal arrangement protects the couple. If one spouse tries to mortgage the farm, they have to have the other partner's consent. If one partner borrows money and defaults, the lender may not file the lien against the "couples" property as the "couple" is a separate legal entity. Marriage is a financial arrangement. The history of this estate originates from the Bible's description of the husband and wife as "being one flesh" or a single entity. Now for a little perspective.

"An estate by the entireties is an almost metaphysical concept which developed at the common law from the Biblical declaration that a man and his wife are one."

United States v. Gurley, 415 F.2d 144, 149 (5th Cir. 1969 (interpreting Florida law

Genesis Chapter 2 verse 24 says, "Therefore, shall a man leave his father and his mother, and shall cleave unto his wife: and they shall be one flesh."

I hope you don't mind this Bible Study, but I think it is important for you to understand that Bible liturgy established modern marriage law, regardless of your beliefs.

Marriage, in its current official make up, financially deals with property disposition after the death of your spouse. The death of a spouse creates an estate. Marriage allows the couple to open joint bank accounts and file a joint IRS tax return. Marriage allows you to receive discounts on life, car, and health insurance. You may sue for your spouse's wrongful death, and you may receive your spouse's Social Security and Pension benefits. (Government and Retirement Spouses have **special communications** privileges. You have a duty to keep your business to yourself as a couple! These marital privileges apply to the courtroom. Spouses cannot legally testify about confidential communications made by their partner. Each spouse must watch each other's back regarding finances. You cannot legally lie to your spouse about finances. You have a duty to manage the Marriage Estate's money responsibly. You may not squirrel away money, send money to a lover, or waste money without the consent of your spouse. Otherwise (if you do these things when the marriage ends, you could be held accountable by the court and ordered to make restitution (pay it all back.

In addition, the **Family and Medical Leave Act** allows you to take unpaid leave to care for a spouse. If your spouse has fallen ill and cannot make financial decisions, the other spouse has the legal right to make surrogate decisions for the other incapacitated spouse.

Marriage and its "Estate" creates and legally protects many rights, privileges, and obligations so that the marriage institution will succeed. It also protects the assets accumulated by the couple and as well create and protect your family legacy and financial stability in a chaotic world. It protects and preserves the family which includes your offspring.

"There's a way of transferring funds that are even faster than electronic banking. It's called marriage" James Holt McGavran

When I worked as an international operator for a communication firm, the back (smoking patio was an amazing lesson in human nature for me. First, my coworkers and friends discussed interoffice romances with openness on the patio. There was no discretion with the ladies. Because of the skewed ratio of men to women employees in this line of work, many married men found many targets of opportunity to "play the field" or "sow wild oats". The ladies reported these events with pride on their smoke break. In fact, on the back patio, I saw the claws come out. I got a front-row seat on the "Scorn of a Woman". Older women counseled younger women on how to take their soon to be Ex, "to the cleaners." Gentlemen, that's a financial term for a major reduction in your net worth! They took no prisoners. Not to leave the men as the only love exploiters, married ladies with children were also "playing the field." Their husbands were not home. They were in the military. Does absence make the heart grow fonder? On the back porch, I consoled a few broken hearts or two. I thought about the consequences the innocent children experienced. I watched from a distance, in disappointment, as a young woman began work at our company with a spark in her eyes and a spring in her step turn into a vengeful, angry, spurned young woman because of a dishonest, impulsive relationship. Was I tempted? Not after what I saw on the back porch. My personal life was staying personal. I wanted to leave the door open to future promotion. Being accused of sexual misconduct and/or harassment doesn't help one's career. Employees equally considered another place I worked, as the "wife-swap" club! Is there a misunderstanding out there regarding the definition of marriage? I think someone important said something about coveting your neighbor's wife. What is a marriage? A legal entity formed by the union of two people as partners in a personal relationship. Most ancient cultures and religions still suggest that the personal relationship stays monogamous. I suggest inviting God to the ceremony. Inviting a supernatural spiritual force into a high stakes personal relationship comprising two flawed human beings may help the relationship last a lifetime. If you disagree, that's fine, but I encourage you to reread my Back-Porch experience mentioned above.

"Ah, yes, divorce ... from the Latin word meaning to rip out a man's genitals through his wallet"

Robin Williams

Marriage is Healthy

Anthropologists disagree, but it seems prehistoric humans began monogamous relationships because of prehistoric STD's (sexually transmitted disease. Having multiple partners and then contracting an STD led to immediate population decline in the mud hut village. They noticed the less social, monogamous couples were still multiplying. In addition, the new baby very much depended on the mom. This placed the role of providing food, shelter and protection to Dad. Dad may have expected fidelity as he was not interested in going into the jungle, risking his neck to provide the needs for someone else's child.

Divorce, Children, and Child Support Costs

According to a 2017 report by the US Census Bureau, over 25% of children under twenty-one have one parent living outside the household. When this happens, the absent parent is legally responsible to provide financial support. From the 2017 census, child support totaled $30 billion. That averages to $3,431 per child or about $260 per month. Sixty-two percent of parents paid on time.

The poverty rate in 2017 of single-parent families was 24% compared to 13.6% for two-parent families.

My personal experience with clients and friends paying and receiving child support is that no one is happy. I would suggest avoiding putting yourself in a situation that may obligate you to have to pay or receive child support. In fact, a US census report estimates only 43.5% of child support recipients receive their full money. Thirty percent receive nothing. The point here is to not depend on paying your necessary expenses with child support. The Federal Office of Child Support Enforcement offers information, and advice on how to collect unpaid back child support. (www.acf.hhs.gov/css)

The price of divorce is high. Unless you are in an abusive relationship, do everything in your power to stick it out. Maintain your relationship, not just for your finances, but for your children. Can you make it work for the children?

If divorce is inevitable

See the book *Personal Finance* by Alfred Mill, and read the chapter *Breaking Apart* to learn how to handle the division of your combined assets back to individual accounts. The chapter covers health care and retirement strategies related to divorce.

In conclusion

Divorce can cause serious health problems. The dreaded "gray divorce," divorce over fifty, is troublesome. Fourteen percent of Americans over fifty divorce and become single compared to two percent in 1960. According to a 2019 Yahoo Finance article, people suffered from higher degrees of depression. "The economic effects are even more stark." grey divorce household income for men drops by 25% and for women drops 40%. It splits family resources. There is no time to recover your financial retirement plan. Women fare worse than men. According to NOLO, a publisher of do-it-yourself legal documents, the average divorce costs $13,000. Added unexpected costs such as real estate fees, financial advice, and therapy fees can approach another $5,000. Uncontested divorces are less expensive. With no complicated financial circumstances and no minor children, the cost can be as low as $500 plus filing fees. Litigation requires each party to hire their own attorney. If you can use an alternative method to litigation like mediation or collaborative practice, you'll save money. I found one website, www.ourfamilywizard.com that offers advice on alternatives to litigation and provides divorce finance advice.

After the divorce, you will need a new post-divorce personal budget. You will need to update your beneficiaries of your retirement accounts. Alimony is tax free to the recipient and not tax deductible to the payer. I have heard stories of deceased divorcees leaving their 401k to their **ex** unintentionally. Readjust your retirement contributions so you can meet your retirement goals on time.

Marriage is hard work. I've heard the platitude many times. I'm sure you have too. Married for over thirty-five years, we raised two well-adjusted children. Find a partner that is financially responsible. Two financially responsible people hold each other accountable and watch each other's back to achieve a financially responsible family.

And they lived Happily ever After!

"We love each other, but we actually like each other and that's an important distinction there," Sting tells PEOPLE of wife Trudie Styler

Chapter 7

Non-Essential Expenses

The waste of money cures itself, for soon there is no more to waste.

~M.W. Harrison

Introduction

The Average American Spends Almost $18,000 a year on Non-essentials, according to an article by the Motley Fool.

Opportunity Cost

When you spend on an unnecessary want, the result is less money available to save and invest. It is necessary for you to save to build wealth. The more money you spend on wants, the less money you save. I call the earnings lost on the money NOT saved and invested opportunity cost.

Chapter 7, Non-Essential expenses or expensive hobbies, considers the many small expenses we justify a million different ways. They make us feel better, look better, or qualify as retail therapy. With a little pre-planning, you can budget these experiences. However, overindulgence results in expenses exceeding income and the result is a broken budget. What follows is a small list of items that to me and many financial coaches are areas that cause problems to lots of people. As a financial coach, I am just a little confused talking to people who have no emergency fund, no savings, have high levels of personal debt, and credit card debt purchasing the items on the upcoming list before taking care of essentials.

Tattoos

Is this a funny subject for a personal finance book? Wait for it.

Tattoos are very personal decisions. Many people add tattoos to their body for many reasons; in tribute, to signify an important person in their life, an event or just to add an interesting dynamic to one's body. Some folks add stars/constellations, nature themes, tribal themes, faces, religious themes and animal themes. They can be a status symbol. Human history regarding tattoos is less friendly. In ancient Greece and Rome, tattoos were used to identify slaves. Beginning in the 1800s, circus sideshows displayed tattooed people. To avoid British impressment, sailors tattooed themselves to prove their identity. Military personnel get tattoos to show their social solidarity, give tribute, and tell their story. A friend in medical school told me that in modern Emergency Room Training, tattoos can signify the patient is the property of another.

Why talk about this in a personal financial book?

How much do tattoos cost? A full sleeve tattoo costs around $1,500. Friends, tattoos are expensive. A tattoo is a very expensive piece of artwork that does not increase in value by itself. It is entertainment that does not earn an income or assist you in paying an expense. Life is expensive. Do you have enough discretionary income (Money left over after all expenses paid to pay for body art?

Let's take a look at the full picture.

1. Tattoos are expensive. Full sleeve tattoos cost about $1,500. Tattoo artists charge by the hour. The normal rate in my area is between $100 and $125. More for a tattoo artist with a great reputation.

2. They are difficult and time-consuming to apply. The average time for an "average difficulty" full sleeve is 10-15 hours. Some complicated full color projects may take 80 hours and entire projects often take multiple sessions taking time periods of many weeks or months! Could you use your time more

productively? I suggest using this time instead for creating another income stream.

   a. Tattoos expose you to unnecessary medical risk. Well, Ken, I thought this was a personal finance book. Now you are discussing medical issues. Medical treatment is not free and takes valuable time to administer. Both reasons are financial in scope.

3. Masks skin cancer - A tattoo may hide skin cancer. Suspicious looking moles can hide behind a tattoo design, making it difficult for your dermatologist to inspect your skin for skin cancer.

4. Infection - Getting a tattoo can expose you to harmful bacterial infections.

5. Allergy - You may have an allergy to a particular color or type of ink. Tattoo ink is permanent, so if you find out you are allergic to the ink, it is possible you will suffer allergy symptoms until you remove the ink. You pay again to get the tattoo removed.

6. Some inks are being studied for their potential role in skin cancer. Inks are unregulated.

7. MRI burning - Tattoos can lead to skin burn when tattooed skin it exposed to MRI scans. It's rare, but do you see the pattern here? There is a lot more going on here than just a pretty design on your "tukis" (rump). In addition, without the possibility of a burn, there still exists the possibility that your tattoo will distort the MRI image you are trying to get to diagnose some other medical "situation". Don't forget to remove your piercings too.

8. Affects how you sweat - doctors have reported tattoos affect how you sweat. Large tattoos don't sound like a good idea. We sweat without interference from an ink coating on our skin.

9. Hepatitis - A dirty needle could pack this bad news.

10. According to research from the International Journal of Dermatology, individuals with tattoos were more likely to be diagnosed with mental health issues and report sleep problems.

I'm not sure what comes first, the tattoo or the risky behavior, but the report suggests a relationship between tattoo application and risky behavior.

11. Open yourself up to unfair prejudice, even though tattoos are mainstream now.

12. Many people who get tattoos end up regretting their decision. Cost of removal is more expensive than application. Removal may take months and multiple laser sessions. I recommended you hire a physician for the procedure to reduce risk of unregulated care (More expense). Amateur removal could cause burns and scarring. Each session may cost you $450. Reports indicate tattoo removal to be more painful than tattoo application.

Solution: Don't get a tattoo. You look great without it!

(Said in Strong, but Loving Teacher Voice.)

Home Gym Systems, Computerized Stationary Bikes, Tread Mills, Gym Membership:

This is a budget item that will exercise your wallet! How about the best computerized stationary bike on the planet! It costs only $58.00 per month for... thirty-nine months! That's $2,262! That does not include the membership fee giving you access to the pretty instructors and your exercise analytics! The membership costs an additional $39.00 per month! Breaking news, 2021 update, now the cost is $64.00 monthly, and the membership is $49 per month!

If you are a rock star, get two! The alternative here is very realistic and a lot less expensive. Buy a real bike. One that you can ride on a sunny day. For rainy days and winter weather, purchase a "trainer" stand that converts your bike into a stationary/spin bike for $90.00. I found one on Amazon. Then set your bike in front of your TV and watch whatever you want! No extra charge! I saved you over $2,100!

Home gyms cost from $1,000 to $2,000. If this is your thing, fine. Most people who buy a home gym system or treadmill end up not using them. This makes sense. The machines are big and bulky, and it's not a lot of fun exercising alone in your home.

An alternative is to take up the right sport. Take up a sport that is fun, promotes exercise, and is entertaining. Tennis is a good sport and inexpensive to start. Many local parks have tennis courts. Many companies sponsor ball teams. If you live in a winter wonderland, try bowling. Jogging is an inexpensive sport. Yes, each of these sports has a small expense but budget them under health, entertainment and social.

If you are not interested in any of these ideas, just walk; 10,000 or more steps a day is a significant form of exercise. The creator made us for walking!

Gym memberships often wind up as recurring charges on your credit card. We often forget recurring charges. This is what I call grey charges. These are subscription charges to your credit card you forgot about, because we are not checking our credit card statement monthly. Your gym company will forget to give you a courtesy call reminding you to cancel.

Twenty percent of Americans go to gyms.

Most people don't make it past the five month mark. Only half of the members go regularly.

Defaulted gym membership contracts can be a cloud on your credit report. When I was selling real-estate, I was assisting a client pre-qualify for a loan. He had an unpaid gym membership, and that was enough for our favorite lender to refuse mortgage pre-approval.

CrossFit can be more expensive than gym memberships. Average prices range from $75.00 to $225 per month.

Solution: Run or Walk on your own for the simplest least expensive form of exercise. For weight training, find the least expensive local gym.

Home Food Delivery

Home Food Delivery cost is another unforced error to your budget and wallet. It is five times more expensive to order delivery from a restaurant than to cook from home. Meal kit delivery services are three times more expensive than cooking from scratch at home. You pay more money for convenience. I know it takes effort to prepare home-cooked meals but, I know you can do it.

According to Wellio, the average price per meal in a restaurant is $20.37, meal kit is $12.53 and home cooking is $4.31.

Boats

"A boat is a hole in the water surrounded by wood in which to pour money." *Anonymous*

"The two happiest days of a man's life—the day he bought the boat and the day he sold the boat," *Anonymous*

B.O.A.T.: Break Out Another Thousand (Dollars).

See where this is going? I have had a lot of fun on boats. They are amazing entertainment. I live in Florida and water surrounds this great state. You cannot see the "real" Florida without getting on the water by boat. That does not give you permission to spend tens of thousands of dollars when a tour boat will do. I have owned two boats in my life, and I paid cash. Borrowing money to buy a boat is not a good idea. They depreciate faster than cars and have no practical purpose. At least I can drive my depreciating automobile to work.

Boating is fun. Most boaters enjoy boating to relax, go fishing, and spend time with family. If you went fishing or boating as a child, you are more likely to become a lifelong boater. According to the NMMA, 142 million Americans went Boating in 2016. During the pandemic, boating became more popular, as Americans looked for alternatives to sitting at home watching the news.

From an older report, the middle class enjoy boating with an average annual income of $100,000. In 2019, average boat prices ranged from $600 to the stratosphere. The average price for a boat is around $20,000. That is from my personal experience.

My point here is that if you are going through a financially tough time, boating should be out of the picture until you are out of your financial situation.

My last "interesting" experience was with my father's last boat. He financed the new boat. Bought at full price from the showroom floor in 2007 at the time the economy was reaching the top of the bubble of the Financial Crisis. The boat's price was about $50,000; $20,000 put down (money from selling the previous boat and financed $30,000. In two years, he was upside down in the boat (figuratively meaning the money for the down payment or his equity disappeared. (In a boat? Equity? Dad stored the boat at a marina, albeit an inexpensive one, incurring further expense. Membership in Sea Tow (the boat equivalent of AAA is another expense. Dad paid additional principal payments on the note to stay financially afloat. Did I mention the expense of accessories? When you buy a new boat, there are additional expenses to consider. Boats need line, anchors, life jackets, electronics (expensive), spare parts, a spare battery, tool kit, first aid kit and on and on.

When Dad turned 80, he ended his carefree days of boating. (Actually, boats require a lot of care. We sold the boat to an investor who shipped the boat to England because this style of boat was popular there.

Instead, if you love boats like I do, consider a boat rental club. They give you several boats to choose from; You pick up the boat at the marina and return the boat later in the day. The marina cleans and maintains it. You don't have to worry about the expensive accessories. Want to own a boat or have a boat, I offer a few tips. Most thrifty boaters do their own boat maintenance. My outboard is very easy to maintain. It's not rocket science, but boat maintenance is expensive if you always take your boat to the shop. Have a place to store your boat free of cost. Marina storage or outdoor storage lots are expensive. I store my boat in my yard.

Clean your own boat. I made a lot of money as a teenager cleaning boats belonging to the wealthy. It's expensive to pay someone else to clean your boat. I take my boat to a freshwater lake, jump in, and clean the above water parts of the boat while floating on the lake!

Learn how to pilot your boat and don't boat under the influence. Check out the US Coast Guard Auxiliary http://www.cgaux.org/boatinged/ for boating courses near you. Boating involves a lot of moving parts and ignorance here can be costly.

RV Life

Driving to work each day, I pass by an outdoor storage facility filled with RV's that are just stored. They never move! Their owners never seem to use them. Why? Why did good folks buy these RVs and never use them?

The Boat and RV Storage Graveyard

Owning a "live aboard" size RV during retirement may be a way to save money and be on vacation full time! Owning an RV to sit in your yard or incur additional expense stored in a storage yard is not good for your budget.

According to https://www.rvia.org, 11 million households own an RV. The typical RV owner is forty-eight years old, married, and an earns an annual household income of $62,000. They spend 3-4 weeks in their RV.

Solution: Try renting an RV before buying.

Check out https://gorving.com/.

RV's run the gamut of price. A pop-up camper starts at $5,000 while a class one motorhome costs over $200,000. My in-laws RV'd full time in their retirement and they had a blast. They were very thrifty. And you can afford to have a nice RV if you sold the ranch! See https://roads-lesstraveled.us/rv-budget/ to research the full-time lifestyle.

Do not buy an RV on a romantic whim, store in an outdoor storage lot, and then forget it. That's a waste of money. Stuff owns us. We do not own stuff. RV expenses include gas, insurance, maintenance, and camp site rent. Plan and create a budget to keep this hobby in perspective.

Cable before Dishonor!

Satellite Dish

It appears that Americans love to sit at home and order food online and binge watch their favorite show streaming also online. On average, Americans spend approximately $23 monthly for TV streaming and/or an additional $90 per month for cable. My suggestion is that you shop wisely and hold your service provider accountable to the level of service your provider promised. I check my internet speed to make sure I'm getting the horsepower I'm promised. Make sure your bill is accurate. Use a service like Ask Trim https://www.asktrim.com/ to renegotiate your fees. Most Americans can save money by cutting the cable connection and relying solely on streaming services, called Paid Per View, on their TV. When you cut the cable, you can expect to save about $100 per month.

My personal story: While my children were home, we did not have cable. Streaming TV did not exist. We had dial-up Internet for most of that time. I paid about $15/month for the Internet and somehow, we survived. We had rabbit ears on our TV to pick up the local channels and when those signals changed to digital, I purchased a digital amplifier and continued to use my 'rabbit ears'. Yes, I am an oddball. An oddball who saved, in my estimate, about $12,000 in cable fees during that time frame.

My point is to consider cutting the cable and use a Payment on Demand (POD) service like Amazon Prime, ROKU or Apple TV.

In fact, you can stream a lot of content free! Another perk is these services do not ask for a credit card number! There are a few conditions, but free streaming is something to consider. Here are a few key takeaways. Make sure you have the right equipment like a Roku or Amazon firestick and a strong internet connection. Be ready to see commercials. That is the tradeoff to a free service like Crackle or IMDb. You won't have access to the latest and greatest content, but you will have more selection than time to watch, in my opinion. So, check out the following free streaming services and save a ton of money! I use Crackle, IMDb and Vudu. I am thrilled with their services.

1. Vudu

2. Crackle

3. IMDb TV

4. Roku Channel

5. Popcornflix

6. Kanopy

One-Third of Americans spend more on coffee than on investing.

This is the headline from a 2018 fool.com article. Obviously, a sound bite, but their data comes from the Acorns 2017 Money Matters Report that used a SurveyMonkey survey. They surveyed 3,010 Americans, women and males between the ages of eighteen and forty-four. I thought the above comment was because we invested so few dollars. According to this survey, the sample group spent over $1,000 per year on coffee. That's $2.74 per day. That's easy to do at Starbucks. My take is that most Americans spend $5.00 per week or $250/yr. A survey conducted by Accounting Principals in 2013 reported that 82% of American work force spend $20 per week or $1,040 per year. Younger workers spent more than older workers. Maybe the older workers were saving for retirement.

We have a love affair with coffee. I like coffee. You like coffee. We all like coffee. **Solution:** I brew my coffee at home, put into a travel mug and off to work I go. Simple, easy, and cheap.

Buying Lunch

According to a popular survey by Accounting Principals that surveyed 1,000 American workers, discovered that respondents paid over $36.00 per week or $1,800 per year for lunch. Another more recent source report that workers spend $173 per month for lunch. That gets us over $2,000 per year.

Solution: Time to learn what a brown bag is. I pack a lunch daily and only eat out on special occasions. Try coordinating eating out with freebies restaurants offer customers for birthdays and other special events.

Rideshare-Uber/Lyft

Estimates differ but seems the "average" American spends between $50 and $100 per month for ridesharing. If you are on business and you will get reimbursed, that's fine. If you need to get across the street because it is raining, well that's just silly, buy an umbrella. I've heard stories of teens hailing Ubers to get to school. Buy a bike. Take the bus.

However, if you want to sell your family's second car to save expenses, then car sharing services could save you money as an alternative.

Sports Season and Music Concerts

I just received a flier for a concert being held in my hometown. Our fair city has a great venue with 6,000 seats. I looked at the ticket prices and almost fainted! I believe I may understand why. According to an article reported by the Economist magazine, as soon as they release music concert tickets, a subsidiary of the "band" buy and resell the tickets at a higher price than face value to enrich the pockets of the "band." It means that the artists scalp their own tickets! According to Live Nation, a concert promoter, admitted to this in July 2019. The artists turnaround and blame legit scalpers, managers and agents. The artists did not want to appear greedy by their beloved fans. Promoters design venue premium memberships and verified fan programs to move as much money from your pocket to theirs.

This recent development of "taking you to the cleaners" is for the changing role of the concert. It is now the major income producer for the artist since sales of albums have disappeared. If you like an expensive music concert scene, I hope you are an heiress, because you will need to be to keep up this expensive habit.

Wedding Expenses

The cost of a wedding does not predict its future success!

A friend told me that after announcing her engagement, wedding vendors, dentists and gyms came out of the woodwork to sell her unnecessary services. Remember, money doesn't care who it belongs to. As a reformed wedding photographer, I have seen countless brides and their families rack up enormous expenses getting ready for the wedding day. According to the Knot, the average cost of an American wedding was $33,000 in 2019. Holy smokes! Be careful of the Wedding Industrial Complex. I find these figures "interesting." I suspect wedding expenses will return to pre-COVID highs as the pandemic moves further away in the rear-view mirror. Parents are financing weddings. If invested over time, such funds could grow into a significant nest egg. I am sure that you can find an inexpensive wedding venue if you look hard enough. If your wedding will be a "show off" event to your friends and family, well, God Bless. Have fun spending that money. One bride's mom told me, after the wedding upon my delivery of the photos, that she spent more money on alcohol than on photography! Because of my experience of photographing weddings, I am sure I could plan one. I know I could create a budget for one. I photographed a wedding at a State Park. You can buy wedding gowns pre-owned! Research, then shop for Flowers, Photography, DJs, and Caterers before deciding. KEEP IT SIMPLE!

Did you buy wedding cancelation insurance? It's out there. I live in Florida, and I have had more than my share of weddings interrupted by the weather. Shop for a good price to protect your prepaid deposits.

Wedding Party Expense

Has your friend asked you to be a bridesmaid or groomsmen in a wedding? Congratulations. This social obligation expense can be a budget wrecker. Is a bachelorette or bachelor cruise or other obligatory pre-wedding festivities necessary? That can add up to $1,000. This is one of the latest fads in pre-marriage traditions. "Cruising for a financial bruising," bridesmaids spend $500 to $1,000 for a bachelorette cruise. Can you afford that? Dresses cost, well, whatever the bride expects. I hope your bride is frugal and does not expect the world of you.

Funerals: Again, if you have enough money, spend the national average of $7,000-$10,000 for a funeral. These fees include services at the funeral home, burial in a cemetery, and headstone installation. Cremation costs half. It is possible to do a direct cremation with no ceremony for less than $1,000. It is possible to buy cremation in advance and save even more. But, be careful if you prepay! Make sure you are dealing with a reputable company that is not going out of business before the death of your loved one. What if you move to an area not served by your funeral agency? If you cannot afford an expensive funeral, consider purchasing a small life/final expense insurance policy of $5,000-$10,000.

"If you have debt, I'm willing to bet that general clutter is a problem for you too.", Suze Orman

I agree with Suze here. Americans used to keep their cars in their garages. According to the US Dept of Energy survey, 25% of people with two car garages don't park in them at all. A third of respondents reported they can only park one car due to garage clutter. About 9% of Americans rent storage space, even though 65% of those homeowners have a garage (Self-Storage Association stat. Even though a large percentage of homes have three car garages, I still see most of my neighbors parking their vehicles in their driveway because their garage is full of clutter. Is it possible to fit two cars into a two-car garage in 2021??

Self-Storage Unit

Step 1: Get a new Credit Card

Step 2: Rent a Self-Storage Unit.

Step 3: Pack it full of worthless stuff while paying $100 a month in storage fees!

Renting a Self-Storage unit for short-term temporary storage of the valuable heirloom furniture during the moving process may be suitable if finding the perfect residence in your new location is taking longer than expected. However, as soon as you have found your new abode, clean out the self-storage unit. Try to use the storage unit for less than three months. They are a tremendous financial drain and encourage collecting and storing material goods that are NOT being used. Sell them. Give them away!

Again, said in loving teacher voice!

SOLUTION: Buy a shed. In my family, we always had a cheap steel shed in the backyard. It was a kit, and you built it yourself. If you are not a kit friendly person, buy an affordable "plastic" sheds from your favorite home improvement retailer.)

Video Game Subscriptions

Video gaming is a big attraction, and you should know the complete cost of a subscription. The gaming industry is a turn style built on planned obsolescence. Once you enter particular gaming companies' "environment," you will be encouraged to purchase expensive updated hardware and pay a monthly subscription price that you have no control over.

Video game subscriptions range from $10 to $20 per month, and that does not include the cost of the PC or gaming controller.

Assorted, possibly unnecessary, subscription packages that can be budget busters.

Subscription Boxes	Monthly Fee
Stitch Fix	$20 Styling Fee, Expensive Clothes
Trunk Club	$25 Styling Fee
Dollar Shave	Up to $9.00 monthly
Harry's	About $80/year
Blue Apron	$10.00 per meal
Hot Sauce of the Month	$12.00 per month
Craft Beer Club	$40.00 monthly

Personal Grooming

Women enjoy the benefits of spending big bucks on a hairdo. Haircare sources estimate women spend $55,000 in a lifetime on hair care.

The average Nail care cost in the US is $1,345 per year.

The cost of manicures, pedicures, haircuts, and blow-outs cost you $1,797 per year. This may be a great place to save money and get your budget back in line!

Gifts

According to the National Retail Federation and a Gallup Poll in 2018, Americans will spend $885 on Christmas gifts. Here is another great budget buster. Put this item in your budget and stick to it. Your children will not love you anymore if you buy them stuff! America spends over $40 billion dollars on games and toys. That is more than many of those same Americans saved and invested! Americans spent a record $16 billion on Father's Day or $139 per person. Mother's Day earned $25 billion or $195 per person. The average wedding gift is $118. Don't keep up with appearances if you are on a tight budget. Consider thoughtful handmade gifts. Do you craft? Are you a carpenter? I always appreciate a handmade gift. Never go into debt to keep up with mega consumers.

Inexpensive Hobbies

When you have downtime, try to spend your time wisely by finding free things to do. Check your local free newspaper or community website to see what free events are happening in your area. Consider reading a book on a topic that interests you. Listen to podcasts. Consider using your free time to volunteer. Check with a local church or checkout Habitat for Humanity. Volunteering gives you a double whammy. You find an activity that is free while getting a good feeling helping others. If that is not a win-win, I don't know what is.

In Conclusion

I know this section is stressful and complicated. It is important to talk about these unnecessary expenses because our economy and culture encourage us to spend more than we should on these goods and services. The people that provide these services are good people making a living providing a service they love to do. That is okay. What is not okay is your overspending and relying on emotion to make a rational decision. Before deciding to spend on an unnecessary good or service, please consult your budget. You will be happy you did after the excitement, passion and emotion of the purchase fades.

Chapter 8

Gambling and Lotto

"Divorce, loss of productivity, bankruptcy, and crime are only a few of the many consequences that can occur."

Gamblinghelp.org

On this bombshell, The Supreme Court, in 2018, allowed states to legalize sports gambling. Online sports gambling surged during the pandemic because most people didn't have anything productive to do. Based on a prediction from a major research firm, by 2027, the online gambling market will be worth 127 billion dollars. The major casinos are changing the casino floor to make gambling more appealing to millennials. They prefer a more video game like experience, called iGaming, than the old-fashioned slot machines. Casinos are scrambling to cater to the new customers.

If you are spending $1.00 per week on your state lottery, I am not worried about you. However, know what is happening in your surrounding culture. Gambling is almost never a good idea.

The "Lootery" (Play on Words)

My wife, while driving home from a trip to Tampa, stopped at a convenience store to get a bottled water. What she saw in the convenience store was interesting. There was a line of tired workers lined up to buy their Lotto tickets. Apparently, the jackpot rose to an amount that attracted more players than usual. Yes, it is their right to buy a lotto ticket and play these "games" for entertainment. It saddens me, though, that most of them do not realize they are wasting their money. To worsen matters, a lot of good people think playing the lottery is a legitimate retirement planning strategy!

The investment app Stash commissioned an online survey of 1,156 people and found that about forty percent of American consumers who responded, including fifty-nine percent of millennials, think winning the lottery could be a good way to fund retirement. What's more interesting, nearly one in four millennials surveyed said they're actually basing their retirement plans from winning the lottery.

https://www.annuity.org/2019/05/30/banking-on-the-lottery-to-fund-retirement/

It is also common knowledge that gambling can cause difficulties in one's home life, financial life, career, and general health.

The odds of matching three numbers and winning $5.00 are one in seventy. That means you will spend $70 to win $5.00. Please understand that the risk against reward ratio for playing the lotto or any other game of chance is working against you. You will almost always lose money.

Most people with a winning "scratch off" ticket will use winnings to buy more scratch off tickets until they own only losing tickets.

https://www.lotto.net/florida-lotto/prizes

The Florida Lottery sponsored a demographic survey by *Ipsos* that stated that the largest segment of players (33% of total lottery revenue) were the youngest segment. 37% of players are 18-34. They are also the least educated with 27% having a High School diploma or less. This segment has the highest participation in other gaming such as Bingo, Raffles, Jai Alai, and "I" gaming (online gaming). https://www.flalottery.com/exptkt/FloridaSegmentationFinalReport.pdf

I suspect these players think their Lotto dollars will support "Education."

Where does the Lotto money go? See this cheerful advertising piece that the Florida Lottery created. So warm and Fuzzy! http://www.flalottery.com/whereMoneyGoes

Is there a discrepancy here? The Florida Legislature created lotto in 1986, under the condition that lotto proceeds were funding the Educational Enhancement Trust Fund (EETF) and used to ENHANCE education. Their literature clearly states the majority of revenue goes to pay prize winners and to pay commissions to the vendors.

According to the Sun-Sentinel November 29, 2018.

"If there's nefarious activity going on here, it's not that lottery money isn't going to education-related budget items, but that it's not supplementing education funding. It's supplanting it."

"Also, the state has other budget priorities, such as health care and criminal justice says, Cheryl Etters, spokeswoman for Florida's education department." [2]

This means the old shell game affects another part of our prized education budget. They use the Lotto money more and more for running day-to-day Florida government operations. https://www.fox4now.com/news/state/where-does-florida-lottery-money-go-here-s-the-breakdown

With my interest in education in mind, I noted that gambling addiction affects the full spectrum of the population. Not just the disheveled laborer. The website www.gamblinghelp.org research department lists materials and studies about Middle and High School Students!

Quote "In brief: gambling is a widespread fact of life among Middle and High School students in Florida. More than half of the students surveyed reported gambling during the last twelve months. Even assuming that recreational gambling is harmless, the data consistently shows a straight-line correlation ranging from students who do not gamble, to those who may gamble very little, to those who are High Risk gamblers for all items analyzed. The High-Risk gamblers are the most likely to have: higher use rates of alcohol, drugs, and tobacco; struggle with depression; engage in antisocial behaviors; have trouble in school; have more risk factors and to have fewer protective factors." --Dr. Louis Lieberman, Dr. Mary Cuadrado June 2006.

Chronic gambling is prevalent in the arrestee community. Folks gamble with borrowed money. Folks gamble with their government assistance payments, and there is a college student gambling problem in Florida.

So, in conclusion, let's list the achievements of Lotto.

1. Entry level game leading to chronic addiction. CHECK

2. Increasing income inequality among uneducated young citizens. CHECK

3. Providing False Hope for the least among us. CHECK

4. Use the funds to skirt a balanced budget amendment by misallocating education funds. CHECK

5. Create another distraction to success by Middle school, High school, and College Students. CHECK

6. Develop advertisement directed at the poor. CHECK

7. Develop false advertising focusing on the public good of buying a lottery ticket. CHECK

8. Create another stumbling block to citizens as a personal budget buster affecting lifelong finances. CHECK

9. Create a financial/political predatory monster that can never be reversed, as the state treasury needs your money! CHECK

10. Underage Gambling. **CHECKMATE**

Solution, what you should do!!

The average American spends almost $220 per year on lottery tickets. Invest that amount in an investment that models the S & P 500 like the SPDR S&P ETF. After 20 years, you could accumulate $10,000.

See this link for a humorous look at lottery life.

https://www.jonathanpond.com/lotteries

Better yet, you can save $100 per month in an S & P 500 index fund. If you earn a conservative 7%, you will have accumulated $240,000 after 40 years. That is a sound investment plan. Gambling is not a sound investment plan.

Please read Chapter 17, Savings and investment.

Additional Resources:

[1]   https://govinfo.library.unt.edu/ngisc/research/lotteries.html

[2]   https://www.jacksonville.com/news/metro/2016-04-07/story/
      florida-gets-f-new-school-funding-report

[3]   https://lawecommons.luc.edu/cgi/viewcontent.cgi?article=
      1964&context=lclr

Legitimate Lottery Concerns as a Winner

Easy Come, Easy Go.

Most winners of the Lotto and other large money jackpots consider winning a curse!

I base the following discussion on my research of lottery winner's stories and events.

Why do you say that winning money is a curse? Your friends will take advantage of you. Believe it.

Expect to have a lot of new friends if you win the lottery. I am not against anyone winning the lottery, but if most Americans are financially illiterate, the chances are good that the winner of a lottery jackpot cannot manage their winnings. Dozens of stories describe the tragic events related to winning the lottery. If I were the King, lotto winners would come with a highly paid advisor with the sole purpose to teach money management and reduce the possibility you will lose your fortune. Remember, you only have to become rich once. The goal after you become rich is not to lose your fortune. It is an enormous task emotionally to manage a large sum of money properly. Become effective at working with attorneys, accountants, financial advisors, and bankers. Newsflash! Not all are honest or looking out for your best interest. I watched from a distance as a group of real estate brokers honestly defrauded a working-class client who inherited a large sum of money because of an industrial accident. The money flowed rapidly from client to real estate brokers! My advice to you is to seek a disinterested party who can refer you to an honest, professional advisor.

A lot of money can damage your relationship.

Your risk of bankruptcy will increase. Because you do not know how to manage money, bankers will aggressively tell you, "You've got great credit!" You borrow money under the idea that you have plenty of money to pay it back! Who needs a budget? I'm loaded.

Your family members, your long-lost relatives, will come out of the woodwork with the most creative "down on your luck" stories that only you can solve with your newfound money.

Here are some links to support this discussion.

https://www.mybanktracker.com/blog/utilize-my-options/winning-the-lottery-curse-19793

It must be an outstanding feeling to check the numbers on your favorite legal game of chance and see that you have won the jackpot! Congratulations! The odds of winning the Florida Lotto jackpot are about 1:23,000,000. In Florida, the probability for getting struck by lightning in your lifetime is 1 in 3000. So that means as a winner of Lotto you have been (probably struck by lightning 7600 times before you won your prize.

The sad story of Jack Whittaker was all over the news in 2012 for winning almost $315 million dollars back in 2002., His granddaughter and daughter died soon after from drug overdoses. They robbed him of excessive amounts of cash multiple times, and they hacked his bank accounts according to one report. He was being sued by Caesar's Atlantic for unpaid gambling debts.

A very sad story involves Abraham Shakespeare, who won the Florida lottery in 2009 to the tune of $30 million dollars. Murdered soon afterward by a new girlfriend who a jury found guilty of first-degree murder in 2012.

How about Georgia native Ronnie Music Jr. sentenced to 21 years in prison for investing in a crystal methamphetamine "business?"

And the stories go on and on.

The stories detail financial tragedy, rags to riches back to rags stories, murder, suicide, bankruptcy, arguments with coworkers, drug addictions, lawsuits, IRS fights and more. Is this what the "government" calls protecting its citizens? It's another nightmare placed upon an unknowing and vulnerable public to pay for ever-expanding government budgets.

If you win the lottery, immediately protect your identity and try to stay anonymous. There are only six states that allow you to protect your anonymity. The government wants the money spread around like flying fertilizer, regardless of if the windfall destroys your life. Don't sign your ticket. Just remember, though, if you lose an unsigned ticket, someone else can find it and legally redeem it. If you sign your ticket early, it may prevent you from setting up the blind trust you need. Make copies of the ticket for your attorney and accountant. Lock the original ticket in a safe place. You should contact a trustworthy attorney as soon as possible to set up a trust. Take your time. There is a window and rushing to the lottery office is not a good idea. Set up a new post office box address and phone number to give to the press. Put together your crack team of financial advisors, bankers, attorneys and accountants. You may hire a public relations specialist. Ask your attorney for a reference. You have become a rock star!

Consider surrounding yourself with close family, friends, clergy, and professional counselors to keep your sanity.

Why do people win multimillion-dollar lotteries only to return to their original net worth or worse? They had no system in place to handle and manage an enormous amount of money. They end up returning to the place they began before winning the prize: broke.

Sports Gambling

Recently Americans did not approve of sports gambling. After government stepped in saying they will regulate the business of sports gambling, there came a change of heart. The average citizen thought more tax revenue from sports gambling businesses results in less taxes owed by me. Now Americans approve of sports gambling online. The Supreme Court reversed 100 years of sports gambling opposition in the 2018 Murphy v. NCAA case. The decision gives states the authority to regulate sports gambling in their states. Ironically, the decision comes nearly 100 years after the 1919 Black Sox baseball scandal.

Like pornography and drug addictions, gambling stimulates the same pleasure centers. Your brain sees a cue that predicts a reward. The cue could be a lottery ticket commercial or an advertisement for an online sport gambling site, and you see dollar signs floating in front of you. You respond to this stimulus by buying a lottery ticket or placing a bet online. If you win, you are hooked. You have just programmed your brain through a craving process to repeat the cycle. The human brain knows how to survive in the jungle, and this thought cycle is great for survival in the "real jungle," but not so much in the "modern" jungle.

I just reviewed one of the large online sports gambling sites and looked at the statistics involved in gambling. If you can understand those calculations, get a job as an actuary, accountant or financial advisor.

If you win a large lottery, CNBC money guru Jim Cramer suggests doing this:

1. Do not invest in anything risky.

2. Take the Lump Sum, pay the taxes now while tax rates are low.

3. Invest in Treasury Bonds.

4. Buy valuable real estate to fight against hyperinflation.

5. Invest in Precious Metals.

6. Invest in High Quality Art.

7. Invest 5% in Bitcoin.

8. Invest in Municipal Bonds.

9. Invest in Dividend-Paying Stocks.

In Conclusion:

If you gamble for entertainment, consider investing the money in legitimate assets. If you are spending $1.00 a week on a lotto ticket, I am not worried about you. However, know what is happening in the surrounding culture. Gambling is almost never a good idea. The big casino, online sports businesses, and state lotto provide invent addictive environments to attract you to their venue. They hope you will stay.

They do not care if you lose all of your money. To them, that is not their concern. They do not care about your finances, and it is a legal way to make money for them. Their single goal is to make as much money for their business, and they do not care how many lives they ruin in their quest for profits.

If you have a gambling problem, please call 1-888-ADMIT-IT (263-4848) or checkout the website: www.gamblinghelp.org
Or https://www.addictions.com/gambling/

Chapter 9

How Addictions Affect Your Finances

"Even in the midst of devastation, something within us always points the way to freedom."

Sharon Salzberg

Back to your Finances Want to go broke quick? Get arrested for a drug violation. Odds are high you will lose money to legal fees. You may lose your job, and possibly lose your mate!

The average cost in legal fees for a misdemeanor drug charge is between $2,000 and $5,000. A felony charge will cost you between $5,000 and $15,000. Can you afford that unexpected expense?

https://personalfinance.costhelper.com/drug-defense-attorney.html

Illicit drug use and abuse is a national tragedy. Nothing can destroy your life and your finances faster than drugs. When I was in high school, in the late 70s, in a small isolated rural town, we separated the school into two cliques: The druggies and the non-druggies. The druggies were cool. They partied. They drank. They did drugs. They had sex. The other half grew up as normal, awkward teens. It was one of many reasons I wanted to get out and away from high school. It was a toxic environment. Even then I asked friends, "Why do you do drugs?" They replied, "I am bored. There's nothing else to do." I need to escape my reality was what they were really saying. It's the same excuse today, just add I'm depressed or I'm unemployed, which justifies self-medication. You choose to be bored. Find something constructive to do. Before there were electronic devices tethered to today's youth, the non-druggies played sports, fished, canoed, met with the neighbors, and worked. As a teenager, I instinctively knew drugs were poison. And I was right. I feel the same way today.

The data show that heavy use of marijuana during adolescent and early adulthood slows development of the pre-frontal cortex. The stuff may turn you into a blithering **idiot**! Decision making takes place in the pre-frontal cortex. Marijuana users report more impulsive behaviors. Impulsive behaviors and lack of decision-making ability could affect your pocketbook! Should we be concerned about the rapid legalization of marijuana in the US?

Health Risks

Many popular drugs like heroin use intravenous needles that exposes an intoxicated drug user to multiple blood-borne diseases. It exposes the needle user to HIV, Hepatitis B and C, tuberculosis, and many more. Be prepared for serious liver, kidney, lung and brain damage. General old infection is a possibility. Make sure you have great health insurance. Regardless, you will max out your deductible. You will need even more resources for a drug treatment center. My point is, your habit may be exposing you to financial ruin.

Drugs and drug abuse are a fast way to ruin. It is a recipe for financial disaster.

If you need help with an addiction, please get help.

Here are resources to find help.

http://drughelpline.org/   **1-877-639-2291**

https://www.addictions.com/

Pornography Addiction

Why here you ask? The addictive forces on the brain from drug abuse resemble the addictive forces of pornography. The chemical in your brain is called dopamine. The visual overstimulation caused by pornography is like the dopamine rush received in substance abuse. Pornography and its related vices are behavioral addictions.

Personal Journal

Homeland Security arrested a co-worker from my High School and charged him with child-pornography for making videos with his cell phone in the girl's locker room. Can you imagine the financial destruction that his family will endure? Pornography's ability to affect our finances negatively, justifies its discussion here.

- Researchers believe that pornography's intense stimulation of the brain brings about significant changes to the brain similar to drug addiction. Simone Kühn, Jürgen Gallinat, "Brain Structure and Functional Connectivity Associated With Pornography Consumption: The Brain on Porn," JAMA Psychiatry 71 (July 2014): 827-834.

A financial coaching client spent family budget money to pay for entertainment by "Private Dancers." This caused lots of stress in his marriage and unnecessary stress on the family's checkbook.

First Things First

If you have a pornography addiction, contact a community like

https://www.therecoveryvillage.com/process-addiction/porn-addiction/#gref

OR   1-866-235-4572

Another great website:

https://www.robertweissmsw.com/about-sex-addiction/information-for-sex-addicts/

One consequence to pornography addiction could be divorce. Please turn to Chapter Six, Divorce, to understand the financial cost. Fifty-eight percent of addicts suffer considerable financial losses. Unemployment can result from porn use at work. Losing your job could be a money losing proposition.

Another problem is men frequenting strip clubs and going into debt to pay for the entertainment. Even as most porn on the Internet is free, the sites are bombarding you to buy additional access.

Instead of looking at problems in the heart and soul, we insist on self-medicating with drugs and controlling our bad feelings through sexual addiction. We engage in escapism to soothe our feelings of anxiety, depression, and unresolved trauma. Drug addiction and sex addiction cause havoc with personal finances and money management. Please seek help to recover from the addictions and heal from the underlying issues that cause your anxiety. You have got too much of an amazing unaddicted life to lead! Let's do this!

"One day they will realize they traded their diamonds for worthless stone."

This quote reminds us life is about more than just money. Life is the legit time we spend with our families nurturing our spouses, children, and grandchildren. It is the authentic friendships we create, not on social media, but in person. Life is far more than anything you can ever see, or hear, or touch, to borrow words from Fred Rogers. Life is not money. It is authentic relationships. What larger-than-life project are we involved, that is bigger than us? Are we taking time to help our friends and families? Do you think there is room for improvement in your life?

Chapter 10

Tobacco and My Favorite, Vaping

Giving up smoking is the easiest thing in the world. I know because I've done it thousands of times.

Mark Twain

Smoking is one of the leading causes of statistics.

Fletcher Knebel

Smoking is an expensive pleasure. Besides the initial cost, consider the expense of chronic health problems associated with smoking. The average price for a pack of cigarettes in the United States is $6.65. According to the CDC, smoking-related illnesses cost the US over $300 billion annually. $170 billion attributed to direct medical care and another $156 billion in lost productivity.

That will put a dent in your retirement savings.

Seeing a cancer/tobacco display sponsored by Moffitt Cancer Hospital at the Tampa Museum of Science and Industry, showing a man with a prosthetic lower jaw which could be removed to see his skull, did not look very appealing. Smoking causes strokes, high blood pressure, many cardiac diseases, and cancer. Some of us still insist on doing it. I hope the stressful nature of this conversation is not a trigger for you to have a smoke. Instead, encourage your friends and family to quit with positive support.

Fortunately, only about 15% of Americans smoke. Which means we should follow the trend that 85% don't smoke! For families that do, it is a costly habit. The average cost of smoking is $337 per month. If you are a smoker, please determine how much you are spending for cigarettes. If you spend $3,000 per year to smoke, consider quitting and save the money instead.

Personal Story: My one and only cigarette experience came at 7 years old when a neighbor girl took me to her house to share the pleasure of smoking with me. We went inside her house, found two butts in the ashtray and lit them using the gas stove. I took one puff, and I almost threw up! I put the butt back in the ashtray and ran out of the house terrorized. That was fortunate for me. I never had a desire to smoke again. My mother passed away from complications of years of smoking. My brother-in-law passed away because of the complications of smoking. It's a terrible habit and, I know from observing my mother, a tough habit to break.

So along comes our savior: E-Cigarettes. The average cost for vaping is $74 to $84 per month. I've seen teen interviews where teens admitting to spending $150 per month for their addiction. They said they sold clothes and other items of value to pay for vaping supplies. Where did the money for those items come from? Usually the parent's money. Was that in your budget?

Studies of vaping revealed higher nicotine amounts causing a higher addiction reaction. Companies and consumers add vaping syrups with their own collection of "unregulated" chemicals. Some teens are not aware they are consuming nicotine. A JUUL cartridge, for example, has 20 cigarettes' worth of nicotine according to JUUL's website. JUUL reports that they only market to adults. One unverified report says that half of the followers of JUUL's Twitter account are underage. I asked my students for their "opinion" on the most popular flavors.... They answered, "Cool Cucumber, Fruit Medley, Menthol and Crème Brule". They changed the names in 2018, but not the product. Mango is big. A quick search of the site Vapor Vapes has Gummy Bear, Cotton Candy, and Do it Yourself Flavors...... Yet the companies claim they are not marketing to kids. One concerning experience in 2019 was consoling a teacher who discovered a group of trusted students vaping in their classroom. Many teachers, myself included, did not know that they shape a JUUL like a Flash drive and kids were charging them in class unknown to the teachers! We all thought they were jump drives! Again, let's get back to finances. A JUUL device is not free. The device costs between $35-$50 and a package of four JUUL pods will cost you $15.99.

How do you get one? Try E-Bay. Search Vaporizer or Vape Pen.

With great empathy, JUUL CEO Kevin Burns apologized to parents in July 2019 for the unintentional consequences his product was causing teens. That's fine; however the e-cigarette business is an example of capitalism run amok. Companies make billions of dollars in revenue exploiting adults trying to quit the tiresome habit of smoking and children trying to look cool.

Since I wrote the above paragraphs, as of January 2020, JUUL had to raise hundreds of millions of dollars in debt to continue operating their business because of increased expenses involving litigation and regulation. Revenues are dropping. Hopefully, the e-cig fad is fading. Americans are fighting back and at the time of writing, states and local governments are passing laws unfriendly to vaping. In fact, in July 2021, JUUL was ordered to pay $40M fine in settlement. The money is to be used by the state of North Carolina to fund vaping cessation and prevention programs. As of September 2021, the FDA delayed ruling on JUUL products and how they affect teenagers. In July 2022, banning the product was discussed at the FDA.

See https://apnews.com/article/health-government-and-politics-business-23de70fa5f6334c27e38dd9dd01452c4

The Surgeon General of the United States considers E-cigarette use an epidemic among youth. A few details remain. One detail is the fact that teens become addicted to nicotine quicker than adults. It may have something to do with the fact their brains are still experiencing physical and physiological changes.

Few addiction treatment options exist for teenagers. According to doctors, nicotine addiction can be reversed through nicotine cessation medications, but that may not be enough. Many doctors suggest therapy besides cessation drugs. An expensive choice to help children break the habit is to send your kid to a substance treatment and relapse prevention center. They last about 4 weeks because that's how long it takes your body to rid itself of nicotine.

My research shows the average cost of a drug treatment ranges from $10,000 to an average of $19,000 for a 4 week stay in Florida.

This would cause an unexpected family expense and a take a large bite out of the family budget.

The vaping culture is incredible. Parents: Beware! There are You Tube videos galore glamorizing the art of vaping that target teens.

When I started writing this book, I knew vaping was a dangerous habit. I am sad to report that vaping is now deadly. As of January 2020, 57 people have died from vape related disease.

The world changed because of the COVID pandemic. One benefit of the COVID-19 pandemic is the reduction in vaping. During COVID it seemed to make sense to steer away from further respiratory illness. The latest vape invention is smokeless vapes. Now students just puff, smoke free, without consequences in class.

If you need help for addictive vaping: https://www.rehabcenter.net/vapes/

For other disorders: https://www.samhsa.gov/find-help/national-helpline

Chapter 11

DUI's and Other Legal Calamities

"A Tree Never Hits an automobile except in self-defense."

Woody Allen

Driving drunk is no joke because drunk driving ruins so many innocent lives. There is no excuse. Over 1.4 million arrests for DUI per year occur according to the National Highway Traffic Administration. According to MADD, Mothers Against Drunk Driving, drunk driving costs the American economy $132 billion per year. Twenty-eight people die every day in the United States because of alcohol-related deaths.

The total cost of the first time DUI in the state of Florida is between $7,500 and $10,000. The Florida amount is similar to the national average. The average time to settle your DUI case is five months. Your second DUI will cost almost the same as the first, but the percentage on the second offense was higher. This increases your chance of receiving a sentence that includes jail time. It is my understanding that it can be pretty difficult to keep a job and still fulfill your jail sentence at the same time.

Prepare for your auto insurance premium to skyrocket. The auto insurance premium increase alone is between $3,300 and $6,000 (after you get your driving privilege back. A friend just told me her insurance rate after one DUI was $5,000 per six months in Florida. In Florida, you must acquire an SR-22; a document that allows you to reinstate your license after purchasing pricey auto insurance. The SR-22, in Florida, has to be in place for three years before you can buy insurance without one. The repeat DUI or DWI offender has to acquire FR-44 insurance. Some say FR-44 is "DUI" insurance. The restrictions are stricter than the SR-22. For instance, if there is a lapse of coverage, the three year term resets to when you reinstate. Leaving the State of Florida does not help your situation. You also must pay the premium six months at a time as there are no convenient monthly payments. According to MADD, 50-75% of convicted DUI offenders continue to drive with a suspended license.

You can hire a high-powered, experienced (read expensive lawyer to request an administrative hearing with your state's Department of Motor Vehicles to appeal the loss of your driver's license.

So, besides a large part of your savings and income committed to pay your debt to society, you may rely on others to get back and forth to work. If your job requires you to have a driver's license, you'll be looking for a new job on your bicycle! This is another area where your finances will suffer from the DUI. Your ability to make a living may change.

After getting your driving privileges back, you may need to install an ignition (interlock safety switch that checks your breath every time you drive to abide by the law. That should begin great conversations with your young children in the car. Interlock Ignition Safety Switch Cost $500-$1,500

Court ordered alcohol treatment classes? $500 - $1,000.

Probation Supervision: $1,000

According to dui.drivinglaws.org, your total first time Florida DUI experience may include the following.

1. License Suspension
2. Ignition Interlock Device
3. Vehicle Impoundment
4. Community Service
5. Jail Time
6. Fines
7. Probation

Florida law requires you to take a breath, blood, or urine test if arrested for DUI. It's called **"implied consent"** and it's on your Florida driver's license. You agreed to it. Check your state laws regarding your home state.

Here is a "subject" where I believe you should learn from **"other"** people's mistakes! The poor choice of driving under the influence could ruin your life! The next time you need a ride after drinking, call a taxicab, Lyft, or Uber.

Introduction to Part II of Get Wallet Wise, Taking Control of Your Finances

Part One helps us heal from the ravages of the Consumer Industrial Complex. I want you to imagine a new you! A new you who is money wise that spends less than you earn, whose debt is less than assets, and content in all things. I designed Part II of *Get WalletWise* to provide you the tools and information you need to take control of your finances. Are you ready? I know you are.

Chapter 12 is where the financial tire meets the road. Create a budget and net worth balance sheet, like a tycoon, to establish responsible spending habits and understand your money.

Chapter 13 addresses Credit Scores and Credit Bureaus. Financial bad habits result in a poor credit score (Your Adult Credit Card) that ultimately results in more expensive debt. Gain understanding of this incredibly important report card.

Chapter 14 discusses Real Estate. Having a roof over your head is important. Know how to navigate the treacherous waters of renting and buying real estate. Not all real estate agents are alike.

Almost everyone needs transportation. In Chapter 15, Automobiles, read about how to survive a real-life shark tank and learn how to buy a car!

Chapter 16, Side Hustles to Make Extra Money dives into the world of self-employment. Well-intentioned workers and budding entrepreneurs find more hype than hope with many popular side hustles. Learn that the average UBER take home after expenses is $10.00 hour. Delivery driving may increase your odds for an auto crash. There are, however, excellent solutions.

We discuss basic savings and investment in Chapter Seventeen. After conquering debt, you can create an emergency fund, fund your 401k, fund your IRA, and invest like the big boys and girls.

Chapter 18 prepares us for retirement. Your money adventure is not over in retirement. This important part of everyone's life needs tender loving care.

Chapter 19 has everything you wanted to know about insurance, but you were afraid to ask. Insurance is vital to the foundation of everyone's financial health. How can a business about risk be boring?

The last chapter, Chapter 20, is about habits. It outlines the behaviors you need in order to achieve financial success. We discuss the habits of highly financially intelligent people. Learn how we live in a physical, mental, emotional, and spiritual world and how this reality affects our feelings about money. I've broken the bad habits and so can you. I reveal the secrets here!

Chapter 12

Money Management and
Your Budget

Having a plan with money doesn't just help you right now, it
also gives you hope for the end goal.

Dave Ramsey

A budget is the most important tool to begin financial responsibility
and ultimate success. It helps you from becoming a victim of financial
fraud, bank errors, predatory sales, and predatory lenders. Ironically,
ignorance of your finances and finances will reduce your freedom and
future opportunities. Budgets are liberators! Budgets are not
oppressive. Unfortunately many Americans think otherwise.

Approximately 40% of Americans keep track of their finances through
the use of a budget, according to a study by U.S. Bank. Another study
by Career Builder in 2017; indicates only 32% of respondents used a
budget. One purpose of this book is to increase that percentage and
help you keep track of your hard-earned dollars. The point is; please
create and use your budget as the best tool to reach financial
independence. Don't worry about what other folks are not doing. It is
important to learn from their mistakes and make a budget for ourselves.

I know it is work, but anything worth having (like money bliss) is worth
the effort.

Let's begin our meeting with your money. You know, a money date!

A Six Step Plan to Understand and Take Ownership of Your Finances.

This plan summarizes the steps to become financially literate.

Step 1: Establish $1,000 Emergency Fund. This may sound like a bad first step if you are in serious money trouble but save $100 per month for ten months and you're there. An emergency fund reduces your dependence on your credit card as a piggy bank.

1. Create Real Budget and a Balance Sheet on paper (I discuss detailed steps below).

2. Check your Credit Reports. See Chapter Thirteen, Check your Credit Reports and Credit Scores.

3. Open a Mint Account (This is a budget app that lives on your phone and computer) that helps you track your money in total.

4. Track and Reduce Expenses on paper.

    a) Sell Expensive assets and use cash to repay debt.

    b) Trim Gift Expenses (Birthday and Holiday gifts can be budget busters).

    c) Take Inexpensive Vacations.

5. Receive Better Prices on Bulk Necessities you always purchase by Joining a Warehouse Club, like BJ's, Costco, or Sam's Club.

6. Increase income (Take on a sustainable side hustle) If this sounds interesting to you, then turn to Chapter 16, Make Extra Money with a Side Hustle.

Step 2: Pay off debt. The "Snowball" method pays the lowest balances first. The Avalanche method pays the highest rate first.

1. Credit Cards.

2. Personal Note.

3. Store Accounts.

4. You can refinance your car at your credit union at a lower interest rate. If you are in serious financial problems, you may have to sell the expensive "high payment" car to remove the expensive car payment obligation and buy a car for cash. (Please see Chapter 15, Automobiles, to learn how to find a good car paid for with cash.

Step 3: Establish Complete Emergency Fund $20,000.

Step 4: Retirement Planning

1. Start saving ten percent of net income after the Emergency Fund complete.

2. Fund your 401k enough to qualify for company match.

3. Increase retirement savings to fifteen percent of net income.

4. Open Roth IRA after you max out 401k match.

5. Max Out IRA Contributions.

Step 5: Save for College 529 Plan, Open a savings account in the child's name.

Step 6: Payoff Mortgage or buy an affordable house with an affordable mortgage.

Time for A Budget!

To access the Budget, Expense Tracker and Net Worth/Balance Sheet templates please see https://www.walletwise.org/ downloadableresources. Click on the XLS file you need to pop it open. Your interactive selection will open in Microsoft Excel.

I created these original resources for you. There are step-by-step examples below to show you how to use them. The Excel file automatically adds and subtracts for you. If you have any difficulty accessing these resources, email me at kenremsen@ walletwise.org and I will email you the forms.

1. List your Income

The income portion asks for net income after taxes. I did this to simplify the budget from having a separate category for taxes.

If your income is a commission style, inconsistent, month-to-month income, or you are self-employed, then use your annual income and divide it by twelve.

Do not consider business expense reimbursements as income.

2. **List your Estimated Expenses**

I've designed a budget with thirteen different expense categories. Please take the time to list your expenses accurately. Each section should total each category automatically. Estimate any expense that does not occur monthly by taking your annual expense of a particular item and divide it by twelve. The budget will total your expenses and subtract them from your income to calculate your "Surplus" (YEAH!) or "Deficit" (BOO!)

I attempted to place the categories in order of importance in a normal budget. Yes, that's right, if you have a balanced budget, charitable giving comes first.

3. **Check the Percentages**

Please keep in mind that the expenses percentages are just a recommendation. Folks with different incomes will experience different percentages. Oh! The guidelines do not add up to 100%. It's like the pirate's code, they are just guidelines. The guideline for credit card and unsecured debt is zero%, but that is rarely the case.

As an additional resource, Dave Ramsey suggests there are roughly ten categories for budgeting: housing (25-35%), food (10-15%), transportation (10-15%), insurance (10-25%), utilities (5-10%), health (5-10%), Recreational (5-10%), personal (10-15%), giving (10-15%), and saving (10-15%). Compare these percentages to yours to see how you rate.

The key is to spend less than you earn.

Budgeting in a Nutshell

Before starting the Excel worksheet consider separating your expense into three clean categories. The 50/30/20 rule is a simple way to get started. 50% of your monthly take-home (net income) goes to essential expenses. These essential expenses include Rent/Mortgage, food, car payments/insurance, debt payments, court debts and utilities. 30% goes to discretionary (fun) expenses and 20% goes into savings. Personally, I would only use this as an overview of your budget. Many famous budget pundits encourage this method, but I don't. This method does not help you manage your money. It is what I call a rule of thumb.

I know you can develop the discipline to take an hour of your time and write down all of your income and expenses on a few sheets of paper. You will thank yourself later for doing the hard work now instead of taking the easy way out.

WalletWise Monthly Budget				
Date of Plan:				
Your Name:				
Monthly Net Income				
Description	Amount			
Monthly Salary				
Child Support / Alimony (Income)				
Interest Income				
Side Hustle 1				
Side Hustle 2				
Commissions				
Retirement Income				
Net Business Income				
Other Income				
	Income Total	0.00		

Monthly Expenses				Percentage
A. Donations and Gifts	Amount			
Local Charity or Local Church			Guideline 12%	
Gifts (Birthdays)			Your %	0
Gifts (Christmas)			Over / Under	-12.00
	Gift Total	0.00		

B. Savings and Investment	Amount			
Emergency Savings				
Auto Replacement Savings				
401k/403b Retirement Plans	0			
IRA			Guideline 5%	
College Funds			Your %	0
Stocks / Bonds			Over / Under	-5.00
	Financial Total	0.00		

C. Home	Amount			
Mortgage				
Property Tax				
Homeowners/Flood Insurance				
Rent				
Renters Insurance			Guideline 27%	
Pest Control / Termite Bond			Your %	0
Lawn Pest Control / Other			Over / Under	-27.00
	Home Total	0.00		

D. Utility	Amount				
Electricity					
Water / Sewer					
Mobile Telephone					
TV / Cable / Satellite/ Internet			Guideline 3%		
Heat Gas / Oil			Your %	0	
Other			Over / Under		-3.00
Utilities Total	0.00				

E. Food	Amount				
Groceries			Guideline 7%		
Eating Out			Your %	0	
Vitamins & Supplements			Over / Under		-7.00
Utilities Total	0.00				

F. Auto/ Transportation	Amount				
Car Payments					
Auto Insurance					
Fuel					
Uber/Lyft					
Repairs/Maintenance/Tire			Guideline 7%		
AAA/Auto Club			Your %	0	
OnStar / Satellite Radio			Over / Under		-7.00
Auto Total	0.00				

G. Credit Cards & Debt	Amount				
Credit Card 1					
Credit Card 2					
Store Credit Card			Guideline 0%		
Gas Credit Card			Your %	0	
Unsecured Consumer Debt			Over / Under		0.00
Auto Total	0.00				

H. Health and Fitness	Amount				
Doctor					
Dentist					
Prescriptions					
Eye Glasses / Contacts					
Deductibles					
HAS / Flexible Spending Accounts			Guideline 5%		
Gym Membership			Your %	0	
			Over / Under		-5.00
Health Total	0.00				

I. Insurance	Amount			
Health Insurance				
Dental Insurance				
Vision Insurance				
Disability Insurance			Guideline 7%	
Life Insurance			Your %	0
Long-Term Care Insurance			Over / Under	-7.00
	Insurance Total	0.00		

J. Children	Amount			
Child Care				
Baby Sitting			Guideline 4%	
Kids Allowance			Your %	0
Music / Dance Lessons			Over / Under	-4.00
	Children Total	0.00		

K. Personal Care	Amount			
Hair Care				
Toiletries / Cosmetics				
Tax Preparation				
Sports / Hobbies				
Subscriptions / Dues			Guideline 6%	
Clothes			Your %	0
Laundry / Dry Cleaning			Over / Under	-6.00
	Personal Care Total	0.00		

L. Pets	Amount			
Pet Food & Supplies				
Veterinarian			Guideline 1%	
Boarding /Pet Sitting			Your %	0
Pet Insurance			Over / Under	-1.00
	Pets Total	0.00		

M. Travel	Amount			
Vacation Motel / Food			Guideline 2%	
Rental Car			Your %	0
Unexpected Travel			Over / Under	-2.00
	Travel Total	0.00		

Monthly	Net Spendable Income	0.00
Monthly	Total Expenses	0.00
Monthly	**Budget Surplus or Deficit**	0.00

Here is a sample budget with a typical income and expenses base on U.S. statistics of personal income and expenses.

Sample WalletWise Monthly Budget					
Date of Plan:	1/1/2021				
Your Name:					
Monthly Net Income					
Description	Amount				
Monthly Salary	5000				
Child Support / Alimony (Income)					
Interest Income					
Side Hustle 1	200				
Side Hustle 2					
Commissions					
Retirement Income					
Net Business Income					
Other Income					
	Income Total	5200.00			
Monthly Expenses				Percentage	
A. Donations and Gifts	Amount				
Local Charity or Local Church	100		Guideline 12%		
Gifts (Birthdays)	200		Your %		11.54
Gifts (Christmas)	300		Over / Under		-0.46
	Gift Total	600.00			
B. Savings and Investment	Amount				
Emergency Savings	100				
Auto Replacement Savings	100				
401k/403b Retirement Plans	100				
IRA			Guideline 5%		
College Funds			Your %		5.77
Stocks / Bonds			Over / Under		0.77
	Financial Total	300.00			
C. Home	Amount				
Mortgage	842				
Property Tax	140				
Homeowners/Flood Insurance	120				
Rent					
Renters Insurance			Guideline 27%		
Pest Control / Termite Bond	40		Your %		21.96
Lawn Pest Control / Other			Over / Under		-5.04
	Home Total	1142.00			

D. Utility	Amount			
Electricity	125			
Water / Sewer	40			
Mobile Telephone	118			
TV / Cable / Satellite/ Internet	120		Guideline 3%	
Heat Gas / Oil			Your %	7.75
Other			Over / Under	4.75
	Utilities Total	403.00		

E. Food	Amount			
Groceries	500		Guideline 7%	
Eating Out			Your %	9.62
Vitamins & Supplements			Over / Under	2.62
	Food Total	500.00		

F. Auto/ Transportation	Amount			
Car Payments	568			
Auto Insurance	120			
Fuel				
Uber/Lyft				
Repairs/Maintenance/Tire	25		Guideline 7%	
AAA/Auto Club	10		Your %	13.90
OnStar / Satellite Radio			Over / Under	6.90
	Auto Total	723.00		

G. Credit Cards & Debt	Amount			
Credit Card 1	250			
Credit Card 2	250			
Store Credit Card			Guideline 14%	
Gas Credit Card			Your %	14.42
Unsecured Consumer Debt	250		Over / Under	0.42
	Credit Card Total	750.00		

H. Health and Fitness	Amount			
Doctor	40			
Dentist	20			
Prescriptions	75			
Eye Glasses / Contacts	25			
Deductibles	50			
HSA / Flexible Spending Accounts			Guideline 5%	
Gym Membership			Your %	4.04
			Over / Under	-0.96
	Health Total	210.00		

I. Insurance	Amount			
Health Insurance	75			
Dental Insurance	25			
Vision Insurance				
Disability Insurance			Guideline 7%	
Life Insurance			Your %	1.92
Long-Term Care Insurance			Over / Under	-5.08
	Insurance Total	100.00		

J. Children	Amount			
Child Care	500			
Baby Sitting			Guideline 4%	
Kids Allowance			Your %	9.62
Music / Dance Lessons			Over / Under	5.62
	Children Total	500.00		

K. Personal Care	Amount			
Hair Care	45			
Toiletries / Cosmetics				
Tax Preparation	10			
Sports / Hobbies	10			
Subscriptions / Dues			Guideline 6%	
Clothes			Your %	1.25
Laundry / Dry Cleaning			Over / Under	-4.75
	Personal Care Total	65.00		

L. Pets	Amount			
Pet Food & Supplies				
Veterinarian			Guideline 1%	
Boarding /Pet Sitting			Your %	0
Pet Insurance			Over / Under	-1.00
	Pets Total	0.00		

M. Travel	Amount			
Vacation Motel / Food			Guideline 2%	
Rental Car			Your %	0
Unexpected Travel			Over / Under	-2.00
	Travel Total	0.00		
				1.79

Monthly	Net Spendable Income	5200.00
Monthly	Total Expenses	5293.00
Monthly	**Budget Surplus or Deficit**	**-93.00**

You may discover that you spend more than you make. It's time to make difficult decisions to get your expenses less than your income. Cancel cable, gym memberships, stop eating out, and whatever it takes to turn your budget around.

I did not include a separate category for income tax because we used net (after tax) income.

1. Track Expenses

Regardless of the budget plan you decide to use, it will be necessary to track and record every expenditure for thirty days. It's difficult. It is certainly not fun. You need to do this, however, to get a handle on what/where you are spending your money. Make a copy of the expense tracker and take it with you daily to mark down your expenses. I keep all of my receipts of the day and add them to the tracker at one time, at the end of the day.

Procedure: Each time you spend money, record the amount in the correct spending category, A-M. The budget items match the expense sheet items.

Download the Worksheet:

https://www.walletwise.org/downloadableresources

Look for WalletWise Expense Tracker and download the file.

WalletWise Expense Tracking

	Budget										0
	% Spent	-	-	-	-	-	-	-	-	-	-
	Remaining		-	-	-	-	-	-	-	-	-

Date	Payment Type	Description	Gift & Donation	Savings & Invest	Home	Utility	Food	Auto	Credit Cards	Subtotal
										-
1/10/2019	2032	ABC Credit								-
										-
										-
										-
										-
										-
										-
										-
										-
										-
										-
										-
										-
										-
										-
										-
										-
										-
										-
										-
										-
	Expense Total		-	-	-	-	-	-	-	-

			Budget		210						210
			% Spent	-	-	47.6%	-	-	-	-	-	47.6%
			Remaining		-	110	-	-	-	-	-	110

Date	Payment Type	Description	Health & Fitness	Insurance	Children	Personal	Pets	Travel	Other	Subtotal
1/1/2019	CrCard	XYZ Supply Store								-
2/5/2019				100.00						100.00
										-
										-
										-
										-
										-
										-
										-
										-
										-
										-
										-
										-
										-
										-
										-
										-
										-
	Expense Total		-	-	100.00	-	-	-	-	-	100.00

Envelope System: Another effective method for getting your household budget in order is the envelope system. Please see the website https://www.wikihow.com/Do-Envelope-Budgeting Free!

Another friend recommended "You need a budget" at www.youneedabudget.com. It has great reviews; however, this app has a subscription fee to access all of its features.

Let's look at how much the average American spends on LIFE. We use this information to show **you** what the average American spends in specific categories to compare it to your situation. I listed the categories in the same order as in the budget. Use this section to help you clarify the purpose of each category. The numbers that I put into the completed sample budget above come from the information I gathered in the following categories.

Cat A: Donations and Gifts

Putting donations and gifts first in the budget may confuse you. "It is my opinion" that you learn financial maturity and wisdom by supporting a charity and its mission. You can embrace the habit of being involved in a "Mission" bigger than yourself.

According to a Motley Fool article written by Selena Maranjian, the average annual household contributed $2,081 to charitable organizations. If you are in difficult financial circumstances, then this category should be zero percent until you make your financial recovery.

According to the National Retail Federation and a Gallup Poll in 2018, Americans will spend about $885 on Christmas gifts! That amount is more than many of those same Americans saved! WOW! Again, according to the National Retail Federation, Americans spent a record $16 billion on Father's Day or $139 per person. Mother's Day earned $25 billion or $195 per person. Men spend more money on both holidays. All I can say is "Keep It Real" if you are on a tight budget. Certainly, never go into debt to keep up with mega consumers.

Cat B Savings and Investment

Just as important as giving to a charity, after you balance your budget, your second most important item is to pay yourself first. According to the St. Louis Federal Reserve, the average savings rate from the first quarter of 2019 hovered between 6% and 7% of disposable income. Based upon the Real Median Household Income in the U.S. of $60,336 as of 2017, this produces a savings amount of $3921.84 per year. Assorted financial advisors suggest that by your 50s you should have accumulated savings seven times your earnings to meet the financial final exam called "retirement." Unfortunately, many Americans don't pass the test. If you earn $50,000 that equates to $350,000. The *median* savings amount for households between 50 and 55 is about $8,000. *Average* savings balance for the same age group is about $124,831. This number is so much higher because of the "uber" wealthy. The median is more accurate.

According to Value Penguin, in 2016 the Median Savings Balance was $7,000. The average savings balance was $30,600 for the average house-hold responding to the 2016 Survey of Consumer Finances. How do you stack up? If you have more debt than you should, **pause saving** until your debt is back under control. It makes no sense to collect, say, 5% in a savings vehicle to turn around to pay out 18% in credit card debt interest.

Cat C Home

According to www.apartmentlist.com, the National median price for a one-bedroom apartment is $959 and $1,190 for a 2-bedroom apartment. According to the BLS, the average household spent $11,895 for shelter. The average American mortgage payment according to the U.S. Census Bureau American Housing Survey is $1,030.

According to Zillow, the median value of a home in the U.S. is $227,700. This where I obtained the numbers to place in the sample budget above.

Be careful to not overspend in this category. It is easy to justify spending more here because this is the roof over your head. A ballpark figure is to spend one week's salary on your housing total expense. If you make $15.00 per hour and you cannot find safe housing for $600 per month, then consider a responsible roommate.

Cat D Utilities

Utility	National average cost per month
Electricity	$125.22
Natural gas	$100.53
Internet (60 Mbps)	$62.33
Cable	$100
Water	$40
Total cost of utilities	$422.08

National average utility cost   https://www.move.org/which-states-pay-most-utilities/

Here is a table showing average American utility bills. Over several years, I have upgraded my HVAC system, replaced my roof, installed upgraded windows, upgraded appliances and hot water heater to lower my utility bills. I used AskTrim (https://www.asktrim.com/) to reduce my Direct TV Internet and TV service and take advantage of employer corporate discounts for call phone service.

There are a lot of options for mobile cell phone plans. At the time of writing AT&T's prepaid plan, Cricket, Mint Mobile, Verizon prepaid, and Straight Talk offered some of the best cell phone deals. AAA offers deals with Affinity Cellular. Metro by T mobile has attractive plans that connect with Amazon Prime. Consumer Cellular offers discount plans to AARP members. Total Wireless uses Verizon's network and is a favorite.

Cat E Food

In the food category, the Bureau of Labor Statistics, American households spent $7,729 per year. They spent $4,363 for food at home and spent $3,365 for food away from home. A great tip for families of four or larger is to invest in a Warehouse Club membership like Costco or BJ's. You will gain a big budget advantage if you buy items in bulk. It saves money! Another big money saver is finding different essential items at Amazon.com, specifically the Amazon Basics brand. I have found a variety of commonly used items, for example batteries, that are economical.

Cat F Transportation

According to the Bureau of Labor Statistics, the average American household spent $9,576 on transportation expenses in 2017. This includes car payments, car repairs, maintenance, insurance, and gas. This category is a real budget buster. Remember, only about 24% of millionaires drive new cars. Only own the least expensive car that meets your needs. Consider paying 20% of your annual income to purchase a vehicle. That's the thinking that builds wealth and reduces unnecessary debt.

Cat G Credit Cards

This book has an entire chapter (Chapter 1 on credit card debt, so I'll be brief here. According to NerdWallet, the "average" revolving credit card debt owed by the "average" U.S. household is $6,741 for $423.8 billion total. The average American household has 2.5 persons. On the surface, this does not look bad. I suspect a small sample of individuals holds most of the debt. Nine percent of Americans feel they can never pay off their credit card debt. The total amount of debt owed by the average American household, including transacting and revolving credit card debt and mortgages, was $135,065 in 2018.

Your goal is $**0.00,** That is why the Guideline is **zero%.**

Cat H Health and Fitness

A 2014 Bureau of Labor Statistics chart shows that the average U.S. household spends $4,300 on health care and fitness related expenses. This category can include gym memberships, insurance deductibles related to healthcare, and dental expenses. Only pay for the least expensive gym membership you can find. See Chapter 7, Expensive Hobbies for a more detailed discussion on this topic.

Cat I Insurance

- According to the 2016 data from the Bureau of Labor Statistics, health insurance costs per person are 7.6% of total compensation.

- According to The Zebra, an auto insurance comparison site, the average American spends about $1,500 per year or about $751 per six-month policy on car insurance.

- The average cost of homeowner insurance based upon my calculation of taking each state average from insurance.com is $1,228 per year. Florida and Louisiana are the most expensive states for homeowner's insurance. Florida's AVERAGE is $3,575. Louisiana's average is $2,979. The average cost of renter insurance in Florida is lower at $300.

- According to Insurance.com, the average non-smoking 40-year-old American pays $578 annually for a $250,000 term life insurance policy. Smokers pay an average of $1,363 for their life insurance premium. A $50,000 whole life policy for a smoker costs $68 per month for a forty year-old.

- Please see Chapter 19, Insurance for a more detailed analysis of insurance.

https://www.fool.com/slideshow/heres-what-average-american-spends-these-25-essentials/?slide=25

Cat J Children / Child Care

In these modern times, Child Care is expensive. The Economic Policy Institute website describes day care expenses by state. https://www.epi.org/child-care-costs-in-the-united-states/

In Florida, the average cost of infant care is $9,238 which amounts to over 17% of the median income of a Florida family. The normal percentage as a part of a family's income is 7%. Keeping childcare expenses below 10% is best. The survey shows childcare for two children, a baby and a 4-year-old costs $16,520 per year or 19.9% more than the average rent in Florida. That's about $1,300 per month.

If you are considering day care for your children, weigh and calculate alternatives. There are no shortcuts here. Consider a trusted family member to provide daycare. Some workplaces provide day care facilities for their employees. Check with a nearby school to see if they have an on-site day care. In my area, it was possible to find an elderly couple who loved babies and children who were looking for a little something to do during the week. This type of day care is less expensive than traditional day care.

Cat K Personal Care/ Clothes

According to the Bureau of Labor Statistics, the average household spends $1,833 per year for clothes. That's $150 per month. I suggest checking out thrift stores and clearance sales. I get my new clothes off the clearance rack at an outlet store. I shop at consignment shops. Here is an opportunity to get name brand, gently used, clothes at a tremendous discount.

Americans love a good Hairdo! They spend $762 per year. Look for hair care coupons, folks. Buy your own razor. Sources state that women spend $80 per month and eleven hours a month on that hairdo! Florida has the longest time blow drying hair at 45 minutes. Who knew! It adds up to $55,000 in a lifetime just for hair products and treatments! That's a lot of dough to invest. Look, I like a nice hairdo as much as anybody, but be aware of the total cost of that "Do."

Cat L Pets

Pets have become a real obsession in the U.S. Pets are very expensive to own. They can become budget busters. A blog post on www.opploans.com tabulated the average monthly expense per pet.

Here's a breakdown of the data per animal:

- **Birds:** $113.89/month

- **Cats:** $92.98/month

- **Dogs:** $139.80/month

- **Fish:** $62.53/month

- **Mice or Rats:** $80/month

- **Rabbits:** $65/month

- **Reptiles or Turtles:** $116.63/month

- **Small mammals:** $251.82/month

I have two fish and I spend nowhere close to these estimates. Reduce your spending in the pet category. I'll say it again. The market and its nonstop bombardment of advertising shames us into believing we must buy fancy food and take our pets to a fancy pet spa. Not true. Be careful of your local veterinarian going corporate and pressing you to follow through on their expensive "treatment plan." If there is a serious problem, make sure you get a second opinion. Like the auto repair business, veterinarians take sales training classes to learn how to upsell.

Cat M Travel

- According to valuepenguin.com, average vacation costs (including lodging, food, entertainment, and transportation) for a four-night Domestic Trip were $581 (or $144 per day) and a twelve day International Trip averaged $3,251, or ($271 per day).

- According to Allianz Partner's Vacation Confidence Index 2019 (the organization sells very profitable travel insurance), Americans' expected spend on vacations this summer is an average of $2,037 for a record setting $101.7 **Billion** in 2019. This tops $2,000 for the first time since 2010 when the survey started tracking spending and marking a 5.2% increase over last year. I suspect that post pandemic spending will be higher than 2019 because of pent up demand.

- According to the 2017 LearnVest Money Habits and Confessions Survey, 74% of Americans have gone into debt to pay for vacations. The average debt Americans racked up is $1,108. **The survey concluded that 55% of Americans don't (Forgot) to put vacation spending in their budget.** https://sctelco.com/learnvest-survey-american-vacation-spending-habits/

- The same survey found that 66% of Americans spent more on their vacation than on one mortgage or rent payment.

- According to an *Acorns* 2017 Money Matters Report, a survey of over 3,000 Americans between 18 and 44, 37% of respondents spent more on vacations than they invested, spending an average of $1.145/year on a vacation.

Stealthy Expenses that were not included in the budget.

Not listed in the above budget are bank late and overdraft fees. I don't pay them. Part of managing money well is to research the best bank account for your financial situation and don't pay bank fees. Sources report bank fees average about $300 per year. Do your best to avoid these fees.

Here is a table from the Bureau of Labor and Statistics on Consumer Expenditures, from 2017. Here you can get a ballpark estimate of the percentages each category should/may have.

Table A. Average expenditures and income of all consumer units, 2015-17

Item	2015	2016	2017	Percent change 2015-16	Percent change 2016-17
Average income before taxes	$69,627	$74,664	$73,573	7.2	-1.5
Average annual expenditures	55,978	57,311	60,060	2.4	4.8
Food	7,023	7,203	7,729	2.6	7.3
Food at home	4,015	4,049	4,363	0.8	7.8
Food away from home	3,008	3,154	3,365	4.9	6.7
Housing	18,409	18,886	19,884	2.6	5.3
Shelter	10,742	11,128	11,895	3.6	6.9
Owned dwellings	6,210	6,295	6,947	1.4	10.4
Rented dwellings	3,802	4,035	4,167	6.1	3.3
Apparel and services	1,846	1,803	1,833	-2.3	1.7
Transportation	9,503	9,049	9,576	-4.8	5.8
Vehicle purchases	3,997	3,634	4,054	-9.1	11.6
Gasoline, other fuels, and motor oil	2,090	1,909	1,968	-8.7	3.1
Healthcare	4,342	4,612	4,928	6.2	6.9
Health insurance	2,977	3,160	3,414	6.1	8.0
Entertainment	2,842	2,913	3,203	2.5	10.0
Personal care products and services	683	707	762	3.5	7.8
Education	1,315	1,329	1,491	1.1	12.2
Cash contributions	1,819	2,081	1,873	14.4	-10.0
Personal insurance and pensions	6,349	6,831	6,771	7.6	-0.9
Pensions and Social Security	6,016	6,509	6,353	8.2	-2.4
All other expenditures	1,847	1,897	2,010	2.7	6.0

Note: Subcategories do not sum to their respective major item category.

Time to Improve Your Balance

The Balance Sheet is a very important as it determines your net worth. In the United States, about 50% of Americans have a negative net worth.

WalletWise Balance Sheet			WalletWise Balance Sheet	
	Insert Your Figures			Insert Your Figures
Assets		LIABILITIES	Liabilities	
Monetary Assets			Short Term Liabilities	
Cash	2.00		Credit Card #1	1.00
Checking Account #1	0.00		Credit Card #2	0.00
Checking Account #2	0.00		Credit Card #3	0.00
Savings Account #1	0.00		Credit Card #4	0.00
Savings Account #2	0.00		Medical Debts	0.00
Savings Account #3	0.00		Past Due Utilities	0.00
Cert. Of Deposit #1	0.00		Past Due Rent	0.00
Cert. Of Deposit #2	0.00		Personal Loans	0.00
Money Market Acc't	0.00		Other	0.00
Other			Other	
Other	0.00		Other	0.00
Total Monetary Assets	2.00		Total Short Term Liabilities	1.00
Tangible Assets			Long-term Liabilities	
Vehicle #1	0.00		Vehicle Loan #1	0.00
Vehicle #2	0.00		Vehicle Loan #2	0.00
Home #1	0.00		Home Mortgage #1	1.00
Home #2	0.00		Home Mortgage #2	0.00
Clothing	0.00		Student Loan(s)	0.00
Furniture	0.00		Furniture Loans	0.00
Entertainment Electronics	0.00		Computer Loans	0.00
Home Appliances & Equip.	0.00		Home Appliance Loans	0.00
Computer Equipment	0.00		Personal Loans	0.00
Computer Software	0.00		Other	0.00
Jewelry	0.00		Other	0.00
Recreation Items	0.00		Total Long-term Liabilities	1.00
Personal Property	0.00		TOTAL LIABILITIES	2.00
Other Tangible Assets	0.00			
Total Tangible Assets	0.00			
Investment Assets				
Stocks	0.00			
Bonds	0.00			
Mutual Fund #1	0.00			
Mutual Fund #2	0.00			
Employer Retirement Account(s)	0.00			
IRA Accounts	0.00			
Life Ins. Cash Value(s)	0.00			
Real Estate Investments	0.00			
Collectibles	0.00			
Other Investment Assets	0.00			
Total Investment Assets	0.00			
TOTAL ASSETS	2.00		NET WORTH	0.00

You may spend a lot more than your income monthly, but if your assets are greater than your liability (debt) then you may have a positive net worth.

Balancing Your Checkbook

Speaking of Balance, do you balance your checkbook monthly? The word on the street is not so much. No wonder we do not have a handle on our finances. I learned how to wash a car from someone who was a chauffeur in the 1930s. The reason to hand wash a car in a time without automatic car washes was to get to know your vehicle intimately. You will find the little dents and find the minor scratches that want touching up. You will notice cuts in the tires. You will see wheel abrasions. The same is true when you balance your checkbook. You will become very intimate with your personal money. You will see where all of it goes. It is essential to balance your checkbook.

Checkbook Statistics

Why should you balance your checkbook? So, you can check for bank errors and theft. That's right. I noticed my balance (which was razor thin) went negative (I am overdrawn) and I incurred an overdraft fee. I looked at my statement (before online apps) and noticed a charge that my wife nor I had started. A little research discovered that a local photographer had gotten the card number to my wife's debit card and charged the card for a bogus transaction. I immediately marched down to my local bank branch and demanded the return of the stolen money and the overdraft fee. If I did not have a handle on my checking account, I would never have known about the fraud. You can balance your check-book. It takes fifteen minutes.

Here is how I do it. You will need your checkbook ledger, your latest bank statement, a calculator, pencil, and highlighter.

If you are not recording every transaction in your checkbook ledger, then it is time you begin. Some folks say they don't use checks much anymore and only use their debit card and/or pay everything online with a credit card. Inaccurate expense tracking may result. In my financial coaching business, I ask for checking and credit card statements on paper to create the budget. To balance your checkbook, we only need to see the expenses you are paying with the debit card associated with your checking account, checks you write out of your checking account, and cash withdrawals you make from your checking account. If you try this exercise and are having difficulty, go to your bank branch in person and ask an associate to assist you in balancing your checkbook.

Here we go!

I match my checking account statement transactions, starting with deposits and moving to withdrawals to my checkbook ledger. I put a tick mark by the item on the statement and the ledger to show I have recorded all transactions properly in the ledger. If you have a lot of ATM withdrawals, they need to be posted in the ledger or otherwise balancing your checkbook gets difficult. In fact, your checkbook ledger is an excellent tool to track expenses. After you have made sure your ledger numbers look identical to your statement, you are now ready to fill out the reconciliation form to see if everything balances. First, fill in the spot where outstanding (unpaid checks go. This is very important. These are items you have subtracted from your balance in your ledger, but the bank has not paid and has not subtracted from your balance. (Therefore, you appear to have more money in your account than you really do. Remove this discrepancy by recording these unpaid items. Locate the bank's account statement ending balance, then subtract the unpaid outstanding items. The result should match your checkbook ledger amount. If it does not, go back to the beginning and recheck your addition and subtraction of the deposits and withdrawals in your ledger. Double check your outstanding items addition. Make sure what you wrote in your ledger matches the bank statement. Do this until both the bank account state-ment and your checkbook ledger match.

Sample Check Ledger

Codes - ACH: ACH Payment | ATM: Cash Withdrawal | BP: Bill Payment | DC: Debit Card | D: Deposit | DD: Direct Deposit | SF: Service Fee | WT: Wire Transfer							
CHECK NUMBER/ CODE	DATE	TRANSACTION DESCRIPTION	(–) PAYMENT/ DEBIT	✓	(+) DEPOSIT/ CREDIT	BALANCE	
		Starting Balance					

Sample Checking Account Reconciliation Form+++

CHECKING ACCOUNT RECONCILIATION FORM

JUST ANSWER THE FOLLOWING QUESTIONS TO "BALANCE YOUR CHECKBOOK".

1. What is the amount shown on this statement for ENDING BALANCE? $ _____

2. Have you made any deposits that have not been credited
   on this statement? Total up these deposits and enter the amount.   + $ _____

3. ADD TOGETHER Lines 1 and 2.   = $ _____

4. Are there any outstanding checks, payments, transfers or other
   withdrawals that are not reflected on this statement? Use the
   table below to add them up and enter the total on the left.   - $ _____

5. Subtract Line 4 from Line 3. This should reflect your
   checkbook balance.   = $ _____

LIST CHECKS OUTSTANDING NOT CHARGED TO YOUR CHECKING ACCOUNT					
Check Number	Amount	Check Number	Amount	Check Number	Amount
			Enter in Line 4	TOTAL ▶	

IF YOU DO NOT BALANCE 1. Verify additions and subtractions above and in your check register;
2. Compare the dollar amounts of checks listed on this statement with the check amounts listed
in our check register; 3. Compare the dollar amounts of deposits listed on this statement with the
deposit amounts recorded in your check register.

CHECKING ACCOUNT RECONCILIATION FORM

Sample Check

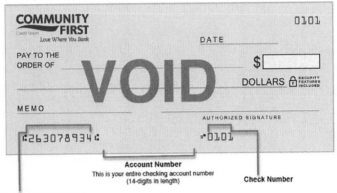

Routing / Transit Number
This is a 9-digit number that identifies the financial institution where your checking account is located

Account Number
This is your entire checking account number (14-digits in length)

Check Number

Other Important Tips

1. Make sure you record automatic deposits and withdrawals in your ledger immediately. It helps keep the records in chronological order and makes balancing your checkbook easier.

2. Record other transactions in your checkbook ledger daily. Waiting a week to record a stack of receipts can lead to errors. When you write a check, you ought to have the ledger with you.

3. Record debit transactions.

4. Log on and check your online checking account entries with your ledger recordings to make sure everything is consistent.

5. Don't forget to subtract fees. ATM fees, check refill fees, et cetera.

https://www.thebalance.com/how-to-keep-a-running-balance-of-your-account-2385978

Motivate yourself by indulging in a reward.

After you have successfully balanced your checkbook, indulge yourself in a reward. Could just be a piece of chocolate, doesn't have to be a whole banana split. Plus, banana splits are expensive in more ways than one.

Automation

Luckily, we live in a connected, technical world that I could not have imagined when I started in the business world. It's easier than ever before to keep track of your money using a digital smart phone applica-tion. My go to budgeting app I use is MINT. The company that sells Turbo Tax, Quicken, and Quick Books (Intuit developed the MINT app. It connects to all of your bank accounts and keeps a running balance for you. Program the application to send you notices triggered by im-portant events. Like you have run out of money. Stop spending! No, seriously, it's like another set of eyes. There are other budget applications out there, but MINT works; it's really free, and it does not upsell you anything.

Another popular app is Truebill, https://www.truebill.com/. It is a great app, but costs about $40.00 per year. Its claim to fame is to assist you in keeping track of unwanted digital subscriptions. Most credit card apps will take you to a page that shows your digital subscriptions. Another method to fight unneeded subscriptions is to report fraud on your credit card.

It usually happens to me organically about twice a year. The credit card company sends you a new card with a new number and expiration date. Then wait; you will start receiving emails from all of your subscription services asking to update your credit card payment information. If you think I'm a rascal for using this technique, that's fine. I call it taking back control of your finances. Renew only the necessary subscriptions.

Online Banking

You will use your computer and your cell phone to access your bank in this era of online banking. You can make deposits using an app on your phone, download statements, check your balance, transfer money between accounts, and pay bills. You can tell (ask) your boss to deposit your paycheck directly into your account. Most employers are on board here because it is easier for them. With online banking, it is easy to set up automatic savings and pay yourself first. With online bill pay, you can pay your credit card bill, utility bills, insurance bills without having to write a check, addressing an envelope or buying a stamp, etc. Online banking allows you to set up message alerts that inform you of any account activity. You can adjust the settings of the alerts so you just hear about the big stuff only. Online banking allows you to download and print your statements to use for balancing your checkbook with pencil and paper.

I recently surfed my online banking portal and found a Spending & Budgeting tool. However, it is not as efficient and effective as doing it with paper and pencil. Why should you use pencil and paper you may ask? The online application is not as specific as our above pen and paper budget. There is something different about your focus on balancing a checkbook or creating a budget with pencil and paper. Changes can be made faster than on a computer. You do not have to have an internet connection (get your statement mailed to you) and you can eliminate most (turn your phone off) electronic distractions.

What is Zelle? With apps like Zelle you can repay friends person to person for money owed, pay your part of a restaurant tab or repay someone for a concert ticket they bought you. You can do similar activities by tapping phones (tap & pay) with the right apps. In fact, mobile phones have themselves become mobile banks. Bank apps on your phone (Citi Card, Apple Pay, Google Pay) create digital wallets that store your credit card information to allow you to pay at participating vendors.

Education

Feel free to use the resources available on my website, https://www.walletwise.org/resources.

Check out www.cashcourse.org .It allows you to sign up for additional financial skill lessons and courses.

Taxes

Taxes are an important responsibility for being a citizen of the United States of America. I don't enjoy paying taxes, but I do like driving on paved roads and traveling on safe waterways and airways. I also heard we have a pretty bad ass defense department. All of it costs money, and we should chip in our "fair" share to make sure the U.S. keeps moving forward. There are consequences to not paying the correct amount of taxes or paying your taxes late. Make sure you have enough "withholding" taken out of your paycheck. When your employer hires you, fill out the Federal IRS form "**W-4**." The form has specific instructions to reflect an accurate payroll withholding amount in most situations.

To do my taxes, I use Turbo Tax. If you use Quicken or Quick Books to directly transfer data to Turbo Tax, well that's your decision. I don't do that. I input my information through the Turbo Tax interface so that I can see what is happening in each important category. Other online software includes H&R Block. com and TaxAct.com. If you dislike digital tax preparation, try your local H&R Block office in person. If you are uncomfortable with numbers, please hire a reputable tax return company to help you with your taxes. IRS liens, garnishments, and seizures are real, and I watched someone else make this mistake (an old boss) and it was not a pleasant experience.

Financial First Aid

If you are in a **financial rough patch**, then you must prioritize differently. Pay for your shelter, utilities for shelter, food, and car payments first.

The next most important is the debt that will immediately affect you if not paid. If you have court judgement debt, criminal justice debt, or child support debts, these **must** be paid before any other expense.

The next important group includes insurance, real estate taxes, federal student loans, and taxes owed to the IRS. This level is important as well, but there may be options to renegotiate payment plans for these items.

Next are the low priority debts. Included in this group are credit card debt, unsecured debt, health care debt, debt owed to friends and family (they can wait), private student loans, debts you owe a cosigner, and then loans against furniture and appliances.

Chapter 13

Know Your Credit Score and Understand Your Credit Report

I have always advocated doing everything possible to pay off credit card balances; it's good financial management and the ticket to a strong FICO credit score

Suze Orman

First things first! Everyone in the United States that has ever borrowed money in any form or simply rented an apartment has a credit report assigned to their identity. Good personal money management is an important skill for you to learn because bad money management results in a lower personal credit score for you. If you score low on this "special" type of report card, you will pay higher interest rates on your debts. Lower credit scores often lead consumers to do business with unscrupulous or predatory lenders. Please remember, The Big Three Credit Bureaus do not work for you, and they may treat you as an inconvenience! The credit bureaus work for the lenders! They do not care if their records about you are incorrect, if your address is incorrect, or they incorrectly marked your credit with a negative rating. They have no incentive to keep your records correct. A negative report justifies the lender charging you more for a loan than if the report was correct, so there is little motivation to correct their mistakes. You decide if that is a conflict of interest. Credit Bureaus collect credit information and credit scores and then resell your information for a fee to lenders, employers, and insurance companies. Utility companies, cable TV, internet and cell phone companies are interested in your credit report. That's the purpose of the credit bureaus. They sell your data to these companies. The companies buying your data are the customer. Credit bureaus are not in the business to help you correct the data of the credit consumers. Monitor he information and correct any incorrect information yourself. It is true that a good credit score can help you get out of poverty and move in to the middle class. It directly affects how much interest you pay on a mortgage. I dislike debt, but debt to build wealth (like a mortgage) is "okay".

Understanding Credit Repair

You have rights to correct errors under the Fair Credit Reporting Act, but you have to do the work.

You can do this! You must update your records, dispute errors, and pro-actively monitor your credit report. Your reward for doing this work is an accurate credit report which will result in you saving money on your debt! The Internet has made these chores easier for you.

Bad credit can stay on your report for up to seven years. So, putting yourself in a bad credit situation makes your life more difficult and expensive. There is good news, though. By monitoring your credit reports regularly, you can dispute legitimate errors in reporting of late or missed payments. The credit bureau will have to respond within thirty days, updating your report. If they do not, rerun your report and file another dispute until they get it right. As I mentioned earlier, credit bureaus work for the lenders. Ask your lenders who are reporting late payments in error to report your payments on time.

Shhh. A little Nugget. If you are making a major purchase like a house or car, your lender may have the power to contact the credit bureau and remove questionable negative files so you and your lender can move forward with the transaction.

Do Not Hire A Credit Recovery Company!

Credit repair companies cannot do anything you can't do for yourself. Remember, only inaccurate information can be removed from your credit report. By law, the three major credit bureaus must correct errors in your report. The three major credit bureaus have instructions for correcting mistakes on your report.

1. www.experian.com

2. www.transunion.com

3. www.equifax.com

What's in the Report?

The credit report is a report card of your credit accounts. Each bureau has a different format, but every report has a list of your open credit accounts, the name of the creditor, the amount borrowed, date of last payment received, length of account, and a listing of any missed or late payments. Credit card lenders, mortgage, car loans, student loans, and other unsecured creditors submit the information to your report. Reports can include public record filings like liens, foreclosures, bankruptcies, court judgments, and civil suits. The reports include any recent applications or inquiries you made for credit. Credit reports keep a detailed description of your personal information. This information includes your current and former addresses, birthdate, Social Security number, and phone numbers.

Order Your Free Credit Report:

It is important that you monitor your credit report by ordering a free copy of your report. The credit bureaus allow you to receive one free copy of each bureau's report once a year.

Get your credit report free once per year from this site.
https://www.annualcreditreport.com/index.action

Make sure you are on the correct site because there are many companies offering free credit reports. However, many are imposters.

If you Google free credit report, "annual credit report.com" is not at the top of the list. The first searches result in legitimate companies offering free credit reports or FICO scores, but they will try to sell you something (credit monitoring and identity theft products you do not need, etc. during your time on their site. "annualcreditreport.com" will allow you to set up one account to access all three credit bureaus. It is wise to ask for one report from one bureau every four months so you can monitor throughout the year at no charge. If a major company or your credit bureau has a large data breach, they may entitle you to a free credit monitoring for at least one year as part of the breach settlement. The three credit bureaus are Experian, TransUnion, and Equifax.

Fun Fact: 57% of consumers checked at least one of their credit reports in 2018. You should too!

Credit Scores and FICO

Besides your credit report, when you apply for credit, lenders pay the credit bureaus for your credit score. Complex computer formulas managed by a corporation called Fair Isaac Corporation, calculate your FICO score and also analyze your credit report history data. www.fico.com.

The banking industry introduced the FICO score in 1989. In the 50s, Bill Fair and Earl Isaac created an automated scoring system that sadly flopped. It took thirty years to make the scoring system acceptable to the banking industry, and that is how the Fair, Isaac, and Company got its start using FICO scores and using numerical ratings to grade your credit worthiness. Lenders use 27 million FICO scores every day and use FICO scores in over 90% of lending decisions.

Here is a link to a great video describing FICO scores.

https://youtu.be/OwIlRGsqxUg

Here is a link to my FICO that shows the interest increase required based on different credit scores. https://www.myfico.com/credit-education/calculators/loan-savings-calculator/

A good "rule of thumb" of credit score ranges

300-629	Bad
630-689	Fair
690-719	Good
720-850	Excellent

Credit Bureaus use the following basic ingredients to grade your credit report and create your credit score.

1. Payment History

    a. Payment History accounts for about 35% of your total credit score and is considered the most important aspect of your credit history.

    b. The easiest way to improve your credit score is to make all of your payments on time.

2. Credit Utilization

   a. How much credit of your "available" credit are you using? If you max out your credit lines, you have no wiggle room or margin.

   b. Borrowers with the best scores use only 6% of their available credit.

   c. This is another reason to be careful closing unused credit accounts too quickly. Closing an old, unused, credit account reduces your utilization ratio and lowers your credit score. Sometimes what seems right (closing account) is not.

   d. Credit Utilization accounts for about 30% of your score.

3. Length of Credit History

   a. Communicates to lenders your history of borrowing.

   b. Accounts for only 15% of your score.

4. New Credit

   a. Only apply for credit when absolutely necessary.

   b. Multiple credit inquiries tell lenders you may be in credit stress and looking to borrow from a new account to pay off another debt.

   c. Be careful. A "hard" credit inquiry on your credit report is reported on your report and affects your credit score.

   d. A "soft" inquiry means your credit is checked without being reported or affecting your score.

   e. When you are shopping for new credit or looking at pre-approval credit offers, demand a soft inquiry until you are serious about applying for credit.

   f. New Credit inquiries account for only 10% of your score.

   g. When making a major purchase, like a home or car, shop for different credit with different lenders in a brief burst of time, so the credit bureaus merge multiple hard inquiries into one reported hard inquiry.

5. Credit Mix

    a. A vague category that shows a variety of credit history.

    b. Credit Mix accounts for only 10% of your score.

A good FICO score is 720. This is a wonderful goal. Good credit scores make it easier for you to borrow money, get credit cards with better interest rates and benefits, better cell phone plans and insurance premiums. Many employers will check your credit. Why? Employers do not want employees receiving stressful debt collection calls at work. They don't want stressed out and distracted employees. Insurance companies check your credit file. Insurance companies know that stressed-out, debt-ridden drivers are statistically more prone to get into an accident thereby causing an expensive claim. "Ain't debt fun"? However, you get to decide who has access to your credit report. All interested parties must have your permission to look at your credit file.

Did you know you have an Insurance Risk Score?

You can get your insurance score! Your insurance score is like a credit score, but a specific score to rate your insurance risk to insurance companies. Check out personalreports.lexisnexis.com to get your auto and home insurance reports.

Checkout this Loan Savings Calculator. I included this calculator here to show you how your credit score affects the interest rate you qualify for. A 620-639 low score borrower gets charged 4.9% while the 760-850 borrower gets charged 3.35% interest. Over a 30-year mortgage loan, that adds up to a lot of money.

https://www.myfico.com/credit-education/calculators/loan-savings-calculator/

Many credit-card companies (Discover, Citi) offer free FICO scores. In fact, FICO lists 170 partners in their FICO Score Open Access Program that allows you access to your score. Just make sure you are not charged by their partner for your credit score.

Here is what a FICO credit score looks like.

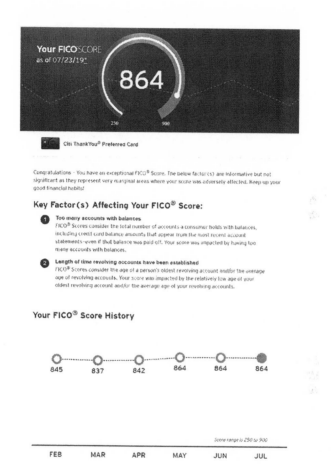

Congratulations - You have an exceptional FICO® Score. The below factor(s) are informative but not significant as they represent very marginal areas where your score was adversely affected. Keep up your good financial habits!

Key Factor(s) Affecting Your FICO® Score:

1. **Too many accounts with balances**
   FICO® Scores consider the total number of accounts a consumer holds with balances, including credit card balance amounts that appear from the most recent account statements--even if that balance was paid off. Your score was impacted by having too many accounts with balances.

2. **Length of time revolving accounts have been established**
   FICO® Scores consider the age of a person's oldest revolving account and/or the average age of revolving accounts. Your score was impacted by the relatively low age of your oldest revolving account and/or the average age of your revolving accounts.

Your FICO® Score History

845	837	842	864	864	864

Score range is 250 to 900

FEB	MAR	APR	MAY	JUN	JUL

To ensure your Credit, Score is High, manage them by:

Pay bills on time.

Pay off Debt instead of moving it to a new consolidation account.

If you have missed payments, get current and stay current.

Avoid having payments go to collection agencies.

Keep outstanding balances low on credit cards.

Don't close unused accounts.

Shop for the best rates.

Do not allow anyone (INCLUDING YOUR CHILDREN) to use your credit card.

Check your own credit reports and FICO score every year.

Checking your own credit report or FICO score does not lower your FICO score.

Try using a credit monitoring app (free with your bank or credit card company) that allows you to check your credit score at no charge in exchange for marketing credit offers for auto loans, credit cards, and home loans to you. This is a great resource if you use credit responsibly. It will compare offers to aid you in getting the best credit product for you. Try https://www.creditkarma.com/, to monitor your credit score.

In the spirit of keeping your credit score as high as possible, the following discussion helps you control access to your credit report and protection from identity thieves. Identity theft can begin by accessing your credit report illegally. Debt accounts opened in your name can negatively affect your credit score. Here are a few ideas to prevent that.

Credit Freeze

A credit freeze is a security lock on your credit reports to prevent someone from opening an account in your name. This prevents identity theft and the consumer credit bureaus from selling and reselling your credit information to encourage credit providers to send you tempting credit offers to you every day in the mail. That's right, besides selling your credit data for legitimate inquiries by apartments, lenders, insurance companies and employers, the credit bureaus sell your data to prospective lenders who use it to directly market unsolicited credit based products to you.

Inform each credit bureau separately to apply the freeze. Credit freeze services are free and mandated by Federal Law. Credit freezes legally protect you from loss.

Do not confuse a credit freeze with a credit lock. They are two different things. They both protect your credit files, but credit locks are not free. They are usually provided by for-profit companies like Credit Karma and LifeLock as part of a paid subscription.

Stay with the Freeze.

Equifax
Equifax.com/personal/credit-report-services
800-349-9960

Experian
https://www.experian.com/freeze/center.html
888-EXPERIAN (888-397-3742)

Transunion
TransUnion.com/credit-help
888-909-8872

They will each provide you a PIN that is a must save to unlock your frozen account. Therefore, it is important for you to protect this PIN. You must have a **reliable method** for saving important documents, passwords and PIN numbers. A credit freeze does not affect your credit score. A credit freeze does not prevent you from getting your free annual credit reports. You can easily unlock your credit freeze when a lender, employer, or insurance company needs to access your files.

You can also start a Fraud Alert on your credit accounts if you lost your wallet or other personal data. The Fraud Alert lasts a period of one year. There is an extended Fraud Alert for those who have experienced identity theft, and this alert lasts seven years. Please read Chapter One, Credit Cards on a detailed discussion of Identity Theft and Fraud.

Please check out this amazing Federal Trade Commission Website that explains much of this:

https://www.consumer.ftc.gov/articles/0497-credit-freeze-faqs#what

OptOutPrescreen.com

Another way to control the distribution of your data is to use the official opt out choice called OptOutPrescreen.com. https://www.optoutprescreen.com

This service is free and allows you to opt out of receiving credit offers for five years. Hallelujah!

For History Buffs. How did Credit Bureaus Start?

Before the era of computers and credit scores, lending in the United States was, well… interesting. They located credit bureaus in each town to provide the service of checking credit on customers of department stores and banks wanting credit. A credit bureau employee would call the local department store you listed on your credit application and ask the owner, "How does Sam pay his bill to ABC Mercantile?" The actual name "Credit Bureau" identifies a list of people in town that are poor credit risks. Eventually credit bureaus merged into larger entities that later became the Big Three Credit Bureaus we have now. Equifax started in Atlanta as the Retail Credit Company in 1899. In 1975 their name changed to Equifax. TransUnion started in 1968 as a Tank Car company. In the late sixties, it started acquiring regional and city credit bureaus. In 1969 Trans Union bragged it stored files on 3.6 million index cards! Experian started in England in 1980. Experian moved into the US in 1996 with its acquisition of TRW Information Systems. TRW was the largest credit bureau in the US.

In 1970, Congress passed the Fair Credit Reporting Act (FCRA) to make sure consumers' credit files were correct.

https://www.consumerfinance.gov/learnmore/

This act is the federal law that allows you to dispute and correct errors, ask for a credit score, and also gives you the right to place or remove a security freeze on your credit history. This is the law that permits you to get a free copy of your report every 12 months from each of the Big Three credit bureaus.

Conclusion:

A good credit report and credit score results in lower debt cost for you. A good credit score does not happen by accident. You must take responsibility for your credit score by making your payments on time, contacting the credit bureau to fix errors, and monitoring your credit reports annually to make sure your credit report information is as accurate as possible. Your credit score is a "special" report card they do not teach you about in school. This report card, if well managed, can save you thousands of dollars in interest over your lifetime.

Chapter 14

Real Estate Rent or Buy?

"Owning a home is a keystone of wealth — both financial affluence and emotional security."

Suze Orman

What are the actual costs of renting versus owning real estate? This chapter is not a complete discussion of real estate. There are volumes of books out there about real estate. This chapter discusses the purchase and sale of real estate and the financial aspects of renting. Use the following chapter as a guideline to make smart decisions for you about renting and owing real estate. Housing costs are our largest expense and require skills and knowledge to make smart choices. I want you to be in a safe, sustainable home. Having a home is the key to less financial and emotional stress.

Source:

1) https://www.cnbc.com/2017/04/07/heres-how-much-more-it-costs-to-own-vs-rent-a-home-in-every-us-state.html

2) https://www.nerdwallet.com/blog/mortgages/cost-homeownership-vs-renting/

Rent or Buy?

Our friends at CNBC say that homeownership is from 35 to 90 percent more expensive than renting. Nerd Wallet says it is 33% to 93% more expensive to purchase than to rent. Researchers base the difference in cost on real estate taxes and maintenance costs from specific locations. Know your state numbers. If you plan to purchase, make sure you can afford all the expenses: taxes, homeowner's insurance, and home maintenance. It appears if you are planning to live in the same area for a period longer than five years, it may make sense to purchase. Home ownership reaps the rewards of financial security, some tax deductions, inflation protection and the opportunity to own a property outright with no mortgage payment. It is important to recognize your home's primary purpose is to provide a roof over your head. Many people think owning real estate is a get rich quick plan. Owning real estate is a foundation to accumulating wealth, but that is not the purpose of your house.

"Don't wait to buy real estate. Buy real estate and wait." *Will Rogers.*

The major headache of renting a home is not being in control over the cost of rent. You could find yourself priced out of a home if you live in a rising rent location.

Mortgages

Fun Fact. The word mortgage is French. The French define the word mortgage as, "death pledge".

Experiment with your budget before you purchase. Estimate your mortgage payment first by researching the prices of homes in the area. Say your mortgage payment will be $1000 per month (based on a $225,000 purchase price). Save an additional $300 per month or add 30% to your estimated mortgage payment while you are still renting to see how home ownership will affect your pocketbook. The total cost of $1,300 will better reflect the total cost of home ownership. It's not just about the mortgage cost! Remember that there are real estate taxes, homeowner's insurance, and maintenance costs to consider.

Find a reputable mortgage broker. Locate a professional mortgage broker to get your mortgage pre-approval. Pre-approval can put you in a better negotiating position compared to more experienced or cash buyers. The mortgage broker must connect you to a competent lender. In a "HOT" real estate market, they must attach your offer to a lender that can close fast. It's another negotiating point in your favor.

McMansion buyers beware! Buy a smaller house than you can afford. Remember, the Realtor and mortgage broker are in a conflict of interest with you. They want you to buy the **most** house you can afford (according to them, not you) and then to borrow the most amount of money they think you can afford. Why? Because the lender receives a commission or additional fees based on production. Therefore, whether you can really afford the property or not isn't their main concern! Think about buying less than you can afford! The Thomas J. Stanley book, *The Millionaire Next Door,* reports that most millionaires in the United States live in modest homes. The folks that live in the mansions want you to think they are wealthy. They are not. They are just "house poor." In 2014 during the housing recovery, in Deland Florida, it was possible to purchase a modest block three-bedroom house in a safe neighborhood for $50,000. If you had cash.

In 2021, those same houses sell for $250,000. Oh my!

http://clark.com/homes-real-estate/price-rent-headed-down/

Online mortgage applications are popular and 50% of prospective home buyers use them. Seventy-five percent did at least a portion of their application online. The most popular include:

- Quicken Loans

- Lending Tree

- better.com

- Rocket Mortgage (a subsidiary of Quicken Loans)

- Chase

- Bank of America, a traditional bank, offers an online component.

Truth in Lending Act

Make sure you read the fine print of your mortgage application. A lot of the chicanery during the Financial Crises was because of shifty clauses in the mortgage applications and the mortgages themselves. Because I owned my business, I ended up with a mortgage with an archaic prepayment penalty. I should have walked out of the closing. I learned about the prepayment penalty at closing and not before. The mortgage broker did not want to take the risk I would not accept. I should have seen this information in the "Good Faith Estimate," but I did not see it until the closing. It was a time when you shuffle and sign papers, but not read them. The "Good Faith Estimate" discloses and reports the expenses related to your new mortgage. Get it within three days of its preparation. Make sure you understand what you are agreeing to before you get to your closing! Insist on seeing your "Good Faith Estimate"!

Due Diligence

If you are renting or buying, visit lots of locations (50 is a good start, really!) and ask lots of questions. If you are purchasing, do the research. Check the Schools. Check the property taxes. Check criminal activity and if law enforcement is on the ball.

Purchasing a house in an unfamiliar location, right before the 2008 financial crises, was a tough choice to make. Home prices throughout the nation were rising with no end in sight. It seemed if you did not buy now, you would never get a home. Unregulated lending practices created the perfect set-ting for a bubble. This happened to a friend of mine who purchased a home that later resulted in foreclosure. They bought an older house that was owned by an investor/ house flipper. An investor bought it and fixed it. The house was in a low-lying area near the water. The Realtor did not disclose the flood issue to the buyer. Every time it rained; the plumbing failed.

Check the house on a rainy day. No kidding. Don't forget to check the basement after a rainstorm. Yup, not everyone lives in Florida (where there are almost no basements).

In fact, if the home you are purchasing, has insurance claims, it may be difficult to insure. Check your property's CLUE report at https://personalreports.lexisnexis.com/fact_act_disclosure.jsp.

I'm sure it overjoyed the bank to repossess this gem back. My favorite part is that when the house was sold, the real estate agent and the mortgage broker were well compensated and lost nothing in the upcoming result. Foreclosure. Be careful purchasing real estate near waterfront. My house has been the go-to shelter for family members during close calls with hurricanes. Remember, if you buy property on low-lying ground near the water, expect to evacuate. If you live near the water, buy high ground.

Consider the Location of Your New Home

Living in Florida, I have seen the devastation incurred by hurricanes. Beach erosion and wind damage turn multimillion dollar properties into splinters. Be careful when you purchase a property. Besides purchasing in a geographically sensitive location, consider traffic patterns, air traffic patterns, and proximity to other nuisances.

- Edge of a cliff;

- Next to a Race Track;

- Next to a popular Tourist Attraction;

- On the Beach;

- Near the Beach;

- Next to a Dry Forest;

- At the bottom of a Geographic Bowl;

- Next to an Airport;

- Next to a Military Airbase;

- On the Flight line of an Airport or Military Airbase;

- Next to a Railroad Track;

- Across the Street from a Bar;

- Next to an Overcrowded School where cars clog the street twice a day.

If you buy a home in an area that experiences floods, hurricanes, and fires, you need additional expensive insurance to protect against floods, mudslides or fire.

Yes, buyer beware. And no, insurance companies are not evil. They are just protecting their investment from the risks man and nature create.

Caveat emptor! Is Latin for "Buyer Beware!"

Don't be shy about visiting your potential new home at a different time of the day. Does that cute school right down the street dismiss at 2:30 which results in cars lining up around the block? Is your new home near train tracks or below a military base flight path?

Make sure there is an accurate survey. If you are financing, this is a requirement. The survey protects the lender, not you. Get a survey specifically for yourself. Rural real estate transactions have special concerns. Make sure legal access "egress and ingress" is described in the title. There is such a thing as being land locked with no "official" access. Read: Very expensive to fix. I've been there, saw that!

Is there a homeowner's association? Almost everything I've heard about them is negative. I've never lived in a neighborhood with one. Lots of rules, other neighbors in your business, and you still have to pay for this luxury. Sign me up!! NOT!

The average American household (about 2.5 people) spends about $56,000 to exist, according to the Bureau of Labor Statistics. Out of that Americans on average spend $18,400 per year or average $1,500 per month on housing. Divide the $1,500 by 2.5 folks per household and you get about $600 per month per person for housing expenses.

Real Estate Agents

Interview multiple realtors. Hire the right agent! In hot markets be aware of bidding scams. Beware of agents giving false hope to novice buyers using their offers to bid up the price of a property, forcing the seasoned deep pocket buyer to offer a higher price on the same property. Never believe verbal promises. Don't waive your right to inspect the property. And yes, pay for your own inspection.

http://clark.com/homes-real-estate/pro-tips-how-to-find-the-best-real-estate-agent-for-you/

Most of the real estate agents out there are professionals, but if you are new to the area, then buyer beware. Hire an experienced agent who is well informed in your area and price range. You may end up with a previously flipped house remodeled by amateurs. The house may be in a low-lying area requiring you to evacuate during a major storm. The Realtor still gets paid their commission, regardless. If you are moving to a new area, rent first, then consider purchasing. We do not find deals, we make them. Remember to calculate taxes and insurance to determine total payment. Houses always need repairs. Budget for this. Buy something less than you can afford. Replacement Roofs, Windows, Flooring, Air Conditioning etc. units don't come cheap.

Other factors that affect ownership include your age. It may be better to rent when you are younger or if you are any age and you know in advance that you are staying five years or less to make it easier to move during career transitions requiring relocation. Another factor is stress. It's stressful buying and selling real estate. Are you up for it?

Check out this "Rent vs. Buy" calculator free from Realtor.com.
https://www.nytimes.com/2014/05/22/upshot/rent-or-buy-the-math-is-changing.html

Don't forget about homeowner's insurance. Go for replacement cover-age. It will cover the full cost instead of the depreciated cost of the damage. I am a big State Farm fan.

When purchasing a home through conventional financing, it is best to put 20% down for your down payment. FHA loans only require a 3.5% down payment. FHA loans are more flexible with less than perfect credit borrowers. **However,** any mortgage including FHA requires PMI insurance for any loan to value ratio less than 20%. After your loan to value drops below 78% then you can refinance to drop the PMI. Under a conventional mortgage, you can drop PMI. PMI is Private Mortgage Insurance required on any home loan with less than 20% loan to value. PMI gives mortgage lenders protection in case of foreclosure. Homes with low loan to value ratios foreclose more often. PMI, on average, costs 1% (per month) of loan value. If you are a veteran, you may qual-ify for a VA mortgage loan. They are zero% down and backed by the US government, so no PMI. They also have less stringent qualification stan-dards. You will only want a fixed rate loan. The uncertainty of variable rates was one cause of the excessive mortgage defaults causing the financial crises in 2008.

I do this! I pay my own real estate taxes and homeowner's insurance. I don't escrow. There is no reason to deposit homeowner's insurance money into your lender's account, earning interest for the bank and not you. Keep control of your money. Just don't forget to budget for these expenses. If you don't pay them, the bank will. That service comes at a high cost to you.

I do this! I pay additional principal each month on my mortgage to pay it off faster and save on interest. I began with a 30-year loan and refinanced it when interest rates came down. I requested to keep the remaining term the same. This means I did not reset the clock to 30 years like many do when they refinance. My remaining term was 24 years, and it was no problem. My payment still went down without extending the term. Do not extend the loan term. I considered refinancing with a new 15-year term. These loans have very attractive interest rates because the bank gets their money back so much sooner. I did not. Here's my philos-ophy. If I accept a 15-year term, I cannot in the middle of things change back to 30. Meaning, if I lose my job or have some other unexpected financial hardship (emergency fund my 24-year payment is less than the 15-year term payment. With a 15-year term I've locked myself into the higher payment no matter what. With the longer term, I can always pay more when everything is good. I started out paying an extra $50.00 per month, which equated to making one additional payment per year. Yes, I know. My mortgage is inexpensive. That's from refinancing at a lower rate a few times. I may do it again.

Now I pay almost double payments. At the end of 2019 my wife retired (not of her choosing and if she does not get a new job that pays as well, we will be okay. Not so okay if I had locked myself into the higher payment 15-year loan. Check out:

https://www.daveramsey.com/mortgage-payoff-calculator

https://www.mortgagecalculator.net/early-pay-off/

Make biweekly payments. Instead of 12 monthly payments, pay 26 bi-weekly payments. Every year you will pay an added month of principal.

If you pay a little extra each month, you will save in the long run. Don't pay your lender to set this service up for you. Do it yourself.

Know how to Read your Mortgage Statement

STATEMENT BREAKDOWN

We'll say it again: Mortgage statements shouldn't require an advanced degree in finance (plus a minor in statistical analysis) to read.

We're constantly listening to your feedback and working to make your statements easier to understand.

Here are the key facts on your monthly statement, with a handy visual guide to finding them.

1. STATEMENT INFORMATION

Here are the basic basics, like the date your statement was generated, loan number, amount due, and your payment due date

2. EXPLANATION OF AMOUNT DUE

A breakdown of your payment, showing the amount for principal, interest and escrow. If there are optional items, late payments or other fees, they will be shown here as well. Click here to see our complete fee schedule.

3. ACCOUNT OVERVIEW

This will tell you your principal balance, escrow balance, and your current interest rate.

4. PAST PAYMENT BREAKDOWN

This section recaps your last payment and also the payments you've made to date this year. It shows how much went to principal, interest, escrow, optional insurance, and any miscellaneous fees.

5. HELPFUL INFORMATION

Here you'll find important explanations and special notices pertaining to your account, plus useful tips for managing your home loan.

6. TRANSACTION ACTIVITY

A basic recap of your recent transactions on your account and the resulting balances, as well as disbursements we've made on your behalf to payees like tax authorities and insurance providers. Want to see more? Sign in to your account.

7. PAYMENT COUPON

If you pay by mail, please fill out, detach, and return this section with your check or money order. It's easy. But the easiest and fastest way to pay is online. Sign in to your account to make a one-time payment or set-up AutoPay. It's free and you never have to lick a stamp.

DO YOU HAVE LENDER PAID EXPENSES?

If you have any expenses that we paid to maintain and process your home loan, like legal fees, repair costs, or property inspections, then you'll see these on the second page of your statement. Click here to see an example.

If you are purchasing and financing a new home and you are in your 40s and 50s, then a 15-year term may be better so it pays your mortgage off by retirement.

Take out a Home Equity Line of Credit (HELOC) for home improvements that maintain or improve the value of the home. I use one. Do not open a HELOC account to pay for European Vacation! I only use it for home improvements and only out of necessity. I purchased a new roof, new HVAC and other important and intelligent upgrades to my house. I justify this because the house is worth more than we paid for it. The investment return exceeds the cost. At the time I started the HELOC, we did not have a "pot to hiss in". (Figure it out. Think snake) We borrowed a reasonable amount of our equity for necessities. Many of my neighbors, in contrast, borrowed as much as they could during the 2008 housing bubble. The market fell off a cliff leaving many homeowners owing more that their houses were worth. Their HELOC payments used variable interest rates and like an Otis Elevator, their payments skyrocketed. As the economy melted, neighbors lost their jobs. They gave up paying their mortgages and HELOCS to live mortgage free until the repo man caught up with them. Welcome to the 2007-2009 financial crises. My wife and I did not lose our jobs. Your combined mortgage balance and HELOC should never exceed your home's worth.

Selling Your House

It requires special skills to sell your house.

Again, hire a reputable, experienced sales agent. Negotiate your sales commission. Yes, the sales commission is negotiable! Spend a little money to make your house look like a home someone would want to buy and live in. No need to hire a professional. Stage the house yourself. Clean out the clutter. Put stuff in storage. Clean the place. Paint the interior. Don't skimp here. If you know potential buyers are visiting, bake cookies! It's always a deal winner. Calculate, before listing your home, the total cost of marketing your house. Make sure the house price is correct. Use a source like Zillow, https://www.zillow.com/, to find out what homes in your neighborhood are selling for, before you sit down with the listing agent. Visit your county property appraiser office. They have a record of the sales in your area and by law; the information is in the public record. That's how Zillow gets the info.

Personal Journal

My preteen experience with Florida Real Estate. Contract for Deeds.

When I was twelve, my family lived in rural north Florida. Retirees populated the community. I made friends with one of our elderly neighbors and was excited to find out that one of his grandchildren was about my age. We had a great time running around the neighborhood doing what kids do. On one of his visits, he mentioned to me in a bratty tone that his parents owned my property. I said politely that you are mistaken. "AM not." Funny thing is that I "maturely" went to his grandfather and asked him what his grandson meant. He said his son, my friend's father, had purchased a tax certificate on our lot. I said thank you and at once went home to tell my father. What happened was, we lived on the lot that was purchased via contract for deed. The price was $25.00 down and $25.00 per month. In the 70s, in Florida at least, this was a very popular way to sell unwanted vacant land. We, however, had improved the property by adding a septic tank and power pole and put our beautiful doublewide mobile home. My parents were very thankful for my report and went to the real estate developer to discuss real estate taxes. When you buy a property contract for deed, the actual warranty deed does not transfer until satisfaction of the contract. Until then, the original developer/owner is still responsible for paying the real estate taxes. The developer/owner may own hundreds of vacant lots owing small amounts of real estate tax on each lot. The game is to wait until the last minute to pay the tax or wait until the developer gets caught not paying them on contracted lots like ours. The developer understood our plight and paid the real estate taxes. Tax Certificate Void. I do not know why my neighbor's son did this to our lot, as there were dozens of parcels in the same subdivision that were vacant and had unpaid taxes. I told my playmate, that no, I was not mistaken, his father did not own our lot. Our friendship waned after that brief episode. Although, that same dad took the neighborhood kids out to learn how to shoot guns. The reward for exemplary behavior was shooting an M1 rifle. Ahhhh...Life in the country! Yes, it was outstanding! I was 12!!

The moral of the story is to be careful of "Contract for Deed" purchases. The advantages are in the seller's favor. If you agree to this type of contract, know the advantages and disadvantages. If your income, credit score, or location of the home is not worthy of conventional financing, then contract for deed could be an alternative.

The property is not in your name until you pay the contract in full. Be careful, it's like "buy here, pay here" car buying situation. Miss a payment and the actual owner will repossess "your" property. They are not obligated in most states to return your paid investment. The actual owner handles the real estate taxes. If the seller wont pay the taxes, you risk losing everything if they sell a tax deed against your property. The property changes possession and you lose your investment.

https://www.trustedchoice.com/insurance-articles/home-family/buying-house-on-contract/

https://www.rocketlawyer.com/article/what-is-a-contract-for-deed-ps.rl

Mobile Home Parks

http://boards.answers.findlaw.com/topic/228727-ad-valorem-tax-passed-on-to-manufactured-home-land-renters/

If you live in a mobile home in a mobile home park, then buyer beware. I just sold a double-wide mobile home for my elderly father and what a carnival! The buyers must be approved by the park management before the sale is legitimate. After the property sold, I am still paying a prorata share of the real estate taxes. The mobile home park owners pass through to the tenant their prorata share of the real estate taxes of their lot. A lot they rent and which they pay lot rent. Yes, on top of the lot rent, they pay a lump sum real estate tax for their share of the property they rent at the end of the year. For property they don't own. It's perfectly legal! If you are shrewd, you should figure out how to become a mobile home park owner! If it's a retirement mobile home park, it's a cash cow! On the back of pensioners!

Who's My Landlord?

Does the house you are renting really belong to the landlord? During the 2008 financial crises, there were many cases where landlords learned they were upside down financially in their investment property. Their mortgage balance was more than the value of the property. The bad economy also pushed rents down resulting in the rental income being less than the debt service (and total expenses to maintain the home in-vestment so savvy owners just stopped paying the mortgage payment knowing that the financial crises resulted in banks taking two years or longer to foreclose on the property mortgage. During the two or more-year period, the "owner/landlord" of the house kept collecting the rent and stuffing it in their pocket. Then when the bank was ready to foreclose, they would inspect the house and let the tenant know they are no longer welcome in the house. The house was in foreclosure and being sold on the market. This happened with no notice and no empathy for the tenant. They were innocent victims. The law (The Protecting Tenants at Foreclosure Act of 2009) states that the tenant may complete the lease or rental agreement. However your new landlord, is the bank. Tenant beware in a poor real estate market!

The Answer to Affordable Housing, The Mobile Home... On Your Land

The mobile home or manufactured home came about because of the original travel trailer. In the 50s and 60s as travel trailers got bigger people lived in them as a substitute for an apartment or small home.

In 1976, manufactured homes meet FHA standards. They manufactured the above mobile home in 1972. I took the photo. It is the mobile home I grew up in. Experts consider mobile homes personal property that depreciate in value like a motor vehicle. Construction standards have improved, and now the construction standards resemble the quality of traditionally built homes. Mobile homes usually depreciate while traditionally built homes appreciate. However, better built, late model mobile homes can maintain their value or increase in value during a shortage in available home inventory. Mobile homes are set up on owner's land or placed in a mobile home park. Mobile homes provide an affordable alternative to traditional homes. Buy a mobile home if you are looking to reduce your housing expenses so you can pay off more debt and then save more. As soon as your finances are secure, buy a traditional house. They rise in value by the rate of inflation. In a "hot market" they can appreciate at a higher rate. Traditional houses are foundations to building family wealth.

Move Often and Lose a Fortune:

Major sources on the Internet say that the average cost of a local move is $1,250. I base this estimate upon a 2-3-bedroom household or about 7,500 pounds of stuff. Moving from state to state is closer to $5,000. A ball mark method of measuring your potential moving expense, including sales commission and moving expense, is 10% of the value of the house. This equals about 6% commission and 4% moving fee.

It will be difficult for you to accumulate savings, let alone wealth, if you move every six months regardless of reason.

Here are some money-saving tips for moving.

1. Get estimates and shop movers who have references and great reviews. check your moving company. There are lots of resources online to help create a moving budget. Reserve about six weeks before moving date.

2. Check out AAA.com/moving to locate moving discounts.

3. Find donated boxes. Don't spend too much on packing supplies. It is expensive but convenient to buy your moving supplies from a rental truck moving center.

4. Create a packing plan. Figure out what you will keep, throw away, give to friends or give to charity. Take only what you need. Moving useless, valueless stuff is not smart. Give stuff away by listing it for free on Craigslist or giving it to charity.

5. Measure all the doorways. Don't pack a box that's bigger than the doorway of your existing place or your new one.

6. Mark the contents clearly on the outside of your boxes.

7. Don't pack boxes too heavy.

8. Treat your movers nicely. This pays dividends later.

9. Don't forget to change your address.

10. Cancel old services and begin new services.

https://www.moving.com/

http://www.merriman.com/family-talk/moving-considerations/

Personal Journal and Conclusion

While still in college, I took a real estate course because of an article I read in Reader's Digest. The article explained how real estate creates the wealthiest people in the world. It sold me. I grew up in a rural and poor community. While taking took the course, I lost my busboy job. I approached my real estate instructor, and he offered me a job. He hired me to clean rental properties and to do research for real estate appraisals. In six months I earned my real estate salesperson license and did property management to earn a base salary. In addition, in my spare time, I performed real estate appraisals and began selling property. Making a living in real estate is not for the fainthearted. The good news is that there is no ceiling to your income. There is also no floor to your income. I learned most of the lessons mentioned in this chapter from the amazing time I spent in real estate while going to college. If I had not read that Reader's Digest article, I would have missed a lot of exceptional experiences.

The Real Estate Office Staff "On Safari" on a 12,500-acre ranch.

I hear personal finance gurus and other celebrities boasting about their real estate finance success. Remember, their success resulted from very hard work. Real Estate investing and being a real estate agent is not an easy-to-get rich path. Both activities require the ability to negotiate fluidly, think on your feet, and possess an extensive amount of knowledge.

I hope this information and the stories I share help you find a home that you love and can afford.

Chapter 15

Automobiles

You Aren't What You Drive, High net worth individuals believe that financial independence more important than displaying high social status.

Dr. Thomas Stanley, author, *The Millionaire Next Door*

The American love affair for the automobile is still insatiable. The cult classic film, American Graffiti, somewhat embodies this strange love affair. My father composed a list of the cars he owned in his life. The number is 40! As we will discuss, cars do not make good investments. This rang true after my mother passed away, leaving my father with an insufficient income to pay the car payment on his 2014 Fiat 500L. He was 81. With a car payment. A month later, we took the car to CarMax, Sanford, Florida, and sold them the car for more than owed.... fortunately. But remember, everyone is not so lucky.

My dad created this record of the cars he owned and the miles he drove them. **Cycling** through cars is an expensive habit.

	Yr	Make	Cost	Mileage		Yr	Make	Cost	Mileage
1.	1953	PONTIAC (1947)	500	5000	24.	1987	VOLVO	15000	48000
2.	1954	HUDSON	2100	42000	25.	1989	JEEP P-UP	15000	40000
3.	1957	VW	1700	19000	26.	1991	FORD P-UP	14000	66000
4.	1958	VAUXHALL	2000	14000	27.	1991	MAZDA MPV	15000	40000
5.	1959	M-B 190d	3400	4000	28.	1993	CHEVY VAN	18000	40000
6.	1961	M-B 220S	4800	29000	29.	1995	CHEVY PUP	12000	86000
7.	1962	PEUGEOT 404	2400	55000	30.	1995	PLYMOUTH VAN	16000	60000
8.	1965	DATSUN	2600	13000	31.	1996	GEO PRISM	16000	98000
9.	1966	TOYOTA CROWN	2230	5500	32.	1999	FORD TAURUS	20000	35000
10.	1967	FIAT 124	1900	29000	33.	2001	MAZDA TRIBUTE	24000	4000
11.	1969	TOYOTA CROWN	3100	29000	34.	2001	MAZDA 626	17900	29500
12.	1970	MAZDA 1800	2100	106100	35.	2002	MAZDA TRIB	23000	30000
13.	1971	RENAULT R-16	2900	55000	36.	2005	SUZUKI FORENZA	17000	
14.	1973	MAZDA RX-2	3900	67000	37.	2006	MAZDA 5	17000	17000
15.	1976	TOYOTA CORONA	4600	56000	38.	2007	SUZUKI XL7	22000	20000
16.	1978	DATSUN 510	5000	13000	39.	2010	GMC	27000	29000
17.	1978	MAZDA RX-4	6800	70000	40.	2014	FIAT	25000	16000
18.	1980	VOLVO DL	9700	265000					
19.	1978	MAZDA GLC	4800	30000					
20.	1986	MAZDA GLC	6800	49000					
21.	1985	ISUZU I-mark	9800	20000					
22.	1986	ISUZU PUP	9600	58000					
23.	1987	FORD AEROSTAR	15000	80000					

The solution is to buy a two-year-old car and replace it after you have owned it four to eight years. Financial experts say you could save enough money, buying a car less often (**cycling**) to retire five years earlier. Ten-year-old cars start to "wear out (literally their welcome" with increasing occurrences of necessary repairs. In addition, you are getting behind in safety technology. The average age of cars in the U.S. is 11.5 years. In my opinion, ten years is a good time to update. Financially, this is golden.

https://www.nerdwallet.com/blog/loans/total-cost-owning-car/

Owning an automobile can be a complicated business for the inexperienced. Car ownership is not for sissies. Get someone with experience to help you navigate the choppy waters of finance related to automobile ownership. You can do this!

Go Online: Buy your car from a reputable online car dealership. Checkout Carvana, CarMax and the new kid on the block, Driveway. Driveway is different because they offer service besides buying, trading, and selling cars. You still have to do your homework. You still have to know your credit score in advance, research the insurance cost of your new ride, and through KBB or Edmunds, determine the value of your trade and the car you are buying. Continue reading for a little fatherly advice.

Automobile expense is the second largest expense for most people. In 2017, according to NerdWallet, average car ownership costs were over $8,000 per year if you drive 15,000 miles. Purchasing a car involves added expenses; insurance, maintenance, repairs, and gas. Many people love that new car smell. That smell is expensive. Most cars lose 25% of their value in depreciation in the first year. I witnessed a situation where the owner of a car totaled their new Chevrolet Camaro. They ended up owing the bank $2,000 because the car insurance paid them the car's value, not the amount of the car note. They lost their car and ended up with a $2000 personal note owed to the bank for the difference. They had to replace the car. Their situation was desperate. Car insurance pays the depreciated value of the car, not what you paid for your car. You get to pay the difference between the insurance company payment and your loan balance. Protect your investment with **gap** insurance. Buy a replacement cost auto policy. Consider this website to investigate **total** car ownership cost. https://autocosts.info/US.

The automobile industry is brainwashing you into purchasing a new car. The automobile industry spent $36 billion dollars worldwide on automobile advertising in 2019. According to Zenith, an ad agency think tank, the US market is worth $18 billion per year. Here's how that affects you. If you take the advertising dollars spent by a vehicle manufacturer, the number ranges from a whopper of $8,500 for each Alfa Romeo sold in the U.S. compared to $250 per Honda or Toyota. GM and Ford together spent over $5.5 billion per year to get you to turn your head.

You are being manipulated! By design!

The Dealership Experience

Personally, avoid the dealership. The only constructive purpose of the car dealership is to test drive a real car. Don't buy the car at the dealership. Hire a car buying service from your local credit union or wholesale club. Check with AAA. Tell them what you want and let them work with the dealership. Buy a car from a private seller.

That's how the wealthiest Americans buy a car. If you are buying a used car, CarMax is trustworthy and no finance manager to pick your pocket. If you must walk into the dealership to negotiate a price, do your homework in advance!

See below related paragraph **I have to Buy a Car from a Dealer**

Know your credit score! Pre-arrange your auto financing. I once got a great deal because I walked in with the check written from my credit union. I negotiated as if I had cash in my pocket. Sorry, Mr. Salesman, I only have $16,800 in my pocket. Not a penny more.

At the beginning of the negotiations, get a number proposal from the sales associate. When the salesperson returns, ask them, "Is that the best you can do?" When the salesperson returns...Look at the number, shake your head and say, I'll have to think it over. Go through the awkward meet the manager routine and LEAVE the property. Come back a month later preferably at the end of the month and test the same model you like again. Repeat this as many times as you can to wear the dealer down and not the other way around! Shop at the end of the model year to secure better deals and higher rebates.

Buying a car is hard work!!!

The Finance Office at The Dealership

Here is a link to a great car loan calculator.

https://communityfirstfl.balancepro.org/resources/calculators/car-loan-calculator

The dealership finance guy is not your friend!

You are, under no circumstances, obligated to buy any product or service offered to you by the finance person. They are there to upsell you and give added profit to the dealership.

Keep silent in this office. Do not nod or move your hands. In fact, sit on your hands. Do not buy the permanent Rain X, Fabric Protector Package, Muffler Bearing Warranty (I made that up), Manufacturer Extended Warranty, Paint Sealant, Rustproofing, Credit Life Insurance, GAP Insurance (most popular product pitched), Auto Insurance, Theft

Protection VIN Etching, and / or Document and Delivery fees. Do not let the finance manager renegotiate your deal. Don't let them change the interest rate, down payment, monthly payment or term of loan unless they change in your favor (Very Rare). If they try, walk away! I have watched finance managers physically shake when I whipped out my... wait for it...my financial calculator and checked the figures. Several times they were wrong. On those occasions, their entire finance contract was retyped or reprinted before we moved forward.

Beware of the Yo-Yo or Spot Delivery Scam. I unknowingly bought a new car off the lot that was sold to an earlier buyer on the Yo-Yo plan. Later in the day, I realized on closer inspection that there was a home-made CD in the Cd player. I turned around to see faint red cool-aid stains on the back seat and the floor. The last straw was the ash tray. It was full...of ashes. I brought the car back at once. It was used and abused.

The Yo-Yo goes like this. You have shaky credit, but the dealer/finance manager has access to subprime car loan money from a financial insti-tution. The dealer tells the customer to take the car home (puppy dog sales technique) before they have signed the final documents. This is before the customer has received financial approval. "The loan is pend-ing". This takes the customer out of the car buying market. It gets the customer excited about their new car. Then the dealer calls back, some-times a week later, to ask you to come back to sign the paperwork, but there is a catch. You are not approved, or your payment has soared. It's Suboptimal! It's immoral, but it still exists in the marketplace. Again, arrange your own financing in advance. Consider financing from a credit union. They offer lower rates and superior customer service. That takes a big hassle out of the car buying circus.

You just have to Buy a Car from a Dealer

Take your time purchasing your next car. Do the **research**. Investigate alternative dealers, cars and lenders **before** stepping on to a car lot. It's all online. First, find the value of your next car through Kelley Blue Book www.kbb.com, and Edmunds www.Edmunds.com. NADA is an-other resource, http://www.nadaguides.com/Cars. Check out Carvana. com and Vroom.com to get a feel for how much you will spend on the car of your choice. If you are brave, use one of these trendy services. The downside is that there is no opportunity for negotiation. The price is the price. You do not see the car in advance. You should reserve this method for mature audiences.

Investigate the auto insurance rate on your car model. The insurance on a Cadillac Escalade may be more expensive than the Toyota Corolla. In fact, car insurance rates jump when the vehicle value exceeds $30,000. The top three least expensive cars to insure according to a Value Penguin auto insurance report are the Honda CRV, Chrysler Pacifca and the Honda Odyssey. Shop between insurance companies. Keep your driving record impeccable. It affects what you pay on insurance. Even minor traffic tickets will affect your auto insurance expense. If you are under 25, then you have no business owning/driving a new car. The insurance premium will be more expensive than the car payment sometimes. Save money on car insurance by adjusting your collision and comprehensive deductible. Compare insurance quotes from several insurers. Start your journey at the Gabi.com or Zebra.com.

Improving your credit score can reduce your insurance premiums. According to a Value Penguin, the difference between a good and poor credit score can affect premiums by 70%.

https://www.valuepenguin.com/state-of-auto-insurance-2021

https://www.valuepenguin.com/best-and-cheapest-cars-insure

Second, negotiate the financing in advance **before** walking onto a car lot, with a lender separate from the dealer. Go to your credit union in advance and get pre-approved. Do not rely on your lender to approve you for a realistic loan amount based upon your budget. They will preapprove you for an unrealistic high loan amount unrelated to your needs. Lenders are in the business to make money, not to help you with your budget! Make sure you plan your auto expense budget in advance. In 2010, they approved me for $40,000. I spent $16,800.

Congratulations Ken, you have the best Auto rate available for your coverage!

Hi Ken,

Gabi compared your current Auto rate against 10 companies and found that you have the best rate available for your coverage—at least for now.

As you know, rates fluctuate over time and insurance companies raise rates periodically. The good news is, with Gabi, the search for a better rate never ends. **We'll continue to monitor Auto rates and contact you as soon as a better rate is available.**

Check your review

You can easily save and switch to your new insurance provider on the Gabi website.

These are my cars. I bought the Hyundai Sonata new in 2010 after the 2009 financial crises for $16,800 with a credit union check. I paid both cars off with lots of life left.

Get a great interest rate when you finance a car. They base your interest rate upon your credit rating. **Know your FICO score.** Order a free copy of your credit report before you go shopping. https://www.annualcreditreport.com/index.action

The auto lenders use an "Auto-Enhanced" score which looks at auto loan specific risk. It is okay if this looks different from your regular scores.

Get copies of the three credit reports at no charge. Don't fall for the first web-site that comes up in the Google search. It says free credit report, but this is not the website you want. Insist upon https://www.annualcreditreport.com. See Chapter 13 Credit Reports.

Third, learn how to negotiate and buy a car at a price below its (depreciated) blue book value. (Should you go to negotiating school first? Check-out www.scotworkusa.com to take a negotiating class. Find a financial coach in your area who will aid you in the car buying process) Remember the seven best words in the world. "Is that the best you can do?" Put the dealer on the defensive. Salesmen take negotiating and sales classes to improve their bottom line at the cost of your bottom line. Money does not care who it belongs to. A good sales associate sees that "their" money is in your pocket. They will use every "professional" trick in the book to lighten your purse as much as possible. Take notes during the negotiation phase. You will refer to them later and this puts the salesperson on notice; Don't fool around with this customer, they write everything. Negotiate each part of the deal separately. What do I mean? Do you have a trade? Negotiate the trade separately from the car purchase. Research the value of your trade online. I negotiate the pur-chase of the newer car first as if I have no trade. If I have a trade, I sell it to a private buyer. It is a hassle, but you will receive the retail price for your trade. This assumes your car is in good shape. If your trade needs a little mechanical or body shop makeover, then a trade could be beneficial to you and the dealer. The dealer can repair your well-worn trade at wholesale in the company garage. Bring the trade in after you have a signed contract for the newer car. A reputable dealer will honor the new car contract and give you a good deal for your trade. You risk another round of intense negotiations using this method and ultimately, no deal. This method is for the seasoned car buyer. An alternative is taking your trade to CarMax and sell it outright for cash. I have done this and expe-rienced a smooth, fair transaction.

The dealership will want to combine everything into a nice, neat package for "your convenience." New car, trade-in and financing wrapped up in a neat little package. The package method is not for your convenience, The package method is for their largest profit. Fourth, learn to be unemotional during the negotiation phase. The dealer will try to convince you that the car you are buying is the last car on the planet. It is not. The dealer will explain that your research is flawed. I have heard statements, "Well, Kelley Blue Book is not here to buy your car" which means KBB's numbers do not show the local market. True, the dealership is not bound by any external auto appraisal service. Don't trust the dealer statement, "Here is the invoice, and you are killing me with such a lowball offer! If I honor this deal, I will have to go out of business." That statement and the invoice the dealer shows you is a joke. Dealers receive monetary incentives behind the scenes that never make it to the invoice. The invoice is a good place to start negotiating.

If this dealer is not in the mood to make a deal, fine. Find a different car at a different dealer. WALK. It is the best negotiation weapon. NO DEAL!

Know what you can afford and don't budge. Everyone in the car buying process will encourage you to "Live a Little." This means, you can afford to spend "a little" more. It won't hurt. Don't cave. Stick to your budget.

At the time of writing over 7 million auto borrowers are delinquent. (Over 90 days late). The banker received their commission, the car sales associate received their commission, and the dealer received their profit. There is little consequence to these assistants to your delinquent loan. Money flows out of your wallet into their wallet. Time for you to pay the piper.

The Best Warranty

The best warranty out here is to buy, reliable, reputable, brand name cars. If you buy used, have the car inspected by your mechanic. I have never bought an extended warranty.

More Automobile Finance

When financing an automobile, I recommend using a credit union. They have the most competitive interest rate, lowest GAP (guaranteed auto protection) insurance rates and best customer service. Go in, open an account, and then get approved for your automobile buy. The credit union will give you a check in advance with the Pay to the order of blank! They make the check amount to a predetermined amount. Negotiate the best deal you can as if you are paying cash. Many credit unions offer buyer services that negotiate an excellent deal for you for a reasonable fee. There are lots of benefits to dealing with your local credit union. If the car you buy offers an added rebate using the auto manufacturer's retail credit arm, then use the manufacturer's finance company and then refinance through the credit union. Sneaky, I know. I have done this several times. In addition, your credit union may have a car buying concierge or buy-ing service. Most services are free; The dealership pays the car broker. your representative negotiates a great deal for you without you having to put up with the hassle of a dealership. My credit union has an easy on-line application! Check out www.AAA.com, www.AutoFinder.com, or www.autonationDirect.com.

Check out www.CarSquare.com

www.usaa.com if you are in the military.

Here's a deal I got in the mail!

The best way to own a car is to purchase it with cash. The best place to buy a car is from an individual. Obviously, do your homework and know the specific car you want to buy and know how much it's valued. Cars selling below $10,000 may be high mileage and more hassle than they are worth. Check out http://www.jdpower.com/ or www.edmunds.com to decide vehicle reliability.

You should checkout your local Facebook Marketplace to find great car deals. I found drivable used cars that had life left in them. Be careful, though, dealers will also advertise on Facebook Marketplace. That may still be okay. They know you want a "buy from an individual" experience and may play nice.

If you plan to buy an automobile with higher mileage, your best bet is Honda. I drove a 1997 Honda CRV with 178,000 miles. It's still in the family. Be prepared for repair bills though. If you chose this route, find a great local mechanic. They are priceless. Try Yelp online. Ask friends, neighbors, relatives for a reference. Try www.ASE.com. Finding a talented mechanic is worth the time and research. http://clark.com/cars/10-tips-to-find-the-perfect-mechanic-cheap-car/. If buying an older car, consider AAA membership. www.autoclubsouth.aaa.com.

Check www.carvana.com. I also like Kia and Hyundai products as they are inexpensive, very reliable, and come with an amazing warranty that is transferable to the second owner. According to Hyundai/Kia, the second owner inherits the 5-year 60,000-mile part of the warranty. Find a model with 40,000 miles or less and you will have a good part of the warranty remaining to make sure you don't end up with large repair expenses. Find a brand you know and stick with it. I have friends who favor Toyota RAV 4's. This is smart. You know how they drive and when it comes time to replace your car; you know what to expect. Stay away from cars whose earlier life was a rental car. I have found cars on Carvana with less than 10,000 miles and in excellent condition. The sweet spot for depreciation is 3 years. You can find a multitude of "cars" (not trucks) coming off of lease contracts that are 3 years old and 36,000 miles on the odometer. Popular terms for car leases are 3 years 12,000 miles per year. The depreciation has peeled off 50% of that new car price and if you choose wisely, you still may smell a bit of new car smell. So, the message here is don't lease… purchase. Buy a car that is three years old and enjoy the three-year depreciation sweet spot. Let someone else pay for the large loss of value to the car. (The lessee paid the depreciation in their payment.) If you are a savvy negotiator and deal maker, look for local deals on eBay. A recent search on eBay produced excellent results, and the cars were in my neighborhood. Check your local credit union for community car sales. The credit union allows approved car dealers to show off their best cars on the lender's property. Since the sale is on the lender's property; the dealers have to play nice.

HMMM. I wonder if banks that lease cars, make profits deducting (for their tax purposes) 50% appreciation…from their corporate income tax burden. This is true.

In fact, most of your lease payment pays your leased vehicle 's depreciation. There is also interest paid and it's called the "Money Factor" or "Lease Fee." It's how they come up with the payment!

https://www.carpaymentcalculator.net/calcs/auto-lease.php Shows Depreciation

https://www.edmunds.com/calculators/car-lease.html Shows Detail

Remember, leasing a car is renting long term. You have fewer rights to the car. Restricted mileage, rigid requirements for auto insurance, sales tax paid every month and what if you want out early? Open your wallet time!

myFico has a calculator you can use to compare the costs between purchase and lease. Using the default information, the buy choice ended up costing $1400 less per year. Plug in your numbers to find out how much more auto-leasing may cost you.

https://www.myfico.com/credit-education/financial-calculators/vehicle-leasing-vs-buying

Check out the Simpson's episode when Homer leased the famed Canyonero?

Car Salesman: Here's how your lease breaks down. This is your down payment, then here's your monthly, and here is your weekly.

Homer: And that's it, right?

Car Salesman: Yup... then after your final monthly payment there's the routine CBP, or Crippling Balloon Payment.

Homer: But that's not for a while, right?

Car Salesman: Right?

Homer:

Sweet!

Look at Dr. Thomas Stanley's nuggets of wisdom donned from his research conducted when authoring his book, *The Millionaire Next Door*. Twenty percent of millionaires are "used" vehicle shoppers. They enjoy purchasing cars via "aggressive shopping among private owners, dealers and leas-ing companies, etc."

When Dr. Stanley wrote this, most people looked in the want ads of newspapers. The Internet was in its infancy. Sites like www.car.com, www.carvana.com, www.truecar.com, now make finding a reliable, easier than ever before.

Be wary of Certified Used Cars. The hype sounds great. Your favorite dealer has done a 1,400-point inspection on your cream puff and "stands" behind your new purchase. Certified pre-owned means they add an additional $1,000-$1,200 onto the price of the car for an **extended** warranty. When shopping for a used car with my daughter, I test drove a car with shaky brakes. They needed to be addressed. It was a "Certified" model. I returned the car to the dealer and said I "may" be interested, but the brakes needed repair. The sales agent texted later telling me their mechanics thought the car's brakes were fine. I am sure he'll find a less informed buyer (sucker to buy the car. Don't be a sucker. ALWAYS get the car checked out by a mechanic before you buy!

Are you interested in an extended warranty? Buy it from your credit union. They sell reasonably priced extended warranties. My credit union website has links to NADA and Annual Credit Report.com. This credit union has budgeting information on the full cost of your car and GAP insurance.

Post COVID note

In late 2021, the automobile market is a seller's market due to an influx of government stimulus increasing demand and a chip shortage hinder-ing automobile manufacturing which reduces supply, rendering most of this Chapter, automobiles, almost obsolete. I predict in few months that the market will get back to normal and Chapter 15 will be fully usable.

Insurance

What is GAP insurance? If you must buy and finance a new car at 100% of the purchase price and the most popular model to impress people who don't even like you, then prepare to owe more money than the car is worth. I knew a tenant that flipped his new Trans Am. The completed paperwork showed they had a $3,000 personal note owed to the bank to pay the difference between the balance owed on the car note versus the insurance payout. AND they had to buy a new car. Genius!

Gap Insurance (Guaranteed Asset Protection

Automobile Gap Insurance is a product designed to ensure the difference between what you owe on your auto loan balance and what the car is worth. It's for car purchases that leave you "upside down" in the deal. You owe more than your car is worth. Your auto insurance company pays, in a total loss scenario, the book value of the car only. When you buy a car new off the lot, its value can drop 50%. Often the value is below what you owe on the car. Have a total loss and the insurance company will pay you what they think the car is worth. **This is an opportunity to negotiate.** You don't have to accept what the insurance company is offering. Remember, these seven words! "Is that the best you can do?" Often insurance companies will increase their payout. Remember they are buying the car from you. Remember they will take your "totaled" car, repair it and sell it, or sell it to a junk yard for scrap. To insure against this situation, you can buy an added **"GAP"** insurance policy. Never buy from the car dealership. Like any purchase you make, **SHOP!** In my experience, the best deal on gap insurance is through your credit union. If you must buy a new car, be a good negotiator. If you need GAP insurance, then you may need to take another auto purchasing negotiating course.

https://www.insure.com/car-insurance/

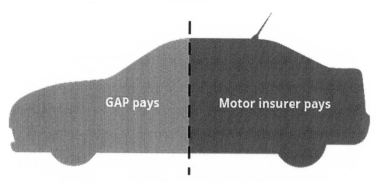

Cover the difference between your motor insurance payment
and the **FULL value of your car**

Oh Lord would you buy me a Z71 4 x 4 Truck?

Look, if you are a construction contractor or towing a full-size travel trailer then blow your children's inheritance on a two story, four door, four-wheel-drive pickup truck! I insist. The United States best seller is the Ford F-150 at over 34 million trucks. The most popular vehicle worldwide is the Toyota Corolla at over 40 million units. There are a few frugal people left in the world. When I was a kid, pickup trucks had a wide bench seat, two doors, two-wheel drive and were used to do chores. And pickup trucks are great for doing chores. But do you have any idea how expensive a modern pickup truck is to own and run. According to https://autocosts.info/US the full cost of ownership for an average new pickup truck costing $45,000 is $15,000 per year. I hope you are a business owner that can write-off this expense. Contrast this with the average $20,000 car costing per year between $6,000 and $8,000 total cost per year to own.

https://www.cnbc.com/2017/09/28/ford-bets-theres-a-market-for-its-100000-f-450-pickup-trucks.html

At the time of this writing, Ford just announced the 2021 Ford F-450 Super Duty Limited 4x4 starting at $91,125. Such a bargain!!!!!!!

2021 BMW 330i

Length: 185.7 Inches, Width 71.9 inches, Track 60.3inches, Wheelbase 112.2 Height 56.8 Inches,

Weight: 3560 lbs., Headroom: 38.7 inches, legroom 42.0/35.2 front/rear respectively, Shoulder Room, Front/Rear 56/54.6 inches.

Price: $ 41,250. Source: bmwusa.com

2021 Toyota Corolla

Length: 182.5 inches, Width 70.1 inches, Track 60.3 inches, Wheelbase 106.3, Height: 56.5 inches, Weight: 2870-3150 lbs., Headroom: 38.3 inches, Legroom: 42.3/34.8 front/rear, Shoulder Room: 54.0/51.87 inches

Price: $ 25,925. Source:www.toyota.com

So how much are we paying for perceived luxury and prestige? The new Toyota costs 40% less than the BMW. I bet you can better deal on the Toyota. LOOK at the dimensions. They are almost the same! In 2018 their sizes were almost identical.

> Too many people spend money they earned...to buy things they don't want...to impress people that they don't like. --Will Rogers

Buy Here, Pay Here.

Okay. Your FICO credit score is below 600 and no reputable credit union or bank will finance you. You have no cash? You have a job or live on social security. You are a sub-prime borrower. What do you do? You may be in the market for a "Buy Here Pay Here lot." It means a used car dealership with 10 to 15+ year old cars with high mileage and a high probability of needing a repair soon. I visited a local BHPH lot, and they have cars that need a lot of TLC. I found a 2000 Saturn SL2. The price was $800 down and $87.50 per week. The car's radio was missing. It had 200,000 hard miles on it. The USC Trojans license plate added to my confidence in this "Cream Puff" as this car spent some time belonging to a college student. They sell cars with no warranty. You buy "as is." The dealer allows you to take the car to a mechanic to inspect. The car may be worth $500 cash. I don't understand why these places exist. The down payment is more than the same car for sale in better condition,

Cash! I found a 2001 Saturn SL for $1,500 that looked great. Car was in good condition and the accessories worked. Check for clean title. That's not always a given.

Put as little as $1,000 down $100 per week and the finance arm of the "Buy Here Pay Here" car dealership will be your new transportation partner. The dealership requires you to make your payment in person...every week. They install a GPS tracker to make repossession easier and a "kill" switch to disable your vehicle. Miss a payment and the dealer will be in your driveway with a tow truck to repossess your new ride. They will take the car, clean it, put it on the lot and start over again. Sell the same car twice, three times or more is a great way to make a living! To avoid this mayhem, you may move closer to work, buy a used bicycle and save enough money to pay cash for a "new" car. ...In my town, Jacksonville, Florida, there are several reputable "**buy here, pay here**" auto dealer-ships. Just remember, "If it sounds too good to be true," it is! Beware of loan contracts contingent on you purchasing add-ons such as extended warranties and your auto insurance. Be careful of the scam called "Yo-Yo." Many times, you think the deal is complete, but after you take the car home (fall in love with it the dealership will call to tell you days or weeks later that you do not qualify for the agreed to terms and must raise your auto loan interest rate or your down payment. **Don't be a victim. Try to buy a good used car with cash!**

In addition, there is legal recourse. When you buy a "Buy Here, Pay Here" car you should receive legit paperwork. Dealerships may obey the Truth in Lending Act. However, Regulation Z states what They must include in the sales agreement. **1:** That the dealership is your financial partner. **2:** The dealer must show the cash price. **3.** The dealer must show the total financed amount.

Be careful of online auto lenders targeting at risk borrowers. They lend you money, and then refer you to a local Buy Here, Pay Here dealer, telling you what car you WILL buy. Beggars can't be choosers! https://www.autocreditexpress.com/

Protect yourself from a used car scam by ordering a vehicle history report from Carfax. Carfax reports the previous owner's location, re-corded accidents, and title history. Title history shows you the salvage, flood, hail, lemon and rebuilt issues. Plug the VIN (Vehicle Identification Number, know this! number into the NHTSA website to research any Safety Issues & Recalls from this government website.

Regular borrowers are not immune from scams. I bought two cars from a local dealer I thought was reputable and received notice of a class action lawsuit. The dealership padded the price by charging a $200 false government document fee. The fee padded the dealership's profit margin. I later received a partial payment in the mail. Thirty years ago, the typical car dealership was a scary place. Hmm. **It still is**. I just visited an Audi dealership. Two years prior, the sales manager reported several cars sold that were not actually sold to enable him to pad the sales numbers and collect a commission. It compromised their VIN numbers. It took them two years to undo the red tape to make them available for sale. And...you guessed it. They were reselling them as new. Not used. The price was okay compared to 2018 Audi prices, but not for a car from 2016. The discounted price was unacceptable. Automobile lenders agreed that the cars were not new cars.

A Suzuki dealer sales manager threatened me to leave the dealership because I had the nerve to reject a car I bought new. Upon further in-spection, I found the car had been sold to a subprime borrower then returned to the dealership after their credit was rejected. This is the "Yo-Yo" effect. The dealer detailed the car and sold it to me as new. The dealership re-detailed it. Now the car smelled like a wet dog. I looked at the detail man (a separate non-dealership subcontractor) and asked, "I'm sure it will smell like new when it dries?" He just looked at me with a blank look. I walked back into the dealership and handed the keys back to the sales manager (politely...not my style and said, "Thank you for the effort, but I came here to buy a new car." The sales manager at once treated me like a regular subprime customer and shouted, "Get the hell out of my dealership and get into YOUR car and leave! Or I will call the police and have you removed!" My response was **uncharacteristically** calm. I suspected the title paperwork was not complete. Their office was incompetent and desperately backed up. It is common in the car business that sales are more important than handling the official paper work! I did not legally own the car. They had not processed the Bank loan paperwork. I said, "Good, when the police get here, they'll find me in that chair over there." I called a friend to come pick me up. While I was waiting, I walked to the "Dog Smell" car to retrieve my belongings. In the meantime, I noticed an auto transport truck behind the building. The same model with the same trim and accessories was on the delivery truck. It was in a color I preferred. I went back inside to wait for my ride when I saw the owner of the dealership breeze into his office. (How did I know this? By reading body language and the fact he walked into the largest office in the building. I asked a salesman if I could see him. He poked his head in the manager's office and he allowed me to enter. I visited the owner and told him my plight. He said if "my" car was untitled, no problem. Thirty minutes later I left with the car I wanted... and it was new! I watched them roll it off the truck. I bought parts and had my car serviced at this dealership. Years later, when I arrived one morning to buy parts, I was surprised to find a friendly policeman in the parking lot. The policeman asked me if I worked there. I said no. The dealership was closed! This came as no surprise to me! And the sales manager (from two years prior) got what he wanted! The policeman (politely) asked me to leave the dealership!!!! Lol!

Here is a picture of my cream puff.

During another car buying episode, I negotiated a very smart deal for myself while shopping a contract from another out-of-town dealer. This time for a Mitsubishi Lancer Sport Wagon. Very well-designed car. Unfortunately, Mitsubishi was having financial difficulties. Banks considered its automobile division the go to brand for subprime buyers. I did not know this. After the dealership agreed on the deal, I took the contract to my credit union and scheduled the closing. Everything was set. The next day the credit union called to say something happened that never happened before in the history of the credit union. The dealer backed out of the deal. They refused to sell the car to me at the agreed upon price. Wow. I knew I struck a hard bargain! However, this was a Godsend. The credit union then told me about the financial difficulties of Mitsubishi Corporation and its sub-prime lending status among lenders. That model of car only sold 3,000 units nationwide that year. A real dud. Thank you, Mitsubishi dealership!

Finally, I am afraid to tell you it is still a "Jungle Out There!" I am reminded by the conversation I had with the sales manager of a local Audi dealer. In an aggressive stance and body language (communicating don't come back and waste my time "Would you have bought that car if I offered it to you for $21,000?" I said, "As I told your salesman...I don't like the car." Let's say the car had a little "baggage."

In conclusion, I find it fascinating to discover that most millionaires don't drive European luxury cars. People who want to "look like" millionaires drive expensive European luxury cars. Only 24% of millionaires own new cars. In fact, the average American spends about 70% of what the typical millionaire pays for their most expensive vehicle. Many millionaires enjoy finding cash deals from private buyers. If you plan on becoming wealthy, do not invest in expensive new cars. Most people who own expensive new cars purchased them with cash after they became wealthy, not before they became wealthy. If you borrow to buy an expensive new car, you lower your odds of becoming wealthy.

Abridged from, Stanley, Thomas J., and William D. Danko. *The Millionaire Next Door: The Surprising Secrets of America's Wealthy.* 1st Taylor Trade Pub. ed. Lanham, Md.: Taylor Trade Pub., 2010.

Learn how to negotiate before walking on to a car lot. Go to a flea market and haggle with vendors. Practice making offers on inexpensive items on eBay to get the feel of compromise or Win-Win negotiation. Take an experienced friend to the dealership to help you negotiate. Remember two things. "No Deal" is always an option. Try Win-Win. If unsuccessful, walk away from the table. Before you do, ask the seven most valuable words in the English language, "Is that the best you can do?"

Automobile Repair

Automobile repair is another opportunity to overspend. Auto repair is another industry with a shifty reputation. Without appearing to be outright scam artists, they encourage service writers to up sell. I encourage you to be familiar with your car's owner's manual with your car's maintenance schedule.

In addition, get more than one estimate if you have a large repair. It's great to have a relationship with a mechanic whom you can trust but be careful. That trust translates into making suggestions to you for unnecessary repairs. Be careful of relying on your car dealership. They make very little income from selling cars. The vast majority of their profits come from the service department.

There is no shame in knowing a little about how an automobile operates. If you are buying a used car, you will need to check for recalls. You need to be on the ball about this because dealers may "conveniently forget" to remind you of this detail because dealerships get a reduced rate for handling man-ufacturing recalls.

https://www.nhtsa.gov/recalls

In working with dealership repair departments, I have had problems. They told me I needed service on an item that my owner's manual said was unnecessary yet. When I showed this info to the service advisor, they were not happy. I did not authorize the service; I walked out the door. Your relationship with a dealership service writer is a conflict of interest. Some dealerships pay service writers a 100% commission.

My Kia was pulling to the left. I took the car to my mechanic to have the alignment checked. That was not the problem. The tire wear was abnormal. Initially I got an estimate for two new tires. I said, no, we need to submit the tires for a warranty replacement. If I had not spoken up, I would have been on the hook for an added $200 plus. If you are a woman, I would strongly encourage you to "borrow" a man to aid you in negotiations. I'm sorry. That's just how the world is today. I taught this technique to my daughter. She asked an acting student "hunk" from college to join her in retrieving her car after an unexpected repair because of negligence. Her mechanic forgot to tighten the lug nuts on one of her wheels. Funny thing was that she was in the shop to get her oil changed. The shop was pressuring my teenage daughter to buy tires. It was unnecessary. You can imagine the conversation between papa bear (me) and the service manager afterward.

Major Items of Interest on Your Car

1. Regular Oil Changes;

2. Inspect and Replace Tires when Necessary;

3. Inspect and Repair Brakes when Necessary;

4. Air Filter Every One or Two Years;

5. Windshield Wiper Blades (Most Auto Parts Stores Will Install them for you, No charge);

6. Change Coolant every two years (Depends on Mileage, Check Owner's Manual);

7. Transmission Fluid Change after 100,000 miles.

That's the most important stuff. These are not usually expensive maintenance items. Integrate these items into your budget as a non-repeating budget item. This topic is discussed in Chapter 12 Money Management.

Extended Auto Warranties

Automobile extended warranties waste money sometimes. The best warranty is to buy a reliable car. Buy an affordable policy from the automobile manufacturer or your credit union. Credit Unions have the best prices. Ignore warranty companies that use telemarketers and direct mail. When you need to make a purchase, you start the conversation.

Here is an unwanted extended warranty pitch I received in the mail. Never purchase anything based on a sales pitch like the one below. Oh look! There is a zero% interest payment option! Whoo Hoo!

Dear Ken,

We have just been advised there will be a Price Increase to our Extended Vehicle Service Plans (EVSP) effective September 1, 2019. After that date we will not be able to honor the service contract quote designed specifically for your 2013 KIA FORTE.

Please call us at ████████, so we can hold your EVSP contract at the lowest program rates.

When vehicles expire out of factory warranty due to time or mileage the Vehicle Service Plan provides coverage beyond the original Manufacturer's and puts your vehicle back under coverage at current Loyalty Pricing. By contacting us now you can avoid the price increase and still cover your investment from the high cost of these unexpected repairs.

We want to make sure we do everything possible to earn your business so please know this program is limited, based on your current mileage and age of your vehicle. At this time No vehicle inspection is required and the 0% payment option is available. Please call before September 1, 2019 for these eligibility requirements to remain valid.

We can be reached between 7 am - 7 pm CST Monday through Friday and between 9 am - 3 pm on Saturday. Call toll-free at ████████

Hybrid and Electric Cars

buy a hybrid or EV (Electric Vehicle) only if you are wealthy! The rest of us should read above to learn how to buy a reliable and affordable, used car.

Hybrids and electric cars have amazing depreciation. Electric and hybrid car owners face up to 60% and 70% depreciation rates over five years. Buy used if you want a hybrid or EV! But be careful. Buy a used one with low mileage to preserve as much warranty as possible. Make sure you receive the transferable manufacturer's warranty. This may be the time for an extended warranty.

Hyundai has a lifetime warranty on its hybrid batteries. Limited transferable warranty.

Toyota Prius is ninety-six months or 100,000 miles. Transferable if car is a certified used vehicle.

Chevy Bolt eight years 100,000 miles.

Honda Insight: **Warning, Warning!** one hundred months (eight years four months) **limited** warranty.

From the 2019 Honda Insight Warranty Handbook:

Warranty Coverage During the first thirty six months (three years) of service, a defective replacement 12-volt battery will be replaced at no cost for the battery, labor, or installation.

For the remaining sixty-four months (5 years and 4 months), you will receive a credit toward the purchase of the 12-volt battery. They base this credit on the then-current retail price:

- Months 37 to 45: 60%
- Months 46 to 55: 50%
- Months 56 to 65: 40%
- Months 66 to 75: 30%
- Months 76 to 85: 20%
- Months 86 to 95: 10%
- Months 96 to 100: 5%

Note to self: Sell the car before it's 36 months old.

I test drove the Honda Insight and I would consider purchasing one. However, their warranty leaves me worried.

The Toyota Prius is the better investment among hybrids. It is the world's first mass produced hybrid starting in 1997. It appears battery replace-ment is a priced maintenance issue when compared to gas cars over the life of the car. However, I have no experience. The Toyota Warranty is not limited. It's ninety-six months 100,000, no prorated warranty like Honda.

2021 Update

Electric cars are becoming more mainstream, but charging station location is still a struggle. The future looks interesting, but I would wait before buying an electric car.

A New Car May Be the Best Choice Financially

Is a used car the only solution to our transportation needs? There are times in the economic cycle of the American Economy when purchasing a new car "could" be a viable option. If you have a recession proof job and you have created a realistic budget to follow, you have funded a healthy emergency fund, and have a positive net worth, it is possible to achieve financial independence and purchase a new car. You must also have an impeccable driving record to keep your auto insurance costs low. New car insurance is more expensive than insurance for a used car. (Fun Fact: This is also because of the cost of the physical materials and extra computers in new vehicles. A lack of claims data on a new model will force the insurance company to hold the insurance premium higher. There is no information, in the world of claims, to determine the likelihood that your car will get into an accident. The insurance company errs to the side of caution charging you a higher rate until reliable statistics become available. Again, this is why I recommend buying a used car. You will also pay higher sales taxes. I'm not suggesting buying a $50,000 Bimmer. I'm suggesting there are many reliable car manufacturers that offer new cars priced close to clean low mileage used cars. I am saying it is possible, if you have amazing negotiating skills, (you are the right person if you are at the right place at the right time, and you can get a deal on a new car close to the deal you could get on a late model used car. Just remember, Americans with the highest net worth buy used cars. Americans with the highest net worth buy their cars by the pound, not by the hood ornament (Status Symbol. When I buy a new car, I keep it at least ten years. $16,800 divided by 10 years = $1,680 auto expense per year. $1,680 divided by 12 = $140 per month. That is a reasonable monthly transportation expense. In comparison, buy a $50,000 BMW. Keep it five years. Your monthly transportation cost jumps to over $1,000 per month. That could limit how much money you are saving for retirement.

Timing: There are times in the American economic cycle when it is possible to get almost as good a deal on a new car as it would cost to get a used car. It's all about supply and demand. A new development is the impact made on the car market by natural disasters. A natural disaster can skew the market for new and used cars because thousands of people are replacing their totaled cars, flush with insurance money. Gas prices affect the demand for gas guzzlers. The demand for sedans (non-pickup trucks and SUV's is soft because gas prices are cheap. If you are lucky enough to have a "recession proof" job, purchasing a new car at the depths of recession can be rewarding. Every year, car dealerships have year-end clearance sales. They have to make room for the new models made available for the least financially savvy, among us, to gobble up like a possum in a cat food factory. It is possible to buy a new car at a price after incentives that results in a purchase price so much less than MSRP (Manufacturer Suggested Retail Price that first year depreciation is a "wash." In 2010, I purchased a new $22,500 Hyundai Sonata for $16,800 tax, tag and title. I financed it through my credit union. When they called me in to sign the final papers, we looked at the possibility of purchasing GAP (guaranteed auto protection insurance. The credit union's own GAP insurance software showed I was far from upside down. In fact, I would stay right side up in my loan for its entire term. I did not need GAP insurance, and I did not have to worry that my auto insurer would leave me stranded in case of a total loss.

Here is a link to a great car loan calculator.

https://communityfirstfl.balancepro.org/resources/calculators/car-loan-calculator

Another resource for automobile financing is World Omni Financial Corporation. http://www.worldomni.com/ . They received the award for best overall customer service experience from J.D. Power.

https://www.jdpower.com/business/press-releases/2018-us-consumer-financing-satisfaction-study

I was able to get such a great deal because the national economy was soft, and the new model Sonatas were on their way. In fact, the 2011 model Sonata was a redo of the model I purchased. I purchased the last model year of that version of Sonata. This is very **important!** The last model year of a version means all the bugs are "worked out". You end up with a very reliable model. Sometimes the improved models develop unexcepted reliability problems because it has no real world experience on the road. Because the economy in 2010 was weak, I purchased a 2010 Hyundai Elantra which was also the last year of that production model. I know, two cars in the same year. Just the way my auto purchase cycle worked out. Hyundai offers a ten year 100,000-mile warranty to the new car owner. In addition, during those trying times, Hyundai offered a program that allowed you to return your car if you lost your job, no questions asked. Well, I'm sure there were a few questions. My wife and I had good jobs, but the extra assurance (the name of their program was a nice security blanket.

From August until the current model cars are sold, cars are **on sale**. For automakers and car dealers this marks the beginning of the big fall sales events to get ready for the next model year cars.

Incentives include cash back rebates, finance and lease offers. Stay away from leases. Combine financing incentives with cash incentives. You get one or the other. Be careful here. It is dangerous to finance where you purchase the car. This gives the dealer another opportunity to cook your books (to rip you off. It is better to arrange financing at your credit union in advance then take advantage of the cash incentives and rebates.

August is the start of discount season and offers you the best selection of auto model options and colors. Similar to a Dutch auction, car prices drop throughout the discount season, and selection becomes an issue. By December (historically the best time to shop for a car the only thing left on the lot from the previous model year is the yellow one with the pink poke-a-dots. Nothing wrong with that.

Ford has their "Hurry Up and Save" sales event, Honda has "The Happy Honda" days sales event. Toyota's Toyotathon is ON! Nissan "Bottom Line Event" or Cadillac's "Made to Move" event.

If you are not ready to purchase a car during the regular fall model year-end sales event, keep a notebook, file or journal and jot down the prices and incentives you see. Later, when you are ready to purchase a car, negotiate a similar deal. It will be more difficult as many of the incentives come from the automobile manufacturer. If the dealer won't budge, find another dealer. Research alternatives.

Holidays: Watch for sales events during Labor Day, during the month of October, Black Friday, and New Year's Day. Monday appears the best day of the week to purchase a car. Fewer customers gives you more time at the dealership to negotiate the best deal and your bank is open for business. If you miss all the Fall sales events, more sales begin on Memorial Day. Remember, a car or truck is a hunk of steel, glass, and rubber. DO NOT fall in love with a vehicle or believe the perfect one you found on the lot is the "Last One." The United States alone consumes over 17 million vehicles per year. Every year. That's a lot of cars and trucks.

Advantages of Buying a new Car: New Car Warranty, No accident or maintenance issues by negligent previous owner, Lower Maintenance Costs, New Car Smell, Latest Safety Tech, Latest entertainment Tech, a lower interest rate.

Disadvantages of Buying a New Car: Immediate depreciation, Limited to purchasing from a greedy dealership, risk paying too much, higher taxes and insurance, risk getting ripped off by the finance manager, and if you do not make a good deal, you may end up upside down financially in your new car. If you buy a hybrid or Electric Vehicle new it will almost always be financially "upside down."

Tires and Battery

I will keep it simple. Go to a Wholesale Club like Sam's, Costco or BJ's. No scams. Just tires. Best prices and they honor their road hazard warranty. Keep in mind for budgeting purposes that tires cost about $600 for a set of four and a good auto battery costs $150.

https://www.edmunds.com/auto-warranty/understanding-tire-warranties.html

Predators Among Us

Be careful where you park. In many cities across America, park a car unknowingly in a "no parking" zone and you will find your car towed and impounded. If this happens to you, retrieve the car immediately from impound As Soon As Possible, before 24 hours expire. If not, unscrupulous tow companies may charge you hundreds of dollars a day for storage. If you cannot pay, too bad. They will auction your car and promise to pay you the balance between what they sold at auction and your storage fees. Another example of Bad Capitalism. Beware!

Chapter 16

Make Extra Money with Side Hustles

"The reason many people do not recognize opportunity is because it usually goes around wearing overalls looking like hard work."

Thomas Edison

Avoid Money Mishaps by Choosing the Right Gig for you! You want to get a side hustle or create multiple income streams. That is a great idea. You may get a second job to just pay off debt. In my community there are several call centers that offer fair pay to work part time in the evening and weekends. If you are looking for an independent contractor relationship, there are many opportunities recently created by the new Gig Economy. Any economy that hires workers for short term "gigs." But, be careful, some independent side hustles can cost you more money than you make. (Think Mary Kay). You will make less per hour than you think after expenses. (Think Uber). Remember, cash flow is not the same as income.

In the past, I delivered pizzas, worked at the very first Blockbuster Video, and I worked as a teacher at Florida Virtual School.

My side hustles include tutoring students in math, photography gigs, and a Financial Coaching Business I just started. I'm an eBay Power Seller. And yes, I work full time. I believe in generating multiple income streams. You should, too.

Treat your Side Hustle like a business. "Aww c'mon Ken, you take the fun out of everything." Are you thinking about working a side hustle? Then make sure it makes money. You will need a bookkeeper. Will it be you? Just like your personal financial life, document your income and expenses. As an independent contractor you handle your bookkeeping, self-employment tax payments, tracking your expenses, proper cell-phone and cell phone plan and making sure you insure yourself for the work you are doing. It's not a game. The world is full of hungry attorneys that don't care whether you are just trying to make a few extra bucks to help pay for baby formula. If you cause an accident while you are delivering a pizza, the accident victims could sue you, and your insurance company may refuse to pay any claims since you are using your personal car for commercial use.

Stay Off the Road!

Look for a side gig in the Gig Economy. Start your own service-based business to provide a service online. This gives you the flexibility to work your own hours, pick your own clients in an in-demand business. You are looking for something that has a low cost of entry, in demand, and high profit. Look for a service you can supply to business owners. Business owners are usually more consistent paying their bills than dealing with the public.

1) Bookkeeper;

2) Virtual Assistant;

3) Proofreader;

4) Transcription;

5) Online Tutor;

6) Copywriter;

7) Voice Overs;

8) Photo Restoration;

9) Buy estate items at a cheap price and resell on eBay at retail (Lots of hidden expenses; shipping supplies, eBay and PayPal fees);

10) Airbnb   Rent out a legitimate space in your home.

Check out FIVERR for Gig work ideas   https://www.fiverr.com/

Pizza Delivery

Many years ago, when my son was first born, I drove for Domino's Pizza until I was T-boned by a convicted drug felon, who was off his ankle bracelet. I was broke (trapped class); hence the part-time job, and now my car was a total loss. I was on the hook for replacing the car. Fortunately, I was current with my car note and I could purchase a new car by substituting the capital on the note. (Reassignment of Collateral is Rare, but a useful procedure to replace the totaled car with another car of equal value to the car loan It worked. Unfortunately, the totaled car was well equipped, and the new car was a base model. So now you know my feelings about pizza delivery. Especially after having a piece of my car's side rear-view mirror pulled out of my eyelid. Fortunately, the glass did not pierce my eyeball, right? The point is, the more you are driving in traffic, at night, in foul weather increases your odds of getting into an accident. I delivered in a friendly neighborhood and on a Navy base, so there was little risk of crime. Now, however, robbery and assault are a real risk. Slip and Fall is a real risk. Traffic accidents are a real risk. Many consider pizza delivery driving (including the Bureau of Labor Statistics) to be perilous.

Uber and Lyft

I thought the ride sharing industry was on to something. Taxis are a little less customer focused than they ought to be. I have used Uber twice and I would use them again. Uber is a disruptive technology innovation. It would never exist without smartphones and apps. However, the truth is somewhere in between. You choose your hours, so great flexibility for the driver. It pays fast. However, if it is so great to be a driver, why are the drivers striking? Uber's Mission is to "Ignite Opportunity by Setting the World in Motion". Sounds like a sales pitch for a multi-level marketing program. The truth is that UBER corporation is not making any money and there is talk it will never make money until its cars are self-driving. In the meantime, the company will squeeze the human drivers by paying them as little as they can. According to the Economic Policy Institute, the Uber hourly wage, after self-employment tax, ranges from a low in Miami of $8.25 per/hour to Seattle at $15.45 per/hour. There are no health benefits or 401k plans. Uber has planned with Betterment to open your own IRA. The average is $10.87 per hour. When I went to sign up as a driver there was a "sort of" a signing bonus statement promising $1,000 guaranteed for your first 150 trips. That's

$6.67 per trip! You will make all that money in return for the opportunity to destroy your car. People, you are squeezing cash (accelerated depreciation) out of your car. In return for the cash, you receive a run-down car. Replace tires, batteries, change the oil more frequently. You must consider the fuel expense, maintenance expense, and your insurance liability. Have an up-to-date cell phone and cell phone plan. You have personal automobile insurance on a vehicle that is being used for a commercial purpose. What happens if you get into an accident? If you are on an Uber run, their insurance covers liability, but you are still on the hook for your collision damage and you will have to file a claim on your personal insurance policy for auto accident repairs. Uber has thought this through for their protection, but I don't think all drivers have thought through the financial risk associated with ridesharing. If the accident is your fault, your insurance company could deny your claims and cancel your insurance. You must contact your insurance agent to see if they offer a ride-share insurance rider to offer additional liability coverage and BUY IT! When something bad happens, everyone is getting sued, no matter who is at fault. Just like the pizza delivery driver, your accident risk increases as your traffic exposure increases. Do you see why this may be a bad side gig?

Regardless of the cons, there is some good news. Uber offers discounts on vehicle maintenance through select repair facilities. Uber also offers discounts on your phone plan. I'm not sure what the ride-sharing policy is on drivers wearing crash helmets.

https://www.creditkarma.com/advice/i/costs-of-driving-for-uber-lyft/

Uber Eats

You can be an auto, scooter, or bike delivery driver. If you are already an Uber driver, you can make Uber Eats deliveries from your Uber ride share app. How convenient. See pizza delivery above.

I thought Dasher was a Reindeer?

No, that's silly, a dasher is a DoorDash Delivery person. Another side gig option that is popular. This option puts you on the road, but you are not carrying passengers. Even in the US, I don't think a Caprese salad can sue you if it's injured in your car. Door Dash looks easy to sign up for and allows a flexible schedule for you. You keep 100% of your tips.

Always remember to report your earnings to the IRS at tax time and take out your own self-employment tax from your profits. Keep in mind you will have auto maintenance and gas expenses as well. Good news! These expenses are legally deductible.

Amazon Flex

An amazon delivery service, started in 2015, allows independent contractors to use their own vehicles to deliver Amazon packages. I suspect this could be lucrative during the Holiday Season as it stretches normal deliveries thin. You load their app, and you accept jobs that are available based on their location, price, and time frame. This idea is better, as you are not responsible for anything except a few packages. Checking out their recruiting website and the results were vague. There was no information about insurance, and I would think your auto insurance company would consider this a commercial use in a personal car. Their site advertises pay rates between $18.00 and $25.00 per hour. I know only one person who tried it and found it profitable. Consider, like driving for Uber, you are putting extra miles on your vehicle and increasing your gas and maintenance costs.

It Sounds like a Simple Plan\

Avoid the draw to sit at your computer to complete surveys for money. These schemes are not designed to help you make money but fill your inbox with marketing nonsense to motivate you to buy unnecessary goods and services!

Freelance Work

If you possess a special set of skills like Graphic Design, Digital Marketing, Writing, Video and Animation, or Computer Programming, consider looking into Fiverr and Upwork, on the internet, to connect with people who need your services. TaskRabbit and Flex Jobs are popular sites. There are lots of options here if you have access to a computer and high-speed internet.

Online Tutoring

If you have teaching experience, this can be a fun and lucrative activity.

Try VIP Kid. https://www.vipkid.com/teach Other popular companies include Kaplan, Tutor.com, and Tutor ME. https://tutorme.com

Child Care or Elder Care

There is a lot of need here. Check with your community to see what prerequisites you need to enter this service business.

Pet or House-Sitting

Pet and House Sitting have a low cost of entry and good demand in most areas of the country. Check with your local community for business license requirements.

Online Bookkeeping

Are you good with numbers? Have a computer and online access? You could become a "virtual" bookkeeper. QuickBooks claims you can earn about $70.00 per hour. There are startup costs, but they are minimal. The high range is about $1,300 to cover essentials like Incorporation or LLC, website, business cards, supplies, and business liability insurance. Remember, bookkeeping and owning your own business are not for everyone. The ballpark numbers, regarding business: 39 percent are profitable, 30 percent break even, and 30 percent lose money. This job is for the reliable, trustworthy, self-managed, and you have to be great with numbers. Are you a good fi t?

Financial Coach

This is an excellent choice for someone with great number and listening skills. A rare combination. It is a doable part time job. Financial coaching is very rewarding as you are assisting others with their financial issues. Disclaimer: Make sure your house is in order, before you give advice to others. See https://www.afcpe.org/

Multi-Level Marketing

This is easy. Less than 1% of MLM participants make a profit in these businesses. Please run away! Runaway fast! I've had friends take part in several MLM organizations. No one is driving Cadillacs or living on an estate outside of Atlanta. Except the founder.

Old School Gigs

- House Cleaning www.housekeeper.com;

- Yard Care https://www.taskrabbit.com;

- General Handyperson;

- Moving Furniture;

- Furniture Assembly;

- Car Detailing.

Other Ways to Raise Cash

Sell that drawer full of unused gift cards.

- https://www.finder.com/cardpool-gift-card-exchange;

- Sell Collectibles;

- Have a garage sale;

- Take your saleable stuff to the flea market;

- List and Sell your Stuff on eBay;

- Sell clothes and sports equipment at consignment shops.

Wrap Up

There are lots of creative and legal ways to raise some cash and supplement your income if you use a little imagination. If you decide on your own business, do the hard work of planning and preparation so you provide an authentic service to your customer. Understand the numbers. Know your expenses so you can deduct them from your business in-come and know that you are really making money. Doing a side gig to lose money is suboptimal. If you are not the "own your own business" type, then consider finding a part-time job.

Chapter 17

Saving and Investing

"If you would be wealthy, think of saving as well as getting."

Benjamin Franklin

Savings is probably the most important aspect of achieving money balance and wealth. I made the mistake of not saving early because I was too busy treading water financially. Instead of saving, I was buying unnecessary stuff. Don't make the same mistake.

Savings has to be painless, sustainable, and ongoing. Savings should be a regular, planned activity.

Regardless of your income, save money. Why? First, to create an emergency fund to face life's unexpected expenses down the road. Do you want to buy a house, start a business, or pay for your children's or grandchildren's college education in the future? You will want to save money to accomplish your goals. Speaking of which, what are your goals for savings. Concrete goals for savings will help you stay on track. Another great reason to save is so we can retire without having to work.

This chapter assumes you have paid off your unsecured debt. If not, go back and read Chapter 1 and Chapter 2. These chapters are at the beginning of the book for a reason. Pay off unsecured debt (credit cards, personal loans, store accounts) before starting a savings strategy.

This is the WalletWise **six**-step plan to savings and investing!

1. Save for an emergency fund by first opening an FDIC or FCUA insured account.

Reduce Expenses to Increase Savings

Do not progress to step two until completion of step one. Go to Chapter 12, Money Management, to create a realistic family budget on paper. The budget will show you where to cut expenses. Open an online and mobile MINT account to track expenses in real time. Make it possible to save by implementing the following:

1. Negotiate Lower Prices on Necessities, like Utilities. (AskTrim);

2. Cancel Expensive Cable Subscriptions;

3. Cancel Underutilized Online Subscriptions;

4. Sell Expensive assets and replace (Can you sell your financed car and replace it with a reliable cash car?);

5. Trim Gift Expenses.

6. Take Inexpensive Vacations

7. Increase Income

A fully funded emergency account is equal to 3-6 months of your annual salary. Let's say $20,000. Safe and sound in a FDIC insured account. Save your money in a FDIC money market account and not in an uninsured money market fund!

2. Invest in your company's 401k until you qualify for your company's full match. Every 401k plan is unique. Check with Human Resources to get company match information. You will need to find the "sweet spot." The amount that triggers the maximum employer benefit. Don't contribute much more. Go to Step 3 if you have deposited enough in your 401k to get your max benefit. If you do not have access to a 401k or 403b go to Step 3.

3. Open a ROTH IRA and invest until you max out at $6,000; $7,000 if you are age 50 or older.

4. Open a Computershare account to accumulate quality dividend paying stocks.

5. Save for College in your state approved 529 Plan.

6. Learn how to Earn.

Estimated Time Frame: This is not a place for immediate gratification!

"The single greatest edge an investor can have is a long-term orientation. Behold the turtle. He makes progress only when he sticks his neck out. Someone's sitting in the shade today because someone planted a tree a long time ago."

James Bryant Conant

WalletWise Savings Timeline

Saving = 0-5 Years	Emergency Fund, Money Market Accounts, Cash
Investing = 10-60 years	401k, IRA's, Mutual Funds, Index Funds, ETFs

"You can never start saving too early, but it's never too late to start."

Ken Remsen

Time Value of Money

It is true the earlier you start saving the better. Why? Because the longer you save, the more time the money earns interest. Then it earns interest on the interest. According to Clark Howard, if a fifteen year-old saves $2,000 per year each year for seven years (leaving it untouched), then it will accumulate to $1,020,430 by age sixty-five! Clark did not mention that these returns depend upon earning 10% interest per year. That's very possible. The point is start saving early!

Here are two cool calculators I found online. Just move the sliders and it calculates the cost of delaying saving.

https://www.fireflycu.org/Calculators/Savings-Calculators/Delaying-Savings-Calculator

https://www.icmarc.org/prebuilt/static/costofdelay/index.html

Personal Note: Hey! Did you start saving at fifteen? Most people don't. I did not. I was too busy paying bills, figuring out how to survive, starting a business, working for a family-owned business with no benefits and did not get serious until I was forty-three . I was not a wonderful role model. The good news is if you stay married to your first spouse or become the victim of a nasty addiction, your survival/ lifestyle expenses go down as you get older, and your children leave the nest. Then you have more discretionary money to save and invest.

Now let's unpack The WalletWise Savings Plan in Detail

Step One Emergency Fund:

Begin SAVING with an Emergency Fund

Okay, after you have created your budget, calculated your net worth, adjusted your expenses so you spend less than you make, paid off expensive credit card debt, then you can plan to **save money**. The first item to create is your **emergency** fund. This is equal to six months' salary.

If, by any chance you got this out of order and you have signed up for an online investment plan or club, or you are investing in your company's 401k or agency's 403b, before paying off all of your credit card debt and high interest debt... STOP IT! I have worked with people who were investing with https://www.acorns.com/ or www.stash.com when they had excessive credit card debt and were insolvent. Pay off credit card and any other unsecured debt first before starting step 1.

You cannot ignore paying off high interest credit accounts. I'm not talking about mortgage payments or even car payments. I am referring to credit card debt and personal loan debt. You are paying 12, 15, 18 percent, and, higher interest to borrow unsecured debt. It is doubtful you will earn that rate of return on your investments over the long haul. Pay off the debt first to reduce the amount of money you are spending on paying interest so you can start saving to earn interest coming to you.

In my less successful years, (and there were many of them! I never understood the concept of an emergency fund. I had some money saved and used that money for emergencies. I never set aside money in an emergency fund. The purpose of an emergency fund escaped me. Make sure you know your emergency fund savings. Treat the emergency fund differently from other savings. The emergency fund is very important because it allows you to take care of emergencies without relying on predatory and expensive payday loans, car title loans, pawn shops, and checking account overdrafts to take care of your unexpected expenses. Most experts agree you should save six months of your household income. If you make $50,000 per year, saving $25,000 is a lot to ask. Start by saving 10% of your income through automation in a traditional bank (FDIC) or credit union (NCUSIF) savings account. The Federal Government insures these accounts. Make sure your payment is automatic. It's called Pay Yourself First! That would be about $350 per month after taxes. If you cannot save this much, I suggest seeing Chapter 12 Money Management to begin the road of spending less than you make. Reduce your unnecessary expenses so you can channel money into savings. It is essential.

Do not invest your emergency fund in the stock market. The emergency fund is not an investment opportunity. The emergency fund should be in a low-risk savings account. Online Bank accounts offer a good safe return and fast access to your funds in case of an emergency. Bank CD's or Certificate of Deposits are okay, but they are more difficult to access in an emergency! This may defeat the purpose of getting money quickly in an emergency.

For Online savings I recommend Ally Bank, Marcus by Goldman Sachs, and Chime to name a few. I've had personal experience saving with Discover Bank. I managed multiple CDs and a money market account for a client. They have excellent customer service and pay competitive rates for an online account.

Consider a Money Market account as this gives you quick access to the funds in an emergency and provides a better than average interest rate.

Step Two 401k:

Now it's time to start and/or restart investing in your **company 401k**.

Fun Fact

Did you know that 401k is the actual tax code number relating to this retirement plan?

Find out the minimum to invest to max out your company match. I love 401k's, but many of them have high fees and limited investment options. I recommend investing the minimum amount to qualify for your full company match. After you are have invested enough to get the largest corporate or company match, we can move on to the next step, step 3. Do not invest your 401k in company stock. It's too risky. If you are under thirty, choose an aggressive growth stock index fund like Vanguard Total Stock Market Index Fund (VTSMX) or Fidelity® 500 Index Fund (FXAIX). (VTSMX) and (FXAIX) is the mutual fund ticker or acronym for the fund or the name of a corporation. For example, Coca Cola is (KO) (for knockout) Facebook is (FB) Apple is (AAPL)) If you wish to be rich someday, you will want to know what these tickers represent. Mutual funds represent a basket of companies to help you diversify. They represent your access to own the world's most profitable corporations. Along with other managers, the CEO of that company now works for you, no matter how small the investment. Companies that pay dividends return those profits to the shareholders in the form of dividends.

Dividends create the passive income for wealthy Americans to live without selling their labor at a regular job. (Nothing wrong with that!. Make sure you select to **reinvest** the dividends. Reinvest the dividends and capital gains automatically to increase your investment return. You should reinvest those gains back into the mutual fund to buy more shares that... wait for it... earn more dividends for you. This is the art of compounding. The act of borrowing money uses compound interest against you. Likewise, investing money puts **compound interest** in your favor!

Locate an aggressive or defensive fund, based on your investing style, from the collection of funds that your 401k allows you to purchase.

It is unnecessary for you to be the sage of Wall Street.

Step Three IRA's:

After you set up your emergency fund, and max out your 401k, it is time to set up your next investment vehicle.

Open a ROTH IRA with Vanguard. In 2021, you can contribute $6,000 per year ($7,000 if you are over 50 into a Roth IRA according to the IRS. It's tempting to open a traditional IRA to offset this year's tax liability but be aware. The **tax savings** you get today may be less than the **tax bill** you get tomorrow. You cannot take the money from an IRA until you are 59½ years old. This is a restriction placed on this account for income tax advantages.

Look at the headlines. The pandemic gave our government permission to speed up spending to prop up the economy at the price of going into deeper debt. We should send a copy of this book to Congress! As of today, July 2021, the national debt is over 28 Trillion Dollars. That's $84,893 per citizen and $223,000 per taxpayer. as of July 2022 the national debt is 30.5 Trillion Dollars. How's that going to get paid? Try higher taxes. I prefer the Roth Ira. Tax me now. Then when I need to take my required minimum distribution (RMD) in retirement, my withdraw is tax free. This strategy assumes that your tax rates in the future are going up.

https://www.usdebtclock.org/

https://www.rothira.com/

https://www.irs.gov/retirement-plans/traditional-and-roth-iras

I prefer Vanguard. Why Vanguard? I like John Bogle. Followers of John Bogle's savings philosophy are called Bogle heads! He founded Vanguard Funds in 1974 based upon the notion that regular folks like you and me could be and should be investing. One quote stated in the below video is Mr. Bogle wanted "regular" folks to have a "fair shake" for investing.

Please take time to watch the video. It will be good for your financial soul.

https://about.vanguard.com/who-we-are/a-remarkable-history/founder-Jack-Bogle-tribute/

https://about.vanguard.com/who-we-are/a-remarkable-history/

Another reason I prefer Vanguard is their low fees. Mutual funds charge fees for management, legal, and accounting expenses. Lower management fees leave more money in your account to make money. They take less capital from you.

If you have trouble imagining a 20% loss in the stock market, you shouldn't be in stocks. --John Bogle

Remember, invest for the long haul.

Yes, there are other reputable mutual fund companies like Fidelity and T. Rowe Price.

Dollar Cost Averaging

Simply pay a constant amount monthly to smooth out the ups and downs of a particular stock price. Do this consistently to achieve a lower price per share. It balances out the difficulties in the market. So, timing the market is unnecessary.

Go to Step Four after you have set up your Emergency Fund, funded your 401K enough to qualify for your company match, and maxed out your IRA's.

Step Four: A basket of Five Conservative Stocks:

What is the definition of "qualified" and "nonqualified" funds? As much as I believe 401k, pension funds, and IRAs are wonderful because they delay taxation on deferred compensation, they come with rules from the government. Pensions, 401k, and IRAs come with rules and provisos (behavior control) in exchange for tax relief. That's not a bad thing. Call it stealth "discipline." These accounts will fund your retirement. There are steep penalties for making early withdrawals. Don't withdraw $35,000 out of your Individual RETIREMENT Account to buy a new Chevrolet Camaro Z28. If you do, you receive hefty tax penalties. IRAs and 401k have an age 59 ½ withdrawal limitation. The IRS considers these accounts "qualified."

After teaching the personal finance part of a low-level math class in high school, I learned about the entity called Computershare. It is a company that manages a collection of a corporation's Direct Stock Purchase Plans (DSPP). https://www.computershare.com/us

We call this investment "nonqualified" meaning unbridled, unrestricted, and to the undisciplined, unmanageable. Withdraw and spend money you invest on the new Camaro with no penalties. And you will then return to that infamous club, the wealth underachievers. Congratulations. Now reread this book.

I discovered Computershare in 2007. I went online, and I realized I could buy individual stocks from an entity called a transfer agent. This is a company that places individual stocks with individual owners and manages the dividend distribution without the use and expense of a stockbroker. SWEET! They design this savings plan for the small investor. You can invest as little as $25.00 per month without a stockbroker commission. There is a fee, but the fee is small, and you pay at set up and through automatic deductions. Research the company you wish to invest inside the Computershare website. Corporations charge high fees for their DRIP/DSPP plan. For example, Ford ticker (F charges a $10.00 set up fee plus 3 cents per share, purchase fee is $5.00 plus 3 cents per share, automatic deposit is $1.00 plus 3 cents per share. Computershare has a research tool directing you to companies that do not charge purchase fees. Aqua (WTR and Abbot (ABT are two companies in the plan I own. In addition, your money invested here is after tax. The new earnings (dividends) are taxed at the lower than income "capital gains" tax. This is non-qualified money unencumbered by the rules of 401k's, and IRAs. You can make withdrawals or deposits as many times as you wish. You have total freedom. I started investing when the stock market was tanking after the financial crises. I kept my investments conservative because I realized how close we came to real national financial collapse. We were close folks. Fortunately, that did not happen, and I could put together a nice portfolio of quality stocks for pennies on the dollar. A once in a lifetime opportunity. I only keep track of a few stocks. You should only concentrate on five. I started with MSFT, NEE, ABT, VZ, and WTR. These stocks are (DRIP) stocks or members of a Dividend Reinvestment Plan. Computershare reinvests the stock cash dividend into more shares of the company. They have worked well in the long term. Remember, this works for me. Decide what works for you. In these accounts I have conservative dividend-paying stocks.

https://www.sec.gov/fast-answers/answersdriphtm.html

Use part of your "investment" time to research individual stocks. Fewer stocks is better. Research a stock with a familiar company. A company whose product you use. Most people use products from Exxon, Walmart, Apple, Samsung, Microsoft, McDonald's, IBM, Verizon or ATT. Computershare handles these companies. Computershare is not the only transfer agent. There are other transfer agents. To keep life uncomplicated, stick with one and the best, Computershare.

> The only place where success comes before work is in the dictionary.—Vidal Sassoon

For Young Computer Savvy Investors

Many online stock brokers like Robinhood and Stash do not charge commissions thereby making it easier to accumulate stocks and purchase fractional shares of expensive shares.

How to Study a Specific Stock: First, I use a site called Investopedia.com to answer any type of general investment question. Then I check out the website of my target investment company. Let's check out Abbott laboratories, https://www.abbott.com. I check out the company's products. Abbott has unique nutrition products for consumers. Inside healthcare, Abbott provides cardiovascular, diabetes diagnostics, nutrition, and a dozen major medicines. I then check the investors tab. Abbott (ABT)) makes available to us the company annual report (important), SEC filings (important, but unnecessary now), and links to receive printed material in the mail that pertains to the company and alerts by email. I sign up for alerts, so I get corporate news as soon as possible (ASAP). You can download the annual report to your computer. The last part of the annual report is the important part. The income and balance statements are found here. Learn how to read these statements.

Oh wait! Shazam! You know how! Remember; you have done this for yourself, right? You have created an income (budget) and balance statement for yourself. Same idea, just bigger numbers. So, big numbers scare you? Look in Chapter 12, Money Management. After you have completed your personal budget (income) and balance sheet, then come back here and apply what you have learned to see if your company is financially healthy. Ask important questions about the company. Is the company making money? Can the company pay its debt? Is the company the top company in its "sector?" Google the company and see what stories pop up. Have they arrested the CEO for fraud? Has your company just secured the cure for cancer? Make sure you use reliable resources. Late-night comedians do not make reliable financial sources. That's company number one, four more to go. Now you see why I only suggest **five** companies. It's actual work.

https://www.nasdaq.com/investing/dozen/	Suggestions on what to research.
https://www.kiplinger.com/	Research Resource
https://finance.yahoo.com/	

Formal education will make you a living; self-education will make you a fortune.—Jim Rohn

Other investment tools.

What's an ETF or Exchange Traded Fund?

An ETF is another investing tool similar to a mutual fund. It holds a basket of stocks like a mutual fund. Unlike a mutual fund, we can trade an ETF like a stock. It is an alternative investment tool to a mutual fund. Mutual funds only report their value once a day. Stock values rise and fall while the markets are open based upon their market supply and demand. ETFs are funds that work the same as individual stocks. You can buy one and sell on the same day (not wise ETFs are in between mutual funds and individual stocks. They are safer than individual stocks because they are a diversified collection of stocks that lessen your individual stock risk. Fees may be less expensive than mutual funds. They are more liquid, meaning you can trade them as individual stocks. ETFs may offer a lower tax liability. They have a lower investment minimum. The news is that you cannot make automatic investments as you can with a mutual fund. Mutual funds allow you to make fixed automatic investments. Workplace retirement plans invest in mutual funds.

ROBOTS in charge

The next big thing is "Robo" (short for robot) investing. It means you can invest money online into vehicles that act as your financial advisor using artificial intelligence. Fees are low and expectations are high. I use Stash to see how it works.

Here are the popular ones.

https://robinhood.com/us/en/

https://www.stashinvest.com/

https://www.acorns.com/

https://www.ally.com/invest/managed-portfolios/

https://www.personalcapital.com/

https://www.blooom.com/

https://www.sofi.com/invest/

https://www.ellevest.com   (targeted for Women)

https://intelligent.schwab.com

https://stash.com

Schwab states that they have a $5,000 minimum and their robot-advisor builds and rebalances your diversified portfolio. You answer a short questionnaire to establish your investment tolerance to risk and to decide your goals. The ROBO advisor creates your portfolio! No calculating, no research (Boo) and no hard work. Not a bad idea, but you won't learn finance. And that may be okay.

Personal Note: I recently started using a Core Portfolio that automatically rebalances and reallocates the invested funds. It currently is earning 17%. Anyway, we'll see how long this good run lasts?

Step Five:
College Savings 529 Plans, Coverdell

Saving for college is not a bad idea. Saving for retirement is more important. The original program was the Coverdell Education Savings Account (ESA). The Tax Cuts and Jobs Act of 2017 makes Coverdell redundant. State sponsored 529 plans are now the "go to" tax benefit/col-lege savings plan. In fact, 529 plans allow you to save for private K-12 tuition (up to $10,000 besides college expenses. A 529 plan, named after Section 529 of the Internal Revenue Code, is a tax-advantaged plan of saving for your child's future college expenses. Individual states sponsor 529 Savings Plans. In Florida, for example, you open this "qualified" account and begin selecting investments that fit your investment style. Use your child's future enrollment date to choose a target date style fund. The investment grows tax free, similar to a traditional IRA. You should set it up with automatic deduction. You can ask your family and friends to contribute through an **eGift portal**. The 529 plan account saves for tuition, fees, books and supplies. It is for room and board when you enroll your student at least half time in a program. They can use the funds for computers, peripherals, software, and internet costs. The Florida plan allows you to attend any qualified public or private educa-tional institution nationwide.

https://www.myfloridaprepaid.com/
https://www.nysaves.org/
https://thecollegeinvestor.com/529-plan-guide/california/
https://www.savingforcollege.com/529-plans/illinois

US Savings Bond or I Bond

Another great tool for saving is the online I Bond. You can buy an "I bond" for as little as $25.00 per month. This savings tool introduces children to savings. There are directions to open a "Minor Linked Account." This is a great way to give an always appreciated gift to children from members of the family. The interest earned is very low but picks up during times of inflation. The I bond is a very slow, steady and very safe savings vehicle.

Treasury Direct is the place you come to later (After you are wealthy or have accumulated more than $500,000) to buy US Treasuries.

https://www.treasurydirect.gov/

Step Six:
Investment Education Resources

If you are interested in learning more about the world of personal finance and investing, please consider the following resources.

An amazing resource for investment education is the Next Generation Personal Finance Program. As a math teacher, I have taught several math courses with a financial component, and this is an excellent resource. Check it out at https://www.ngpf.org/. It's full of info.

My credit union, Community First Credit Union, has an amazing financial education program called moveUP

https://www.communityfirstfl.org/move-up

https://www.cashcourse.org/	(Great Financial Management Starter Course)
https://www.aaii.com/	(Investing Education Resource)
https://www.investoreducation.org/	(Awesome for Investor Education)
www.investopedia.com	(Investing Education)
www.finra.org	(Financial Regulatory Authority)
www.nasdaq.com	(Exchange and Research Resource)
https://www.sipc.org/	(Investor Protection Resource)

Is there a **Step Seven?** Yes. After you accumulate about $300,000 in assets, hire a professional money manager. Not a topic of this book. If you achieved this goal, Congrats!

> *"Compound Interest is the eighth wonder of the world. He who understands it, earns it... he who doesn't... pays it."*
>
> *Albert Einstein*

In Conclusion, INVEST in Yourself!

Please take time to start adulting! The wealthiest people in America take time out of their busy schedule to educate themselves, and manage and watch their savings, investments, and finances. This means you may have to adjust your video game and TV watching schedule. If you spend six hours a day at the local bar complaining about your poor lot in life, then you may find that adjusting your schedule and changing that habit may reap financial rewards. You reap what you sow. Farmers know this. It's called the "Law of the Harvest." For a crop to be successful you will need good seed, fertile soil, and enough moisture. If you sow (save) generously, you will reap (reward) generously. Conversely, sow sparingly, you reap sparingly.

Ken's Favorite Mutual Funds

- VDIGX Vanguard Dividend Growth Fund

  ○ Minimum Investment $3,000 www.vanguard.com

- VGHCX Vanguard Health Care Sector Fund (Held up well in Pandemic)

  ○ Minimum Investment $3,000

- VTIAX Vanguard Total International Stock Index Fund Admiral Shares

  ○ Minimum Investment $3,000

- VEIPX Vanguard Equity Income Fund Investors Shares

  ○ Minimum Investment $3,000

- PRSCX T. Rowe Price Science and Technology Fund. (Did Well in Pandemic)

  ○ Minimum Investment $2,500

- SWSSX Schwab Small-Cap Index Fund schwab.com

  ○ Minimum investment: $100

Warren Buffett's Favorite 5 Vanguard Mutual Funds

https://finance.yahoo.com/news/buffett-advice-5-vanguard-funds-194833003.html

Required Legalese!

Folks! I, Ken Remsen am **not** offering investment advice in this book.

INVESTMENT RISKS:

Investments, including real estate, are speculative and involve a large risk of loss. We encourage our readers to invest carefully. We encourage investors to get personal advice from your professional investment advisor and to make independent investigations before acting on information published here. Much of our information derives from information published by companies or submitted to governmental agencies on which we believe are reliable but are without our independent verification. We cannot assure you that the information is correct or complete. We do not warrant or guarantee the success of any action you take in reliance on our statements or recommendations.

Past performance is not indicative of future results. Investments carry risk and investment decisions of an individual remain the responsibility of that individual. There is no guarantee that systems, indicators, or signals result in profits or that they will not result in losses. Investors should understand risks associated with any investing they do.

Hypothetical or simulated performance is not indicative of future results. Unless noted otherwise, return examples provided in our websites and publications are based on hypothetical or simulated investing. We make no representations or warranties that any investor will, or is likely to, achieve profits like those shown, because hypothetical or simulated performance is not indicative of future results.

Don't enter any investment without understanding the worst-case scenarios of that investment. You may lose your entire investment.

Resources

<u>Internet</u>

<u>https://www.aaii.com/</u>   (Total Financial Education Resource)

<u>https://corporate.americancentury.com/en.html</u>   (Great Mutual Funds)

<u>https://www.bankrate.com/banking/cds/cd-ladder-guide/</u>   (CD Laddering)

<u>https://www.bankrate.com/cd.aspx</u>   (CD rates)

<u>https://www.collegesavings.org/</u>   (College 529 Plan 411)

<u>https://www.computershare.com/us</u>   (Transfer Agent to Purchase Stocks Direct)

<u>https://www.fidelity.com/</u>   (Great Mutual Funds)

<u>https://www.fdic.gov/</u>   (Check that Online Bank is Legit)

<u>https://www.morningstar.com/</u>   (Resource to Research Mutual Funds and Stocks)

<u>https://www.rothira.com/</u>   (Research the Amazing Roth IRA)

<u>https://www.troweprice.com/corporate/en/home.html</u>   (Great Mutual Funds)

<u>https://www.usaa.com/inet/wc/investments-usaa-mutual-funds?akredirect=true</u>   (Great Mutual Funds for Veterans)

<u>https://www.usdebtclock.org/</u>   (National Debt Statistics)

<u>https://investor.vanguard.com/home/</u>   (Great Mutual Funds)

<u>https://about.vanguard.com/who-we-are/a-remarkable-history/founder-Jack-Bogle-tribute/</u>

<u>https://about.vanguard.com/who-we-are/a-remarkable-history/</u>   (Vanguard History)

<u>https://finance.yahoo.com/</u>   (Yahoo Finance)

Chapter 18

Retirement Planning

"Begin with the End in Mind,"

Dr. Stephen Covey

Dr. Covey hits the nail on the head. You are never too young to think about retirement. This chapter is helpful to those just entering retirement, but if you are young and just starting out in life, I suggest you read this chapter, too.

According to the GAO or Government Accounting Office, half of households aged 65 and older relied solely on social security income. 48 percent of Americans 55 and older have no retirement savings.

Yes, it is possible to survive on Social Security. But you will only survive. We set up our economy for you to work for 40 years, and while working, save a portion of your salary to create a "Nest Egg". The Nest Egg is the money that earns or makes enough money for you to retire. Your goal is to create what the experts call passive income. Passive income creates income generated by your savings and investments.

Financial gurus of many stripes complicate the world of retirement financial planning. I say those reports and TV ads are making retirement planning more complicated than necessary. Please plug this and that number into our complicated calculator. You may be interested to know that many on-line calculators may offer you a financial product to buy. I'm sure it is a coincidence.

Congratulations! You're right on track!

You're doing well! We estimate your savings will be enough to give you $13,066.54 per month in retirement.

Estimated Monthly Income
$13,066.54

Needed Monthly Income
$12,762.58

Monthly Surplus
$303.96

Tell me more about how my estimate was calculated.

$13,066.54 — Estimated Monthly Income
$303.96 / $12,762.58 — Needed Monthly Income

Our calculations account for a 3% annual inflation rate, 6% annual rate of return on investments, and are shown in present day dollar values. Social Security payments are not included.

Send Me My Results   Edit Selections

It's simple, if you are not an heiress, if you don't save money for retirement, or do not take part in your company's 401k, 403b plan (if you are a government employee) then in your old age you may eat peanut butter crackers for breakfast, lunch and dinner. This book's theme is to help you achieve financial success by spending less than your income. This will increase your ability to save. First, create an emergency fund, second, take part in your employers' 401k or 403b plan. Next, take extra income and windfalls and fund your IRA. See Chapter 17 Saving and Investment to get the details.

Let's look at a simpler way to calculate your retirement money finances. Time to buy a calculator that does exponents. I know, scary!

Let's do an example. You make $40,000. Multiply by 80%. Retirement life, all else equal, should be less expensive; about 20% less expensive. You will eat out less, have less dry cleaning, and lower transportation costs. So now we are at $32,000. Multiply this amount by inflation. We will err high and use 3% per year. Next, calculate your remaining years until retirement. Let's say you're 40. You've got another thirty years to work and save. Here's the hard part. It's time for exponents. 1.03^ (number of years until you retire). Here, 30 years. 1.03^30=2.4272. $32,000 income adjusted for inflation is $32,000 times 2.4272. That equals $77,672.40. That's your future $32,000 income adjusted for inflation. From the $77,672 subtract $22,800 because of social security. That leaves $54,872. You'll need enough savings from your 401k and IRA and non-qualified investments to create $54,872 of income. Take $54,872 and multiply by 20 **(20 and 5% rule, based 5% withdrawl rate divided into 100. 100/20=5)** to get the total amount you will need to earn this income. $1,097,440. Assuming you earn nothing on your money, you can withdraw your funds at a rate of 5% per year for the next 20 years and die penniless at 90. Sweet!

This is why it is important to budget! You will need to budget your income and expenses for your entire life.

I mention this now and later because it is so important for you!

Create Your Online Social Security Account Now! https://www.ssa.gov/

Does it work? Yes, it does. Take the $1,097,440 and multiply that by a low 3% return. Most high-quality divided stocks earn 3% dividends and less risky treasuries earn about 3%. So, $1,097,440 times .03 or 3% = $32,923.2. Add your Social Security of $22,800 for $55,723 (close to $54,872 We adjusted the calculation for inflation on retirement income. Then you pass away in your sleep and leave a cool million to your heirs!

Retirement Math Calculations				
		Inflation Multiplier		
40,000	Annual Income	1.03^30=2.4272	32,000	Net Income
0.8	Retirement Multiplier		2.472	Inflation Multiplier
32,000	Net Income		77,672	Future Income after Inflation
77,672 - 22,800 = 54,872	Income Minus Social Security		54,872	Net Net Income
			20	20 and 5% rule Multiplier
			1,097,440	Future Nest Nest Egg Amount

I told you it was easy.

Here is a list of reliable free retirement calculators.

https://www.myretirementpaycheck.org/

https://www.marketwatch.com/calculator/retirement/retirement-planning-calculator?showsmscrim=true and

https://retirementplans.vanguard.com/VGApp/pe/pubeducation/calculators/RetirementIncomeCalc.jsf

https://www.personalcapital.com/financial-software/retirement-planner

Here is the Social Security Benefits Calculator Link https://www.ssa.gov/OACT/quickcalc/

How long will you live? The folks at Lincoln Financial Group do. https://www.lfg.com/public/lifeexpectancycalculator/landing

Good news! You may not need to save a million dollars. If you have a pension (rare and getting more so) subtract that amount from the $77,672 above besides subtracting social security. Most companies have a 401k plan instead of a pension plan. If you took part, when you retire, convert the 401k to an IRA and allow it to create an income stream. At 70 ½, you will take RMD's or required minimum distributions. We subtract this income stream from the above $77,672.

In addition, you can use the multiply by 25 and 4% withdrawal rule or the more conservative multiply 33 and 3% withdrawal rule. These figures are Rules of Thumb! Notice these rule-of-thumb numbers when multiplied equal 1.0!

Even Simpler! Every $100,000 you save, invest, and then return 3%, results in $250 per month of income. That's a great RULE of Thumb! So yes, that means $1 million can create an income of about $2,500 per month.

Long Term Care Insurance: This insurance helps pay your nursing home bill. The alternative is that your adult children may have to take care of you. The other alternative is that they will admit you into a nursing home and you will pay the bill. The average, assisted living cost is $48,000 per year. The average nursing home cost is $95,000. How much will it cost when you will need long-term care?

The nursing home pays your bill from your remaining assets. After they deplete your assets (there are provisions) you will be a ward of the state, with your fees paid by Medicaid. Sobering thought. I know families who take care of their elderly parents until they pass. This has been normal for humans for the past 5,000 years. Long-term care insurance is expensive. You should shop for it in your early fifties. Find an affordable policy. You may not afford a policy that pays 100% of your expenses and provides perfect inflation protection. Buy a policy you can afford. Something is better than nothing.

Look for your 401k:

Corporations provide (and continue to offer) monetary incentives and matches to encourage you to invest in their 401K plan. A 401k plan is a tax-deferred savings account designed to save for your golden years. If you work for a company that does not have a 401k plan, you can open a solo 401k plan.

Don't put all of Eggs in One Basket!

A good friend of mine, a retired banker, relayed a sad retirement tale to me. The tale resulted from putting your eggs in one basket. After leaving a successful stint at a New York bank, he moved his family to south Florida in the mid-1980s, working for the very prestigious Southeast Bank based out of Miami. After joining Southeast Bank, they recommended he rollover his retirement nest egg into Southeast Bank (bank stock. My friend did so only to watch the entire accumulated nest egg become worthless after overzealous federal banking regulators shuttered the bank and sold it to First Union Bank in 1991. Southeast bank stock value went to zero. Only top management could get money from their stock portfolio leaving middle management and below unable to recoup their investment. The final settlement protected the pension.

The lesson here is to be careful about saving too much of your nest egg in one company's stock. You must diversify. Do not invest everything you have in the company you work for. Even if you think that company is completely bullet proof. Sure, invest some of your nest egg, but only a small percentage just in case. Another example of inappropriate behavior involved Enron. The employees invested their pension in Enron stock. In fact, employees had 60% of their 401k assets invested in Enron stock. Enron prohibited employees from selling their Enron shares.

According to FINRA, 57% of employees with 401k assets, invested in Enron stock. The stock fell 98.8% in 2001. It is better to buy a diversified mutual fund.

Planning for retirement can be difficult because life throws curve balls. The good news says we can adjust our stance so we can still hit the ball out of the park. For instance, you may move to a less expensive area to live. Many retirees sold houses in high price markets and moved to another state with a lower cost of living. This can free up much needed cash for under-funded savings. Many states in the US have lower real estate taxes and no income taxes to make your financial life easier.

Part of planning for retirement is to have your house paid off. A Merrill Finance study found 80% of Americans over sixty-five own their homes. Seventy-two percent of Americans own homes with no mortgage. If you are sixty and still don't have enough saved for retirement, there is still hope. Reduce your expenses, live frugally, and save as much as you can for five more years.

The Family Bank

It is common for adult parents to give monetary resources to their adult children. The average amount of financial help is $6,500. That takes a bite out of your retirement savings. You should consider the opportunity cost of your gift. How much could you have earned on the money instead?

According to Merrill, the most common cause for giving money to adult children is to help them pay for housing and buy a car.

In the Millionaire Next Door, Dr. Stanley calls this financial phenom "Economic Outpatient Care." Sometimes our children need help, but it is important to teach our children to be responsible with their money. It is not our job as parents to inflate our children's standard of living. It may wreck your retirement savings plan. It may begin a spiral of expectation that produces an unproductive and dysfunctional adult.

https://www.federalreserve.gov/publications/files/2018-report-econom-ic-well-being-us-households-201905.pdf

I have received the panicked text message of a family member who totaled their car in an accident not their fault. There were no emergency funds to buy a car while the insurance company procedures ran their course. What do you do? Sometimes the right thing to do is to help, sometimes not. Every situation is unique. Here, I decided not to help, and everything worked out okay. It was a very tough decision. Get ready to make tough decisions. If you want to guarantee a successful retirement.

Please refer to Chapter 17, Savings and Investments, to develop a savings plan.

According to a report created by www.accountingprincipals.com employee spending habits revealed a large tendency for people to raid their retirement funds.

Raiding your retirement fund is not a good idea. Many people did so during the COVID-19 pandemic to make ends meet. Understandable, but what this really communicates that a lot of Americans wealthy enough to have retirement savings were not budgeting and did not have an emergency fund. You adjust your spending habits and use your emergency fund to bridge the gap, not your retirement funds.

The report created by the online group "Accounting Principals" found that 16% of employees raided their retirement fund for non-essential leisure expenses including home remodeling, buying a second home, vacationing or the real retirement sinker, (pun buying a boat.

For many people, their retirement fund becomes a cash ATM. Over 28 percent of workers have withdrawn money from their retirement account. Many workers made withdrawals because of unemployment.

https://www.accountingprincipals.com/employers/employer-resources/workonomix-spending-habits/

Pension/Annuity

I know pensions are less popular, but they are still out there, especially in the government job arena.

Do not waive the Qualified and Joint Survivor Annuity option if you are married. Don't leave your spouse without something if you, the pensioner, die first. My parents thought the guy dies before the gal. That may be true. You should still plan for the unexpected. My mother opted to receive the larger benefit of a juicy government pension without providing a survivor benefit to my father. Guess who died first. Mom.

Leaving Dad with no survivor's portion of her pension. There are several survivor options.

A Few Pension/Annuity Payout Options

Life Income: Monthly income is paid to you for your lifetime. Your cash payments end at your death. If you are married, your spouse gets nothing. Life Income is an excellent choice if you are not married. You will receive the highest payout.

Life Income with Ten Years Certain: Monthly income is paid for life. If the pensioner dies before their tenth retirement anniversary, then their spouse receives the same payment for the rest of the ten years.

Joint Income with 75% to the Survivor: Monthly income is paid to you and joint annuitant. When either spouse dies, the survivor receives 75% of the joint Life Income.

Life income with 50% to Beneficiary: That is the best choice. Monthly income is paid to the pensioner for life. If you die first, your spouse receives 50% of the benefit for the rest of their life. If your spouse dies first, then your payment stays the same.

Working in Retirement

Working in retirement should be for pleasure. Work gives us a positive routine and gives purpose. Retirees who work at a pleasant, part-time job often report being happier. The following story inspires me to save well. I'm reminded of the elderly house painters I met. They are wonderful men, pillars of their community. They worked most of their life for a local mining company. The company provided no 401k or pension. A foreign company; they came in one day and thanked the employees for their services, and that was that. Mine closed. No savings, No pension. These two brothers from different mothers started a new house painting business to supplement their retirement income.

Retirement Income, Social Security, Pensions and RMD's

Before you retire, you must create a plan to manage your retirement income. Your retirement income may be a combination of Social Security, Pensions, Annuities and Required Minimum Distributions (RMD) from your IRA. Take an inventory of all the assets you have accumulated and saved to prepare for retirement. Make sure you consider any savings accounts not visited in years or savings bonds filed away, but not seen. Get it all out on the table! Then create your new retirement budget. This is a great time to reassess your expenses relative to retirement.

RMDs

Take RMD's on time. Required Minimum Distributions are small withdrawls the IRS requires you to take from your traditional IRA, 401k, and 403b accounts after you turn 72 1/2. Other employer-based retirement plans include 457b, SEPs, and Simple IRAs. The IRS wants you to take the withdrawal so they can tax that income. Remember, the money in the IRA was pre-tax (untaxed) dollars allowed to grow and compound without being taxed for many years. Now the IRS gets its chance to tax that money. Roth IRAs do not need an RMD while you are alive. According to the IRS, you may calculate the RMDs from each of your accounts and then withdraw from just one account or any combination you see fit. You may not want to take money out of an account that is performing well. I mean withdrawing from an account that earns a great "return on your investment." (ROI) The penalty for not withdrawing the RMD money and making it available for tax is 50% of the amount not withdrawn. OUCH!

When you are ready to retire, merge your multiple retirement accounts into one account for ease of management. Most investment advisors and brokerage firms will allow you to combine your accounts (money market, brokerage, and IRAs into one account. I use and recommend Vanguard.

Then it's time to decide if your RMD withdrawl added to your pension and added to your social security is enough to pay the bills. If not, rethink your budget. The ballpark drawdown figure by most money managers is 4% (The drawdown rate is the amount you deduct from your savings annually. You may have to drawdown less if the market is doing poorly and your nest egg is not growing. Calculate a withdrawal equal to 4% and see if this satisfies the RMD minimum. If your RMD is greater than 4% then save the difference as non-qualified money. (Unqualified funds or non-qualified funds means funds unprotected from taxes or after-tax dollars. Qualified means tax protected or pre-tax dollars or money in retirement accounts).

Remember This!

Qualified Savings or Pre-Tax Dollars = Employer Sponsored Retirement Plan, Traditional IRA, Pension, 401k, etc.

non-qualified or After Tax Dollars = Everything else (Roth IRAs are non-qualified)

Investment Strategy in Retirement

You should reserve one year of cash to cover retirement expenses in a Money Market Fund.

Create a CD or Treasury Bond Ladder with two to four years of expenses. Start a treasury bond ladder at https://www.treasurydirect.gov. A ladder reduces your risk by investing one-third of your money in treasuries that mature in one to two years, another one-third that mature in three to four years and the last one-third mature in five years. When the one year matures, invest in the five-year CD. When the two CDs mature, invest in the four, three for three, and when the four-year CD matures buy a two year CD. When the five-year CD matures, invest in the one year to keep the mix the same. You can use this same strategy for Bank CDs.

Bond or CD Ladder

Matures		Purchase
1 yr.	-----------------	5 yr.
2 yr.	-----------------	4 yr.
3 yr.	-----------------	3 yr.
4 yr.	-----------------	2 yr.
5 yr.	-----------------	1 yr.

Invest the Rest of your qualified nest egg in Reliable Mutual Funds.

Invest your "non-qualified" nest egg in reliable dividend-paying stocks. If you prefer investing in a diversified dividend fund or ETF, then consider Vanguard Dividend Growth Fund (VDIGX), SPDR S&P Dividend ETF (SDY), or Schwab US Dividend Equity ETF (SCHD).

As you grow older, increase cash assets. When you reach eighty, I suggest 30-50% in cash. Then invest the rest in conservative stocks and bond funds. Do not invest in long term bond funds. They expose you to interest rate risk.

"In this world nothing can be said to be certain, except death and taxes."

Benjamin Franklin

Taxes don't stop in retirement. Social Security could be taxed if you have added sources of income. Withdrawals from 401ks, 403b's and traditional IRAs are taxable. You will pay taxes on investment income in the form of dividends. Capital gains tax rates stay the same as before retirement.

Social Security Step One! Create your Social Security account online to access your personal information, no matter your age! Stop reading and do it now! The Social Security Administration has a friendly website filled with lots of retirement planning information. https://www.ssa.gov/

The best advice I can give if you are born after 1960 is to delay applying for benefits as long as possible. You will qualify for delayed retirement benefits under the current plan. The rules will change. At least make it to your birth year's Full Retirement Age or FRA. Just remember, everyone in the financial business is still talking about the "claim now, claim more" later strategy that only applies to people born before Jan. 1, 1954. For married couples, strategies exist for spouses who did not work and for spouses that earned an equal income. Financial gurus have written entire books about Social Security strategies. It should not be so complicated. Just wait as long as you can before filing for your Social Security. If you are not healthy, retire early. The decision to delay benefits is up to you.

Mortgage and Car Debt Free

By the time you are ready to retire, have your house and cars paid off. If you are young and reading this book, consider driving only paid off cars. If you are nearing retirement, it's time to stop accumulating and begin saving. If you are facing retirement with a car payment, consider selling the car, pay off the note and buy a good used car with cash. See Chapter 15 Automobiles.

Pay off your mortgage before you retire. Do what you need to do to make this a reality. Watch mortgage interest rates and refinance when rates drop. Do not reset the term of the loan, nor cash out to pay off unsecured debt. Keep your mortgage balance clean. Do not borrow using a HELOC or second mortgages. Double your payments to increase the principal paid to pay off the mortgage sooner. If you cannot afford to double your payment, then add enough extra each month to add another payment by the end of the year. This minor act can save interest expense in the long run. If that does not work, consider selling and downsizing. Take the existing equity you have in your home and use that to buy a smaller property outright.

Stay away from reverse mortgages. It's just another way for the big guy to end up owning the assets of the little guy. If you are considering a reverse mortgage, then you may own a home that is just too big. Consider selling and downsizing. Reverse mortgages come with restrictions for the borrower, lots of regulation for the lender, in what appears to be a foreclosure opportunity of your house.

Retirement Health Care ABC's and Sometimes D Lucky you. You live in the USA. When you reach sixty-five, sign up for Medicare. That will take care of most of your medical expenses. There are two Medicare plans, the Original Medicare or a Medicare Advantage Plan. The government pays for Original Medicare. Medicare Advantage Plans are offered by private companies approved by Medicare. Medicare Part A is Hospital insurance, Medicare Part B is Medical Insurance and Medicare

Advantage is part C. Your retirement health insurance ABC's! Part D is the prescription part of Medicare. You will shop for this plan separately. Government insurance is a government entity and subject to constant change.

Each Medicare Advantage Plan has different benefit plan and program costs, so you have to shop before you join. Many Advantage plans include vision, dental, wellness, and Part D prescription benefits.

You may purchase a Medigap Policy. This is a policy to supplement services and supplies which original Medicare does not supply. If you choose original Medicare, pay for a Medicare supplement plan. My elderly clients have one, and I recommend them. These policies help pay co-payments and deductibles. When you have Original Medicare and a Medigap policy, Medicare will pay its share, then Medigap pays its share. Make sure you shop for and secure your Medigap policy as soon as you turn sixty-five. This opens the Medigap Open Enrollment Period that allows you to buy a policy regardless of your health conditions. Purchase a separate Medigap policy for yourself and your spouse.

You will need to plan for prescriptions, vision, and dental. The Medicare website is very user friendly and will offer you plans that fit your prescription needs for your location and health situation. If you are not comfortable on the computer, find a trustworthy grandchild to help you!

Financial managers estimate you will need between $200,000 and $250,000 to cover out-of-pocket medical expenses in retirement. I find this figure high. Most Americans that retire don't have this much money saved. I don't see thousands of medically starved retirees in the streets. It has been my experience, depending on the retiree's financial status, that they will charge a financially humble retiree with the Medicare preset for their healthcare, leaving little or no balance. This is especially true if you have a Medicare supplement or Medigap plan. Vanguard quotes a figure of $3,600 per year for a Silver Medicare plan, plus supplemental F. That's not terrible. The Medicare system bases your Medicare premium on your income. Sounds fair. In 2021, Part A Medicare Premium is free unless you paid Medicare taxes for less than 40 quarters. Then you may pay $259 per month. If you paid less than 30 quarters of Medicare taxes, your premium goes up to $471. Part A has a $1,484 deductible based on a sliding scale based on days in hospital. The Part B premium is $148.50

(or higher based upon income Part B deductible is $203 per year. After that you handle 20% of the Medicare-approved services. This is another area Medigap kicks in. My point here is that a retiree in average health should be able to handle their medical expenses without busting their budget. It is manageable.

https://www.aarp.org/retirement/planning-for-retirement/info-2019/health-care-costs-calculator.html

Caring for very elderly parents

This is tough. Caring for elderly parents can be a financial "situation." Everyone's "situation" is different when dealing with caring for an elderly parent. I remember my grandparents taking care of my elderly great-great aunt. It did not help their financial situation. If your parent has financial assets, you may hire an assistant. Consider checking out the site of National Council on Aging's Benefits Check Up. https://www.benefitscheckup.org Fill out a simple form online and they will send you benefit information for your specific situation.

Consider a Home Monitoring Device. I have experience here and they work as advertised. I use Medical Alert for my father.
https://www.medicalalert.com/

Try splitting up responsibilities with other family members, friends or church family.

If your parent is a veteran please see, https://www.benefits.va.gov/persona/veteran-elderly.asp to see a comprehensive list of benefits. If your loved one is a veteran, there are care benefits available.

Legal: Will and Trust

Hire an elder care attorney and consider creating a living will and trust if you have assets over $500,000. A Last Will and Testament, proper Durable Power of Attorney and Healthcare Directives should do the job. If you have less than $500,000, you can use nolo.com and use their templates to create your own will.

Quicken WillMaker Plus does an outstanding job preparing these documents for you if you have a simple situation. Then after you have prepared the documents, run them by a trustworthy, affordable attorney to make sure you have don't miss any details that apply specifically to you.

Remember! Everyone should have a will. Otherwise, you die intestate, and the court decides who gets assets.
What you need.

1. Will;

2. Health Care Directive (Living Will and Power of Attorney);

3. Durable Power of Attorney for Finances;

4. Final Arrangements;

5. Information for Caregivers and Survivors.

In conclusion, you must live on less money than you spend. Saving for retirement is more important than saving for your children's college, buying a second home, or buying a boat. You must be frugal and smart with your money. You should not use your retirement fund to subsidize your adult children's lifestyle. It ruins their ability to learn how to live on a budget and prevents you from making earnings on your money so you can retire and not have to rely on your children to support you in old age. Hakuna matata, the real circle of life! In addition, it is a good goal to have more money left at the end of your life than the other way around.

Chapter 19

Insurance

"I don't want to tell you how much insurance I carry with the Prudential, but all I can say is: when I go, they go too."

Jack Benny

What is insurance? Insurance is a financial contract that comes in many forms that protects you from the unexpected. Don't risk more than you can afford to lose! However, don't spend more than you can afford on insurance.

Insurance is risk protection. Another name for insurance is risk management. What risks do you have? If you own a car, you must have insurance, more insurance if it's financed. Home, mobile home, or renter's insurance is important if you own a home or rent. If you are alive, most of my readers qualify, have a family that depends on your income, then consider life insurance. Everyone should have health insurance. Insurance is an important part of your financial picture. It protects your finances from life's unexpected events. Without insurance, you may be expected to pay for another person's lost wages and hospital expenses suffered in an automobile accident. If your house burns down, can you afford to replace it out of pocket? Probably not.

Insurance allows policy (contract) holders to spread the risk of a predictable event through the entire population of policyholders. Insurance pays you for unexpected financial losses and damages caused by a particular set of hazards. Insurance insures specific things of value: home, car, health, or your life. Insurance insures against specific hazards such as fire or illness. Insurance companies charge you a premium (fee to protect you. That premium is tiny compared to the value of the potential financial risk the insurance company takes.

How can they do this? Insurance companies use very specialized statisticians called actuaries who calculate the odds that certain risks take place to a certain population or pool of potential policyholders. Insurance companies use that information to calculate a premium that covers the potential dollar amount of claims paid plus profit.

To keep the insured honest, the insurance companies insist on the insured paying a deductible, so the insured suffers financial pain to prevent excessive or fraudulent claims.

Fun Fact: In 2017, every 41 seconds, someone steals one vehicle. That's only 771,000 vehicles per year. Charming.

In this chapter, I discuss auto, home, health and life insurance. The idea here is the same through the book. Get the best deal. Shop for the most effective insurance at the best price. Learn to use insurance "aggregators" to assist you find the best policy for you at the best price. Learn what is a necessity and a luxury in the insurance business.

Auto Insurance

I'll start with auto insurance. Auto insurance is the first insurance I purchased. Yes, the black stripe made it go faster! Don't tell my insurance agent. Shhhh.

I split auto insurance companies into three categories.

1. Online;

2. Direct to consumer;

3. Brick and mortar.

Go online and compare quotes. Try https://www.thezebra.com/ or https://www.Compare.com/auto-insurance. These sites, called aggregators, allow you to make comparisons among dozens of insurance companies competing for your business. Companies that sell direct offer competitive rates because they drop the middleman, the agent. GEICO and Progressive are the largest. The insurance industry splits brick and mortar insurance agents into two categories. Independent agents that represent multiple companies and "exclusive" agents who represent the company whose name is on the door. For example, Esurance is the online version of the brick-and-mortar agency, Allstate. I use the old standby State Farm Insurance company because I receive a high level of service. They are a sound company, and I don't expect any surprises if I make a claim. The rates stay stable. Know that insurance companies may attract your business by offering an artificially low rate only to sock it to you, raise the premium next season now that you're "in the family." It is advisable to ask trustworthy friends and family to recommend a local trustworthy agent who represents a trustworthy insurance company.

Deductibles: To control the cost of your auto insurance rates, take the highest deductible you can afford. Have the deductible available in savings. The insurance company does not pay the claim until you pay the deductible! Higher deductibles reduce your insurance premium.

Bodily and Property Damage Liability Coverage: Required in every state, Bodily Injury and Property Damage Liability coverages are expensive. You pay for specific limits. My theory is, make sure the coverage is large enough to motivate your insurance company to hire and use their attorney. Each state has its own minimums. Those minimums are not high enough to protect you. Consider at least 100-300-100. That stands for $100,000 each person, $300,000 each accident, and $100,000 Property Damage. Get higher limits if you can afford it. If you are a teenager and do not have any assets, then the smallest is fine. If you are an adult with money in the bank, raise your limits to qualify for a

$1,000,000 liability umbrella policy. Just remember, if the accident is your fault and serious and your coverage does not cover the damages and settlements, they could still hold you responsible. Buy as much as you can afford. We live in a litigious society.

https://www.nasdaq.com/article/do-i-have-to-pay-if-my-liability-limits-are-exceeded-cm122655

Comprehensive: This coverage pays for damage not caused by a collision. Comprehensive coverage covers, theft, natural disasters, fire, and vandalism. Financed cars require this coverage. I own it on my paid off cars. It is the least expensive of the auto coverages.

Collision: This coverage pays for collision damages to your car. It pays if you hit another car or another object, like a tree. The lender requires this coverage if you finance your car.

Uninsured Motorist: If the other driver is at fault, but not insured, your company pays the claim, including hit and run. They do not require this coverage in all states, but you should have it. They estimate that 15-20% (depending on your state of drivers are uninsured. Your car starts and runs whether or not you have a license or insurance. Depending on your insurance policy, if you have multiple cars, uninsured coverage is stacked. This means limits of both cars are added together.

Personal Injury Protection (PIP, Medical Payments, No Fault:

This coverage pays for you and your passengers' medical bills if you are injured in a car accident, regardless of fault, hence the "no fault" name. Check with your specific state for your status.

Underinsured Motorist: This insurance protects you from the teenager running around with the legal liability limits but causes damages over his policy limits. Then your underinsured coverage comes to the rescue and pays the balance.

Extras: Many auto insurance companies will sell rental car coverage while your car is being repaired and Emergency Road Service coverage. Rental coverage is not a bad idea, just an added expense that may not be necessary. I prefer AAA for Emergency Road Service.

Read your auto insurance policy declaration page. It outlines your coverages for each car. If you are an A-B student in high school, you may qualify for discounts.

Note to Self

Get your homeowner's and auto insurance at the same insurance company to score a discount.

Homeowner Insurance

Dwelling: This insurance coverage amount is the value placed on your home. This item requires a decision between replacement cost or actual cash value. Most homeowner policies are replacement value, but you need to check. Make sure you have enough coverage to rebuild your house in case of catastrophe. If you do not have enough coverage, then you pay the difference out of pocket.

Personal Property: This coverage is usually a percentage of your home's value. It includes coverage for your home's appliances, furniture and personal possessions. Make sure you have a personal property inventory list including photographs to make the claim process go smoothly. www.iii.org. Keep it simple. Just grab a legal pad and go room by room listing your personal belongings. You can make a video of the interior of your home. You should store this information in a safe place. Digitize and store it in the cloud. Most personal property policies are actual cash value and not replacement cost.

Living Room			
Item	Price	Purchased	Make/Model
Furniture (e.g. sofas, bookshelves, tables)			
Electronics (e.g. television, stereo and speakers, DVDs)			
Room Decor (e.g. art, carpeting, lighting, blinds and curtains)			
Miscellaneous (e.g. other small items)			

Loss of Use: This coverage helps pay temporary living expenses in case your home is unlivable. Many policies cover temporary residence, moving bills, laundry, and pet boarding.

Personal Liability: This is liability insurance to protect you from your guests suing you.

Deductible: In Florida deductibles vary based on the cause of the catastrophe. I have a regular deductible and a special Hurricane deductible. Review your deductibles with your agent. Make sure you can afford to pay your deductible if an insured event occurs.

Self-Storage Facility: Your homeowner's policy covers your personal items stored in your self-storage unit.

Endorsements, Riders, and Floaters: If you own a valuable baseball, coin, or china collection, you may purchase a rider to cover specialty items. The insurance company usually requires an accurate appraisal of your valuables.

Flood Insurance: Does what it says. Buy it thirty days in advance as your policy will not take effect if the hurricane is right off the coast when you buy flood insurance.

Renter's Insurance: This is for the folks that are renting their habitat. This insurance covers your personal property inside the rented structure. It is very inexpensive.

Important! Do not make small claims on your homeowner's policy. Homeowner's policies are for catastrophic events. Nickel and diming your insurance company for small claims may cause an increase in your rate or cancellation of your policy. Your multiple small claims are showing the insurance underwriter that you are a bad risk.

Recommended Insurers

Amica Mutual earns top customer satisfaction ratings from J.D. Power. USAA tops the list but is only available to military personnel and families. State Farm, Auto-Owners, Erie Insurance and Auto Club of Southern California Insurance Group round out the top five.

Homeowner Insurance Shopping Tips

Buy a policy with the highest deductible that you can afford. Is that deductible realistic? Deductibles can be paid from your emergency fund. Become familiar with your policy exclusions. Many homeowner's policies exclude:

- Mold
- Sewer backup
- Sinkholes
- Flood

- Earthquakes
- Stolen/destroyed cash
- Trampoline accidents
- Dog attacks
- Pool accidents

Buy an insurance rider to cover these added risks. Flood insurance is a separate policy; not a rider.

Check your homeowner's policy to see if it covers the belongings of your boarding school or college student.

Health Insurance: Entire books have been written about health insurance. I recommend a brilliant book that covers many types of insurance. Insurance for Dummies, by Jack Hungelmann.

To protect your financial ecosystem, you must have health insurance. A few of the main health insurance companies include AETNA, Blue Cross, Blue Shield, Cigna, Humana, Kaiser, and United Healthcare.

https://www.webmd.com/health-insurance/types-of-health-insurance-plans#1

Let's start with a little alphabet soup.

HMO: Health Maintenance Organization

Delivers a full menu of health services through a network of healthcare providers and facilities. Little paperwork (no claim forms, low copay, but the least freedom to choose your doctor. A primary doctor directs your care. Going outside the network means you pay the full bill!

PPO: Preferred Provider Organization

Better access to choose your own doctor. Higher out of network copays and deductibles if you go out of network, and more paperwork than HMO. This plan is the most common. You may see specialists without a referral.

EPO: Exclusive Provider Organization

No coverage for out of network healthcare. You are on your own. May have a deductible. Very little paperwork.

POS: Point-Of-Service Plan

A POS is a combination of an HMO and a PPO. More freedom to choose than an HMO. Paperwork if you go out of the network. A primary doctor directs your care.

Catastrophic:

If you are under the age of thirty or have a hardship exemption, you can purchase a catastrophic health plan. You get three primary care visits before the deductible kicks in. Free preventative care. A catastrophic health plan, as of 2020, has a deductible of $8,150 for an individual. After your deductible is met, you are covered 100%. If you intend to use this plan, it is important to have an emergency fund with enough money to pay your deductible! Save your healthcare receipts for this program.

HDHP with HSA: High-Deductible Health Savings Plan with a Health Savings Account

High Deductible Health Plans (HDHP are like catastrophic plans. The plan may be an HMO, PPO, EPO or POS type of plan. They resemble Preferred Provider Organizations with a high deductible. You will encounter higher out-of-pocket expenses. After you reach the expense limits, the plan kicks in at 100%. If you have an HDHP, you qualify for an HSA.

An **HSA** is a government regulated pre-tax savings account you use for medical expenses. To qualify for an **HSA,** you must have a plan deductible of at least $1,400 per individual. The money can accumulate in your account and when you retire, you may use your HSA funds to pay for Medicare premiums and other approved medical expenses. The account must be used for medical expenses, or they may charge you a penalty of 20% and expose you to income tax. The maximum you can deposit in 2021 is $3,600 for an individual and $7,200 for family coverage. Keep your receipts so you can receive reimbursement smoothly.

FSA: A Flexible Savings Account is another pre-tax government sponsored savings plan that allows you to deposit pre-tax money into. It is unique, in that the account is pre-funded. This means when you sign up to pay twenty pay periods in the amount of $50.00, it immediately credits your account $1,000. That money is available to pay expenses. They deduct the money from your taxable income. There is a big catch! Use the money in the account during the plan term, usually one year. Any money you don't use disappears. Your company, however, can transfer up to $500 to next year or give you an extension so you can use your money. You can use the money for many medically related expenses. You can use the funds to pay for doctor visit copays and deductibles, and you can use the FSA to pay for eye doctor appointments and pay for your glasses and contact lenses. The funds can take care of dental expenses and prescription drugs.

If your employer offers health insurance, take it. Many employers offer a flexible plan or cafeteria plan. The difference between the cost of your plan and the employer credits you receive come out of your paycheck. So choose wisely. Employer sponsored health plans offer the least expensive alternative to getting health care. Even if the employer plan is not a great policy, an average health insurance policy is better than nothing if catastrophe strikes. Medical bills cause many bankruptcies in the United States. Make sure you have an emergency fund to pay deductibles even if you have health insurance.

Affordable Care Act: if your employer does not offer a health care benefit or you are self-employed, consider the Affordable Care Act or Obama Care. Set up an account at HealthCare.gov. The site will deliver the options for which you qualify. If you do not qualify for subsidies, checkout various health care insurance sites (aggregators like Health*plans*.com or eHealthInsurance.com.

Medicaid: https://www.medicaid.gov/ Insurance for lower income individuals, families, and seniors. Protection is available for people with disabilities. States administer Medicaid individually and state programs differ from state to state. They base eligibility on your income level compared to the federal poverty level. In Florida, if you qualify for Supplemental Social Security, then you qualify for Medicaid. Enrollment is available at HealthCare.gov.

CHIP: Children's Health Insurance Program provides low-cost health insurance to children who are from low income homes, but with more income than qualifies for Medicaid.

Fidelity Bonds: This insurance is protection from fraudulent acts by specified employees. It protects a business from dishonest acts from its employees. Over 30% of business bankruptcies are caused by employee theft.

Disability Insurance: It is possible that you could be injured and require time off from work. Disability insurance helps pay your lost income while you get better from your injury. Some say a thirty-five year old worker has a 50% chance of becoming disabled for a ninety day period. This is another reason why you should have an emergency fund. Disability benefits kick in between one month and one year after you file a claim. The typical long-term disability policy covers 60% of a base salary. Check out PolicyGenius.com for competitive rates.

Life Insurance

The Life Insurance Salesman's Wife:

A woman asked me to manage a mobile home on a canal in a small town. Peter and Anne retired and moved to a cute little mobile home on a canal in a very quiet little town in North Florida. Peter was a retired life insurance salesman. Peter then unexpectedly passed away. To my surprise, she told me her husband was a life insurance sales associate. He neglected to buy a policy on himself to protect his own wife!

Anne could no longer afford to stay retired. Anne was off to a nearby city to get a job and another place to live. She hired me to rent her retirement home so it could make an income.

Why do you need Life Insurance?

1. Life insurance can help your beneficiary (s) payoff your mortgage. Use your mortgage balance as a foundation for establishing how much life insurance you need.

2. You may want to leave a particular lifestyle to your partner. As I mentioned in the story about Anne and Pete, Pete did not

leave Anne enough income after Pete's death to support her lifestyle.

3. If you have children, life insurance creates an estate that can help your children live in the manner they're accustomed to and also help them to get through college. How much will it cost to raise them after you're gone?

4. Life insurance companies design policies to cover funeral expenses. They call this final expense or burial policies. They have a lower policy amount resulting in a lower premium.

5. Your life insurance policy may just leave an inheritance.

Who Needs Life Insurance? Folks that have other folks depending on them. Babies do not need life insurance (yes, an agent tried to sell us a life insurance policy for our first child. Teenagers do not need life insurance if they are not yet parents. Most teen parents cannot afford life insurance. Young couples starting out may have life insurance provided to them by a company group policy. That's okay. The purpose of life insurance is to provide an estate for your family before you have an estate. After you have an estate (assets/money, then life insurance is an optional vehicle to leave an added inheritance to your children. Only consider whole life insurance if you have maxed out your tax deferred investment vehicles and have considerable net worth. (over 500k. "Whole Life" insures you for life and costs five to ten times the cost of term insurance. Whole life policies accumulate cash values you can borrow against and repay. The point is, whole life insurance is off the table until you are very wealthy. You should steer clear of Universal Life Insurance.

Term insurance is inexpensive and allows you to "rent" a decent financial estate while you are creating a real one. It guarantees life insurance for a fixed time period. I suggest that a twenty year term is best. Term insurance has no cash value. Check out SelectQuote.com or Amica.com to research competitive rates. Amica.com has multiple product lines. They insure autos, homes, Life, Condo, Renters, Boats, Motorcycles, and offer umbrella policies. SelectQuote.com shops dozens of insurance carriers to get the best rate for you. Inspect their website to research the variety of term insurance policies. Dave Ramsey recommends https://www. zanderins.com/. Another great resource.

How much Life Insurance? The correct coverage amount for life insurance depends on how much debt you have. Insurance experts suggest ten times your annual income. The point is to have enough insurance to invest and produce enough income so your family can pay their bills after you pass. The policy should cover your total outstanding debt. This prevents your spouse from being responsible for an unpaid debt. The better plan is a policy amount that covers your mortgage, car notes, unsecured debts, college education expenses for children, and enough money for your spouse to live in the same standard of living for five years. Consider reducing insurance amount by your partner's cash value of retirement plan (rare and 401k plan. They will no longer need extra insurance money to retire. I suggest checking out free insurance calculators online to find your insurance need. In addition, at the time of this writing, State Farm Insurance is a highly rated life insurance company with high customer satisfaction.

Do not buy declining balance mortgage insurance. It is a terrible investment compared to term life insurance. Unless you think you will keel over soon!

Free Life Insurance Calculator:

https://www.nerdwallet.com/blog/insurance/how-much-life-insurance-do-i-need/

Universal Life: This product offers large commissions to insurance agents and big incomes to insurance companies. They disguise it as an investment living inside a life insurance policy that earns a return large enough to pay the premium in the future. Most reputable insurance companies do not sell Universal Life. Please don't buy Universal Life Insurance.

Unnecessary Insurance

Rental Car Coverage: If you have car insurance on your car, you may not need additional auto coverage to their car rental. This is a very profitable product for rental car companies that overlaps coverage you have in your personal auto coverage and possibly coverage you have when you pay using your credit card. Check your credit card details to see if they automatically covers rental car insurance. However, lately, popular credit cards that used to cover car rentals no longer do so. I recommend checking out Chase Sapphire Reserve or City One Spark Miles. They still have rental car coverage.

Flight Insurance This is a very expensive life insurance that is unnecessary. If you die in a commercial plane crash, there will be a settlement for your family.

Pet Insurance: This insurance may be unnecessary. You need to be practical with pet care expenses. The trend is to offer state-of-the-art health care to the pet equivalent to human health care at about the same cost as human health care. The choice is yours. Your vet is not on your budget's side of this discussion.

Smartphone Insurance: If you're clumsy, then you may need this insurance. This is insurance is very expensive for the coverage you get. It carries a high deductible to protect the insurance company from some people that are careless and klutzy. Don't buy!

Identity Theft Insurance: I discuss Identity Theft Insurance in other chapters of the book. Join AAA for vehicle road hazard insurance and sign up for their ProtectMyID program. This is a free AAA benefit offered in partnership with Experian.

Extended Warranties are Insurance Policies too: Extended warranty insurance for appliances is expensive for the coverage you receive. However, if you are purchasing a new kitchen appliance or washer and dryer, purchasing through a big box retailer like Home Depot and Lowes an extended warranty may be a good idea. I bought a new refrigerator and the internal circuit board had to be replaced and I bought a new dishwasher and the internal circuit board had to be replaced. I bought a new central HVAC, and the compressor disintegrated. The technicians said the same thing. Manufacturers are stretching the boundaries of existing technology to squeeze the greatest amount of energy efficiency out of our appliances. The technicians replaced circuits in the refrigerator and dishwasher, redesigned from the original circuit boards. The warranty on my HVAC replaced the outside cooling unit with a new unit. New unit arrived with the same brand and model number, but the unit was a redesigned size and shape. Consumers are beta testers for new technology imbedded in what used to be old-fashioned mechanical technology.

In Conclusion

Your Insurance Budget

Insurance expenses will make up a significant part of your budget. In the budget included in Chapter 12, Money Management, in this book, insurance costs may be about 7% of your total budget. This is just a ballpark amount. The point is, insurance is a necessary part of life and you need to plan and create an insurance budget. Your insurance budget is as important as your overall budget. Life insurance could run between $500 and $750 per year. Automobile insurance should run approximately about $1,250 every six months per car, and homeowner's insurance should run between $400 and $500 per year. Hopefully, your employer deducts your health and disability insurance from your paycheck. Because this chapter summarizes insurance, I recommend *Insurance for Dummies* by Jack Hungelmann so you can know more about the many details of insurance.

Chapter 20

The Habits of the Financially Successful

"There are many in the world who are dying for a piece of bread, but there are many more dying for a little love. The poverty in the West is a different kind of poverty — it is not only a poverty of loneliness but also of spirituality. There's a hunger for love, as there is a hunger for God."

Mother Teresa, A Simple Path

Most personal finance books show you how to fix the numbers, but most neglect how to fix your habits about numbers.

Remember the saying, "It is better to give than to receive?" It means give good, respect, hope, trust, positive vibes, and you will receive these in return. No, the quote was not just about material things. You can give greater gifts that cost you no money. This reminds me of a story. A co-worker of mine, Cameron, was tallying his sales on his Excel worksheet after receiving his commission check. After checking the numbers, he realized the boss underpaid him. Looking at the numbers more closely, he realized it was probably deliberate! He asked nicely for a short meeting with our sales manager and calmly explained the situation. The sales manager agreed with Cameron and was most apologetic. The two went to lunch later, had an adult beverage, and buried the hatchet. Would you have handled that situation the same way?

It's time for a cool change:

If you want to succeed in this financial life, have a positive attitude. This is a strong suggestion. Develop a HEALTHY plan to deal with the stress of life and finances. You cannot respond to negative life events (they are going to happen with knee-jerk reactions. You cannot respond to stress with behaviors that will ultimately cause more stress! It's difficult, but you will have to reduce the negative emotions. You attract the emotion you are giving. You can build resilience. Have a little grit. I know you can do it! Be tough in the face of adversity. You can succeed at being financially in control. The Universe is on your side.

I know you can change. If you want to have a household with a balanced budget, you may have to make big changes. Change is possible. You may have to reduce expenses and increase income.

I know you can develop the skill set to change your behavior. If your behavior does not change, all the advice in this book will be worthless.

How do we see the World?

When you face adversity, how do you respond? The way we explain the difference between resilience and helplessness is how we see the world. According to Karen Reivich and Andrew Shatte, in their book *The Resilience Factor,* "Pessimists are people who explained their adversities with 'Me, Always' (I cause my problems 100% of the time 'Everything' (This will affect **every** area of my life style tended to become helpless and depressed. Optimists (those with a 'not me, not always, not everything' style) remained resilient and depression free."

As an example of resilience, a friend of mine, Tim, drove an old (paid for car and the transmission was misbehaving. This problem was certainly not his fault, but definitely a stressful situation. Tim drove the car to the local transmission mechanic and got the transmission repaired. He had enough money in his emergency account to pay for it and he did not get depressed. He did not blame himself. Tim remained resilient and took care of his problem successfully.

If Stupidity got us into this mess, then why can't it get us out?
Will Rogers

If we continue to solve the same problem in the same way without a positive result, what is the result telling us? Find a different solution. If you are out of ideas, ask reputable, intelligent people for their advice. Hoping the problem will solve itself may not work. If you cannot afford a counselor, find a trustworthy pastor. If that is uncomfortable for you, then learn to get comfortable accepting help from trustworthy people. You can change. If you wrestle with anger, sadness, guilt, and/or embarrassment about money, then challenge your belief system. You can choose to be happy and content. You can change and you have the power to make the right choices. You can choose to not be angry with your boss. You can choose to be content with your car. It is truly up to you. You have the power to change. I believe in you!

Rich people believe "I create my life." Poor people believe "Life happens to me."

"Poor people see a dollar as a dollar to trade for something they want right now. Rich people see every dollar as a 'seed' that can be planted to earn a hundred more dollars... then replanted to earn a thousand more dollars."

~ T. Harv Eker, author of *Secrets of the Millionaire Mind.*

You can't fake this. Good intentions don't work here. Develop discipline to save for the future. Have discipline to manage your finances.

Does this quote sound familiar?

"Quit making excuses, putting it off, complaining about it, dreaming about it, whining about it, crying about it, believing you can't, worrying if you can, waiting until your older, skinnier, richer, braver, or all around better. Suck it up, Hold on tight, say a prayer, make a plan and JUST DO IT."

I recommend a couple of great resources. *Secrets of the Millionaire Mind* dives into determining your physical, mental, emotional, and spiritual relationship with money. I highly recommend this book to you if you want to get in touch with your attitude toward money.

How do you feel about money?

You may have a negative image of Wall Street tycoons from movies and TV not based on reality. Gordon Gekko was a fictional character. In the actual world, there was a really bad guy, Charles Ponzi. There was a real Bernie Madoff. However, the vast majority of people in the financial industry, including Wall Street, are/were very honest and hard-working people. I was lucky enough to have such a person in my family. My great-uncle, Alfred B. Averell, began as a messenger on the New York Stock Exchange before the Wall Street crash of 1929. I asked him if folks were jumping out of windows (as reported in history books. Uncle Al taught me there was a lot of media hype and not as many people jumped as reported. He said he worked in the less exciting bond business. Mr. Averell, trustworthy, took care of investing money from my grandmother's inheritance. She received a small portion of an estate in England. He put my grand-mother into the best conservative stocks available. Uncle Al told me the best quote ever. "<u>Money does not care who it belongs to</u>." After he told me that, I had a better attitude toward money. I suspect a bank robber could say the same thing to justify theft, but that's not what it means in the real sense. It means in a capitalist society there are opportunities to accumulate wealth. And it's okay.

Ask yourself, "Are you afraid of money?" It's understandable.

Are you angry with rich people?

If you live in the USA, compared to the vast majority of the world... you are wealthy! See Stats Below.

Comparing ourselves to others is not always healthy. We compare ourselves to a small group of people who are better off than we are. Consider this!

If you make $7.25 per hour or $15,080 a year, you would be in the top 10% of global income.

If you make $25,000 per year, you are in the top 2% of richest people in the world by income. Do you make $50,000 per year? You are in the top 1% of the world.

If you had a net worth of just $1,000, you would rank in the top 69% of the world's wealthiest people!

To break your bad money habits it has to be done gradually. If not, you will not heal and you will restart the bad habits again.

Let's shift gears and take the momentum to do the right thing and figure out why we are not doing it. I hope you have learned from this book that mass marketing may be brain washing you to do the wrong thing!

This book discusses common, money bad habits. I do not discuss these habits to pass judgment, but to show you the financial fallout from the bad habits. Do you have any of those bad habits? What are you going to do to correct them? It is up to you. How do you change habits? How do you create your financial recovery? I can tell you it is hard work, but I know you can do it. You must muster the courage, desire and good intentions into real motivation, focus, attention to detail and grit. If you read this book and set it down, then your financial situation will not change. Wishing for financial freedom is not enough!

If you google the advertisements by E*TRADE, making fun of the 1% or uber wealthy class you will see what I mean. Don't get mad, get E*TRADE. What's a non-trust fund baby to do??

It's Time to Get in Touch with Your Feelings!

Simply following a financial guru or reading a book will not solve your money problems. What is your relationship with money? Are you fearful of money? When did you form your feelings about money? Did you inherit those feelings from your parents? Do you have the reverse "Midas Touch?"

I encourage you to find a trusted friend, pastor, or psychologist to see if they can help you answer these questions honestly. I recommend a brilliant book, *Financial Recovery*, by Karen McCall. This is a great resource to learn how to have a healthy relationship with money. Another book that addresses the psychology of money is *Mind Over Money, Overcoming Money Disorder*, by Klontz & Klontz.

The 10 Habits of the Financially Successful

The financially successful are reliable. I put this habit first because without this habit the rest won't matter. If you are unreliable, then the forces of heaven and earth cannot help you. The mediocre and worse will pass the most talented person in the world if the talented person is unreliable. Please choose to be reliable.

The financially successful are honest. The best way to create a miserable life is to be dishonest. You will get away with a little dishonesty, but it is best not to make dishonesty a habit. You are untrustworthy. No wise person gives a good job to the untrustworthy. No one lends money to the untrustworthy. The Hollywood theme in the Pirates of the Caribbean, "Take what you can, give nothing back," is so ...sick. Most scholars agree that real life pirates lived a miserable life.

It's not the honors and the prizes, and the fancy outsides of life which ultimately nourish our souls. It's the knowing that we can be trusted. *Fred Rogers*

The financially successful are good with numbers. Are you uncomfortable with math? Do you just think you are bad at math? Studies show that people good with numbers are financially literate. Those that can work with numbers, but are not confident with their number skills, are less financially literate. Then there's everyone else. The folks that are least comfortable with numbers and are not financially literate. Where do you fall? If you are afraid of numbers, connect with someone good with numbers who is willing to assist you. Would it not make sense to hire a bookkeeper, daily money manager, or an accountant to help you grasp your finances? Find a trusted family member or financial coach. Then hire them or retain their services.

If you cannot afford help, find a helpful math teacher at your local high school. You should go to your credit union and ask an officer to sit with you and teach you how to balance your checkbook and start your budget.

The financially successful learn from other people's financial mistakes: I have listened to countless stories of people's financial mistakes and have learned from them. I have made my own mistakes and learned from them, too. Get your head out of the sand, look around. See what is happening. Notice what the financially successful and the financially unsuccessful are doing and start repeating the habits of the financially successful.

The financially successful are resilient. There is that word again, resilient. The financially successful person sticks to the plan. If knocked down by any of life's inevitable setbacks, the resilient don't stay down. They get back up, dust themselves off, and get back on a course to succeed. Mistakes are learning experiences. Up against the ropes? Don't stay there. Move forward, no matter how little. Life is full of adversity, so don't respond to it negatively. Despite adversity, the financially successful stay positive. Surround yourself with people who are positive and support you. Nothing is more deadly to success, and being able to develop meaningful plans, than having a negative attitude and have having people around you who are dragging you down. I am reminded of the story of the pot of crabs being boiled for dinner. The crab on top sees a way to crawl across the crabs below and get to the edge of the pot and escape. What do the other crabs below do? Grab on to the one that has the chance to escape. If we go down, you go down too. Moral of the story. Stay away from the crabs. Know what you want and fight to get there. It will take longer for you to reach your goals than you think. Don't quit. Stick to the plan.

The financially successful believe in self-education about money. Don't be a victim any longer. Learn the habits of being competent financially. The financially successful are open minded and open to learning new skills and on the lookout for the next big idea or the next big thing. Read books; and magazines. Watch videos about finance. Watch TV shows and reports that discuss the financial picture of the world and apply it to your individual financial situation. Ask questions to better learn and understand the complex world of personal finance and money management. The financially successful invest time managing their money. Go to the library and read Money Magazine. If you don't understand every-thing in the articles, that's okay. Reread them and research online any terms or discussions you do not understand.

The financially successful do not covet and suffer envy. Envy causes misery. Envy is the emotion that leads us into accumulating debt to impress those that could care less what type of car you drive or what brand of watch you wear. Do not worry about what people think about how you spend money. Align your purchases with your financial goals and systems you have put in place.

The financially successful know about the Law of the Harvest: You reap what you sow. If you invest money in a credible and legitimate in-vestment, expect to reap a reasonable return on your investment. Then take the return and reinvest that. That is the foundation of compound interest and compound returns on investment. If you invest your money in fast cars, girls, and party narcotics, then you will reap the reward you harvest. The successful create their own opportunities. They do not depend on handouts from their parents, their family, or their govern-ment. They take initiative. Plant the right seeds in the right soil that will cause financial success. Any farmer will tell you: it is what is under the ground that determines what grows above the ground. This philosophy is true with investments, your time and your thoughts.

The financially successful have a System to Achieve their Goals: The financially successful have a written financial plan. They have a written budget, and they follow it. A budget not followed is worthless. They have a written balance sheet. They develop a plan to pay off debt and increase their savings, and they put the plan into play. They set career goals and monitor their progress. Their goals are specific, measurable, attainable, and timely. Their goals create a framework to construct a system of processes that supports genuine change. Goals without pro-cess systems are dreams, thoughts that never become a reality. Enact a plan of action to realize your goals.

The financially successful are frugal: They spend less than they earn, regardless of their income or status. They tend to not be greedy. They don't use credit cards to buy something they cannot afford. A sign of greed. They don't buy cars on credit that they cannot afford. They do not envy other peoples' lifestyles, tempting them to one up their friends or neighbors. They do not believe life owes them a particular standard of living maintained by borrowing money for unnecessary wants. They shop for their needs and negotiate a good value. They spend as little as possible so they can save and invest. Then they make an income on their investments. Then they earn money on the money they earned! The frugal do not buy fancy cars or boats, fancy clothes, and fancy jewelry. They appear less rich than they are.

I recommend the book written by James Clear, *Atomic Habits,* to learn more about changing habits. His philosophy will help you build great habits. Below, I summarize his philosophy.

Creating Good Habits	**Eliminating Bad Habits**
Law One: Make it Obvious	Law One: Make it Invisible
Law Two: Make it Attractive	Law Two: Make it Unattractive
Law Three: Make it Easy	Law Three: Make it Difficult
Law Four: Make it Satisfying	Law Four: Make it Unsatisfying

Let's use the mind-numbing chore of balancing your checkbook as an example.

Make it Obvious: If I plan to balance my checkbook, I can program my online banking app to notify me that my (monthly) statement is ready. If I cannot stop what I am doing to balance the checkbook right then, I will create a task reminder on my cell phone and create a deadline. The task reminder will set off an alarm, say by the weekend, to remind me to balance my checkbook.

Make it Attractive: Create a healthy reward for your efforts. After you balance your checkbook, eat something tasty and healthy that you enjoy. Fix yourself a special non-alcoholic drink you enjoy, like a root beer. Or a banana split!

Make it Easy: Have digital access to your checking account so you can print your statement. Put your calculator, highlighter, pencil, checkbook, and ledger in the same place so you do not have to do a scavenger hunt through the house to prepare for balancing your checkbook. Print the balance ledger so it is ready to go when you are ready to balance your checkbook.

Make it Satisfying: Is it not great to know that you have accomplished a very important task in your personal, financial life? This activity/habit is consistent with the goals you have set to be financially literate. The act of balancing your checkbook gives you a unique insight into your income and spending habits. Yes, you are making sure your checkbook ledger matches your checking account statement, but that act involves getting intimate with the individual transactions you make every month. No other activity accomplishes that goal. You should feel a sense of sincere accomplishment. If not, go have a root beer. See Law Two, make it Attractive.

Habits require specificity. This means defined action, and a specific time in a specific location set aside for financial tasks.

Plan of Action Poster

I will (Action_____ at

(Time_____ in (Location_____

https://s3.amazonaws.com/jamesclear/Atomic+Habits/Implementation+Intentions.pdf

For example, regarding finance, you will need to define an action like balance your checkbook (what) at 4:00 p.m. (when) Friday at my dining room table (where) by me (who).

Develop Good Decision-Making Skills:

1) Establish Goals for your decision;

2) Prioritize by level of Importance;

3) Consider Alternatives;

4) Consider Existing resources;

5) Consider the positives and negatives of each decision;

6) Decide what is best;

7) Test the Results.

Set Financial Goals example

Make a List to put the Behavior in Play:

a) Establish a $1,000 Emergency Fund.

b) Create a Monthly Budget and Balance Sheet on paper.

c) Check your Credit Report. See Chapter Thirteen, Check your Credit Reports and Credit Scores.

d) Establish Spending Reduction Plan. Use an app like MINT to manage your income and expenses.

e) Track and Reduce your Expenses.

    a. Sell Expensive assets and use cash to repay debt.

    b. Trim Gift Expenses (Birthday and Holiday gifts can be budget busters).

    c. Take Inexpensive Vacations

f) Buy bulk necessities by joining a Warehouse Club, like BJ's, Costco, or Sam's Club. Walmart is not a club, but works well too.

g) Research Additional Income Streams, See Chapter 16, Making Extra Money with a Side Hustle.

h) Create a Credit Card Debt Repayment Schedule (six months to three years)

i) Create a Personal Loan Repayment Schedule (six months to three years)

j) Manage your Insurance. Check your Health Insurance and Disability Income Insurance. See Chapter 19, Insurance.

k) Research Investment and Savings Strategies, See Chapter 17, Savings and Investment.

l) Plan for Retirement. See Chapter 18, Preparing for Retirement.

m) Save for your children's college education. See Chapter 5, Student Loans.

n) Payoff your Mortgage.

Set multiple financial goals. Set goals about how you will pay off your credit card debt and personal loans. Develop an action plan to get out of your cycle of debt. These decisions will be painful, but they will put you back on the path of financial success. Can you sell your financed car for more than you owe, then buy a car for cash? If not, when will you be at the breakeven point of the amount owed versus the car's value? Is your housing expense reasonable? Do your expenses compare well with the guidelines established in the budget in Chapter 12, Money Management? What can you do to earn extra money and keep your sanity? These are just some important questions you will have to ask yourself.

Smart Goals (Financial)

Smart Goals is a popular method of goal setting and a great way to monitor your progress. When you make the goal to reduce credit card spending, track your progress. Use pencil and paper. Use an online calculator to assist you in your goal. https://www.bankrate.com/calculators/credit-cards/credit-card-payoff-calculator.aspx is a great calculator to help you plan your credit card debt repayment plan. For a financial goal to be reached, it has to be realistic. The goal has to be something that you can achieve or attain. Set a deadline. If you have not met your goal, but you have made progress, that's okay. Reset your goal aim and start over. That is okay!

Here is what S M A R T stands for.

S-Specific

M-Measurable

A-Attainable

R-Relevant or Realistic

T-Timely

SMART Goals Related to Credit Card Debt Example

Specific - Pay Off Credit Card Debt Balances.

Measurable - In three years I want to be out of Credit Card Debt and have zero credit card balances.

Attainable - I have time for a side hustle to make extra income to pay credit card debt.

Relevant - It's essential I get my money management in order

Timely - My Goal for Eliminating Credit Card Debt is three years.

After you have your financial goals in writing the next step is to create a plan of action. For example, let's say you want to save $100,000 by the time you're forty is a great goal. Just saying that does not make it happen. Recognize and change your bad habits, which are preventing you from reaching your goal. Create good habits. For example, after your budget is sustainable and there is money left over for savings, set automatic deductions for savings from your checking account. Set up automatic deductions for IRA investments and non-qualified retirement savings. That is a process that helps you reach your goal. I have heard the adage, "Save first." No. Not until you spend less than you earn! People starting out in life have very little money left over to save. Be frugal when you start out so you have a little money left over to save. Then you can save first, by setting up the process of automated deductions.

Self-Image: To begin with new good habits, change your self-image. If your self-image is smoker, and you want to quit, change your self-image to non-smoker (even though you are still trying to quit smoking). If your self-image is that you are poor with finances and you want to change that self-image, tell yourself, I am good with finances. Uncomfortable with math, then hire someone good at math. If you cannot afford help, find a math teacher at your local school to help you. The point is… Get some help! That is problem solving by being open to distinct possibilities. Having a new, mental perspective trains both the subconscious brain and conscious brain to think before acting. If you need a couch for your apartment, don't be enticed by the offer on the television tempting you to get a new couch for low money down, and low monthly payments. See Chapter Three, Payday Loans, Rent to Own and More. Instead, buy a used couch for cash.

Goals, without a system, accomplish little. Have goals but create an environment that allows you to attain those goals and plans in your normal daily routine.

Your New Process: Instead of heading to the buy-here, pay-here, furniture store, you can check FaceBook Community sales, Craigslist, Yard Sales, and Thrift shops. I once bought a beautiful dining room set from a local Goodwill store for $100 cash. The point is, slow down and take a breath. The advertising industry produces a barrage of advertisements through catalogs in the mail, TV, Facebook Ads, radio, newspaper, magazine, billboards and other methods to communicate you can have everything you want and need by simply signing your name on a dotted line. Like the popular food TV advertisement, "I want it ALL. I want it NOW."

That's you they are talking about. Don't fall for it. Do not be impulsive.

Advertising draws you in to create a belief in yourself that you are already part owner of the product that they are trying to sell. If you think you are already part owner, you will place a higher value on the good or service because it is already "yours."

Instead, be disinterested in the product you "need" to purchase. Be cold, calculating, and unattached to your purchase with no emotion. This takes time and talent to learn this skill. But, you can do it!

Know the Difference between a Want and A Need

To make a turn in the right direction, distinguish between your decision motivators (what floats your boat):

1. Need - it's essential for survival   (Food, Water)
2. Want - something you would   (Eating Out, Chocolate Latte) enjoy
3. Consumerism - unwise spending based on impulse or attractive marketing

Knowing what's motivating you will help you make better financial decisions.

Instant Gratification: In my experience with teenagers in the class-room and adults in the business world, I have observed a deficit in a very important character trait: patience. Everyone expects imme-diate gratification! In reality, repairing your broken, personal financial situation may take over six months to repair. It may have taken many years to get into trouble. A reasonable time frame to fix credit card debt is three years.

After year one, you still may see little progress. Don't quit.

Self-Control: Only you can control yourself. Please develop a better sense of self-control. To develop self-discipline is a lifelong goal. Part of developing self-control is to have a plan. Create a budget, establish life goals. Use the above-mentioned SMART goals for most areas of your life. The SMART goal system can help you lose weight, begin an exercise plan, or create a travel destination wish list. We all have weaknesses. Recognize those weaknesses and remove the temptations. The result will be that you make better decisions faster. That will cause you to achieve your goals faster and faster. This allows you to set new, higher goals and ultimately continue on a positive cycle.

An Entrepreneur magazine titles an article about self-discipline,

"Like everything else that brings progress, the greatest struggle is al-ways within ourselves. That's why you need to learn self-discipline."

Speaking of time: According to Health and Human Services, children spend over seven and a half hours per day in front of a screen. About six hours with the TV and one hour with video games. Why do I mention this? Because those hours are crammed full of advertising. Advertising directed at children encouraging them to be better consumers. More screen time means you receive more advertising. More advertising translates to more likelihood to act on the advertising and buy something.

https://www.hhs.gov/fitness/resource-center/facts-and-statistics/index.html

Did you know Mr. Rogers spent his life creating a TV show for children that did not exploit them to be future consumers? Mr. Rogers testified to Congress in 1969 to communicate how his program differed from mass bombardment television associated with child focused advertising grooming them for over consumption.

Priorities: Instead of spending too much time in "time wasting" activities, spend a little of your spare time on your money management. If your finances scare you now, avoiding them will not help the situation. Break up large tasks into small ones to make the task easier to accomplish. If working on your finances produces negative thoughts and emotions, step away and take a breather. Have a cold beverage. Jot down your positive thoughts. Your brain is a perfect guidance system. Perception is everything. Feed your brain with positive thoughts, then you will return more positive thoughts and emotions. Remember the positive moments you experienced. Remember to be thankful for your blessings.

See your future self as a confident, money mature person. Your money and debt under your command and control.

Get Organized: You must have a quiet, personal space to work on your finances. Your space must be comfortable. Get your office supplies that may include pencils, highlighter, stapler, tape, scissors, paper clips, post-it notes, calculator, and paper in one place and organized. Buy an old desk at the thrift shop. Put your laptop on it. Have a two-tray system - just like in the movies. One tray for new stuff or the "In" Box and one tray for completed work in the "Out" box. Make sure you have a small file cabinet, bankers box, or even a file box to store important papers. You will need a shredder to shred credit card statements and other documents that contain sensitive personal information. Have a trash can.

Filing System

No matter your circumstances, have a filing system to store important documents. It can be simple. An expandable file folder works just fine.

Here are a few sample categories:

Car Your filing system should have a section for your car. In this file you should have folders for Certificate of Title, Purchase Agreement and Loan Agreement. I keep a separate file of car maintenance expenses and receipts. If there is ever a warranty dispute, I want documentation.

House Keep your rental agreement. If you own your home, keep finance paperwork, closing documents, mortgage application, mortgage statements and any home improvement receipts. Tax receipts. Home inventory for insurance.

Credit Cards Keep your credit card application, credit card agreement, and the last 12 months of credit card statements to track expenses and then readjust your budget.

Insurance This is easy. Keep your policies. Keep policies for auto insurance, home insurance, and life insurance.

Personal Documents Keep Birth Certificates, Family Death Certificates, college transcripts, any personal legal documents like judgements or criminal justice reports. File Marriage certificate and military documents.

Savings Keep the statements. You'll need them for tax purposes.

Taxes: Keep your tax returns and tax related forms for 5 years.

This is not a complete list. Everyone's filing system will look different. Having stacks of papers throughout your house is not a filing system. Again, if you cannot do this, get someone you trust to get your filing in order. Check out this outstanding book and resource, *Get It Together* by Cullen and Shae.

Get Guidance in Areas of Weakness: Please get counseling if you suffer from an obsessive-compulsive disorder, from an addiction, marital concerns, or mental illness that is preventing you from financial freedom.

Find a Trustworthy Mentor: Find a trustworthy friend who has had similar experiences to receive suggestions.

Spiritual Guidance: Please see a pastor, priest, imam, or rabbi for counseling if you suffer from an obsessive-compulsive disorder, from an addiction, marital concerns, or mental illness that is preventing you from financial freedom. If you don't know a religious professional find one at your local church. If you don't have a church, mosque, or temple, find one in your local area. They are very interesting people and I suspect you will come away from the experience much richer, spiritually!

A friend of mine, Howard Dayton, wrote a book *Your Money Counts*. He says, and I believe, there are over 2,300 biblical scriptures related to money. There are 500 verses on prayer and faith In the Bible. Sixteen out of the Thirty-Eight parables of Jesus were about money and material possessions. The only scripture that God asks us to challenge him pertains to money. If you don't believe in God, I understand.

The first step to living an amazing life is to get your financial house in order. I hope that "*Get WalletWise*" has opened your eyes to your potential to be financially literate and then financially successful beyond your wildest imagination. Just remember to Live the Simple Life.

'Tis the gift to be simple, 'tis the gift to be free
'Tis the gift to come down where we ought to be,
And when we find ourselves in the place just right,
'Twill be in the valley of love and delight.
When true simplicity is gained,
To bow and to bend we shan't be ashamed,
To turn, turn will be our delight,
Till by turning, turning we come 'round right.

Elder Joseph Brackett

Index

Please Leave a Review

Please leave a review for this book on Amazon! Your feedback is important to help make the next edition better for those who want to achieve financial freedom.

Please review on Amazon:

https://www.amazon.com/dp/
B09FY91V6Y#customerReviews

https://www.walletwise.org/

Made in the USA
Coppell, TX
22 December 2022

90534180R00176